Looking Left

RENE

DA

D0973688

GAYLORD			PRINTED IN U.S.A.

LOOKING LEFT
Socialism in Europe after the Cold War

edited by

DONALD SASSOON

THE NEW PRESS

ISBN 1-56584-428-9

Published in 1997 by I. B. Tauris & Co. Ltd, Victoria House, Bloomsbury Square, London WC1B 4DZ, in association with the Gramsci Foundation, Rome
Published in the United States by The New Press, New York
Distributed by W.W. Norton & Company, Inc., New York

The New Press was established in 1990 as a not-for-profit alternative to the large, commercial publishing houses currently dominating the book publishing industry. The New Press operates in the public interest rather than for private gain, and is committed to publishing, in innovative ways, works of educational, cultural, and community value that might not be considered sufficiently profitable. The New Press's editorial offices are located at the City University of New York.

Set in Monotype Ehrhardt by Ewan Smith, London
Printed in the United States of America

9 8 7 6 5 4 3 2 1

Contents

List of tables   vii

Notes on contributors   ix

Introduction   1
Donald Sassoon

1   The British Labour Party since 1989   17
    Colin Leys

2   The Italian Left after 1989: Continuity and
    transformation   44
    Giulio Sapelli

3   The Left and the crisis of the Third Hellenic
    Republic, 1989–97   64
    Vassilis Fouskas

4   The PSOE: Modernization and the welfare state
    in Spain   88
    Paul Kennedy

5   The French socialists: Towards post-republican
    values?   109
    François Hincker

6 The transformation of German social democracy 124

Thomas Meyer

7 The post-communist socialists in Eastern and
Central Europe 143

Peter Gowan

Notes 177

Index 196

Tables

2.1 Chamber of Deputies: share of the vote 1987–96 (Italy)   49

2.2 Seats obtained by party coalitions in the Chamber of
    Deputies 1994, 1996 (Italy)   49

3.1 Electoral results 1989–96 (Greece)   87

3.2 State aid to manufacturing (Greece)   87

4.1 The Spanish general election results 1989–96   97

6.1 SDP share of the vote in selected *Länder* elections, West
    Germany 1978–96   132

6.2 SDP share of the vote in the new *Länder* (former GDR)
    1990, 1994   133

7.1 The share of the vote in East and Central Europe 1989–96   144

7.2 Communist Party transformations   151

Notes on contributors

VASSILIS FOUSKAS is the author of *Populism and Modernization: The Exhaustion of the Third Hellenic Republic 1974-1994* (Athens, 1995) and various articles on Italian and Greek politics. He completed his doctorate on the transformation of Italian communism at Queen Mary and Westfield College. He is the founder and co-chair of the Association for the Study of Southern Europe and the Balkans (ASSEB).

PETER GOWAN is Principal Lecturer in European Politics at the University of North London and a member of the editorial board of *New Left Review* and of *Labour Focus on Eastern Europe*. He is the author of numerous essays on Eastern and Central Europe and co-editor of *The Questions of Europe* (Verso, 1997).

FRANÇOIS HINCKER is Professor of History at Université Paris-I Panthéon-Sorbonne and author of *La Révolution française et l'économie: décollage ou catastrophe?* (1989), *Le PCF au carrefour* (1981), and, more recently, 'Le PCF dans l'élection présidentielle' in Pascal Perrineau and Colette Ysmal (eds) *Le vote de crise. L'élection présidentielle de 1995* (Presse de la Fondation Nationale des Sciences Politiques, Paris, 1995).

PAUL KENNEDY is Lecturer in Iberian Studies in the Department of European Studies, Loughborough University. He is completing his doctorate on the PSOE and European integration and has published in the *International Journal of Iberian Studies*.

COLIN LEYS is the author of *Politics in Britain* (Verso, 1989), *The Rise and Fall of Development Theory* (James Currey/Indiana University Press, 1996) and co-author (with Leo Panitch) of *The End of Parliamentary Socialism* (Verso, 1997). He is Emeritus Professor of Politics at Queens University (Kingston, Ontario) and a contributor to *New Left Review*.

THOMAS MEYER is Professor of Political Science at the University of Dortmund. He is the author of *What Remains of Socialism* (1990), *Die Transformation des Politischen* (1994) and *Fundamentalismus. Aufstand gegen die Moderne* (1994). He is Director of the Political Academy of the Friedrich-Ebert Stiftung, and drafted the Declaration of Principles of the Socialist International (1989) and the Berlin Programme of the SPD (1989). He is Vice-chair of the Basic Values Commission of the SPD.

GIULIO SAPELLI is Professor of Economic History and Cultural Analysis at the State University of Milan, Director of the Feltrinelli Foundation and President of the Centre for the History of Enterprise. His recent publications include *Economia, tecnologia e direzione d'azienda in Italia* (Einaudi, 1994), *Cleptocrazia* (Feltrinelli, 1995) and *Southern Europe since 1945: Tradition and Modernity in Portugal, Spain, Italy, Greece and Turkey* (Longman, 1996).

DONALD SASSOON is the author of *One Hundred Years of Socialism: The West European Left in the Twentieth Century* (I.B.Tauris, 1996 and Fontana paperback, 1997), which was awarded the 1996 Deutscher Memorial Prize. The second revised edition of his *Contemporary Italy* (Longman) was published in 1997. He teaches history at Queen Mary and Westfield College, University of London.

Introduction

DONALD SASSOON

The fall of the Berlin Wall and the subsequent collapse of the USSR and of the communist system coincided with the development of two contrasting tendencies. The first was directly connected to post-communism: a conspicuous increase in political unpredictability – the uncertainty principle. The second had begun before the end of communism: a pronounced trend towards homogeneity – the convergence principle.

The old bipolar world, though always in precarious equilibrium, was a relatively well-regulated system: spheres of influence, different social systems in East and West, military alliances, controlled competition between the two sides, low level of conflict between the protagonists in the two camps, a steady increase in material wealth favouring the western camp (where voters required governments to deliver prosperity) – all contributed the informal rules for the coexistence between East and West. Regular and manageable crises in both camps provided indispensable stimuli for constant yet controlled development. The collapse of this world order has created a climate of unprecedented uncertainty whose most unstable variable is the fate of the Russian Federation and the other members of the Commonwealth of Independent States. No new security system has evolved to guarantee the continuing coexistence of the former opponents. The victory of Boris Yeltsin in the 1996 presidential elections did not bring stability. It is not clear whether the Chechnya conflict is only the harbinger of further fragmentation or a local difficulty which sensible politicians will eventually be able to resolve or at least to contain; a sort of Russian version of the Irish 'Troubles'. No consensus has emerged on the economic prospects confronting the Russian Federation and the other post-USSR states. The optimists assure us that an economic miracle is round the corner, poised to deliver capitalist prosperity. The pessimists contemplate a further aggravation of the tragedy which has plagued the Russian people for generations: the transition from an illiberal and often despotic form of socialism to a 'jungle' capitalism where a few quasi-gangsters enrich themselves at the expense of the overwhelming majority. Though the first scenario is unquestionably and infinitely preferable to the second, the consequences of either are equally unfathomable. Would a prosperous and competitive Russia constitute a further threat to the economic stability of the West, as its large resources, its skilled population and high level of literacy might suggest? Would an impoverished Russia give rise to dangerous and uncontrollable forms of nationalism, forcing the West into a second Cold War, a new iron curtain and an arms race more unpredictable than the first?

The whole matter grows even more complex if we bring other variables into the equation: from the effects of global 'liberalization' and the accompanying dangers of protectionism, the future of the Asian economies (especially that of China), the population explosion and the ecological crisis, to the emergence of masses of potential economic refugees out of the desperate predicament endured by most of Africa, and much else besides.

Compared to such momentous changes, the prospects for Europe may appear relatively tranquil and serene. Yet the fate of Russia – still 'a riddle wrapped in a mystery inside an enigma' (Churchill) – impinges on Europe's future more than on that of any other region. No one can predict with confidence whether monetary union and expansion will reinforce or undermine the European Union.

Yet the strength of the principle of convergence should not be underestimated. The breakdown of communism has eliminated the most influential non-capitalist model of economic development which was particularly appealing to less developed countries deprived of native capitalism. Everyone is, in some shape or other, openly or covertly, a signed-up member of the capitalist club. At this time, the last 20 years have witnessed the effective termination of the main European model of capitalist regulation: 'national Keynesianism'. This consisted in the assumption that national economic policy could be relatively effective in determining the main economic variables of the nation-state: the balance of payments, interest rates, prices, growth and employment. The consequence of this double collapse is the extraordinary ideological success of the proponents of the liberalization of market forces. Irrespective of separate national traditions, economic particularities, contrasting social structures and cultural differences, the nations of the world are being enjoined to deregulate labour markets, to lower or eliminate tariffs, to privatize state property, to eliminate subsidies and, in general, to let market forces operate with as few impediments as possible. An international communication system, largely originating in the West but global in its reach, envelops the entire planet. Consumption patterns are rapidly internationalized: similar fast-food outlets, items of fashion and television programmes are now available in New Delhi, Tokyo, Rome, Paris, Moscow and Cairo. Those who do not have them, want them. Contrary to what post-modernist theorists appear to preach, a 'grand narrative' of global proportion, unequalled in earlier times, has established itself. As Marx had predicted more than a century ago, capitalism has become a worldwide system. Resurgent or new forms of nationalism or the rise of different varieties of religious fundamentalism appear as local reactions rather than as international countervailing forces.

The European Left – and by this I mean the mainstream socialist, social-democratic and labour parties, including the former communist parties – shares the central defining features of this turmoil. It too endures the consequences of the uncertainty principle. It can no longer rely on theoretical instruments, such as Marxism or Keynesianism, enabling it to find a way out of the present impasse. The point Colin Leys makes in his contribution, that Tony Blair's 'New Labour Party' cannot rely on the contribution of noticeably original or creative thinkers (one thinks of Keynes or Beveridge) could be made of the rest of the European Left. Marxism – of great value as an explanatory theory, of little service as a guide to public policy – was effectively discarded either long ago (for example, by the German SPD and the Swedish SAP) or in the 1970s (either openly, as with the Spanish PSOE, or in practice, as with the Italian PCI), or very recently (the post-communism of eastern and central Europe). In the case of the Labour Party, Marxism, of course, had always been of minor importance. In any case, it never provided the socialist parties of western Europe with any significant practical counsel in government. More significant has been the fall from favour of the real guide of western European socialists in power: Keynesianism – so insubstantial as an analysis of capitalism yet so effective, and for so long, in managing it.

Deprived of their pathfinders, the parties of the Left have adopted, more or less overtly, a defensive strategy. Its basic coordinates are an acceptance that market forces can be regulated but not eliminated; that such regulation must often be coordinated with other countries; that the growth of public spending should be curbed; that the welfare state can be defended but not extended; that privatization may be unavoidable and, when it eradicates monopolies, desirable; that equality, though still appealing as a goal, may be tempered by the need to preserve incentives and competition; that the power of international financial institutions – and, above all, of financial markets – may be contained, if at all, only by international agreement and not by unilateral state policies. Further indicators of political convergence are the generally positive attitude of the Left towards European integration – at least compared to the position of many of their opponents on the Right – a dilution of their previous commitment to state centralism and, consequently, a significant acceptance of the values of devolving power.

Of course, differences remain. Political parties continue to respond overwhelmingly to a national electorate. They are inevitably constrained by the weight of their own traditions and those of their own countries. They react to the persisting differences in the levels of development and structural characteristics of their respective economies. The size of the working class may have been shrinking everywhere, but the rate of de-industrialization is highly uneven: it is far higher in Sweden and in the UK than in Germany or Austria; Greece is more inflation-prone than Germany; unemployment in Spain is far higher than everywhere else; inward and outward investment ranks highest in Britain as does resistance to taxation. Opposition to cuts in welfare spending is more significant in France and Germany (where, however, it takes different forms) than in Britain. Social indicators suggest other differences: a higher rate of divorce and family break-ups in Britain; a lower demographic growth in Italy, Greece and Spain; a lower female participation in the labour force in Holland; more part-time female work (and concentrated among the less skilled) in Britain than in France. Ecology plays a far more important role in politics in Germany and Sweden than in France or Spain. Feminism has greater strength in western than in eastern Europe.

Yet there is no denying that the principle of convergence has accelerated with ever greater momentum in the years since the end of the Cold War. Before 1989 it would have been perfectly permissible to divide the parties of the Left in Europe into three large 'families'.

The first, quite distinct from the other two, was made up of the communist parties of the so-called socialist camp of eastern and central Europe. They shared with the Left in western Europe some generic features: a commitment to social equality and a disdain for market forces with the consequent assumption that states did better than markets especially in health and education. The differences – above all in the domain of democracy and civil liberties – are too obvious and well mapped out to warrant further elaboration.

The second 'family' consisted of the 'northern' social-democratic parties, with those of the Scandinavian countries offering the most celebrated examples. At the cost of stretching the idea of 'North' unduly – in politics, geography should not be taken too seriously – one should also include in the northern model the Austrian and German social democratic parties as well as the Labour parties of Holland and Britain and, perhaps, the Belgian socialists. All these parties came to power, usually in coalition, in relatively well-developed capitalist countries. Their task was not the modernization of capitalism but its management and the proper distribution of the wealth resulting from its growth. Most of them, especially the Swedish, German and Austrian, were strong, working-class-based parties with a large membership. Their fundamental aims were full employment and the establishment of a sturdy welfare state.

In the third category we find the socialist parties of southern Europe. Their main characteristic, especially evident in the instances of Spain, Portugal and Greece, was that their principal objective was modernization and the development of welfare policies where none or few existed previously. Because they came to power after a long period of dictatorship (Spain, Portugal) or quasi-democracy followed by military rule (Greece), these parties also played an important role in the consolidation of democracy. Having entered government after the mid-

1970s, when the '30 glorious years' of post-war capitalist development
had come to an end, they were not able to enjoy the full fruits of
capitalist prosperity, but had to prioritize economic development.

Italy sits somewhat uneasily in this category, its own transition to
democracy having been achieved long ago, as a consequence of the end
of the Second World War. By the mid-1970s, Italy was already, to all
intents and purposes, a fully fledged member of the club of the most
advanced countries. Yet the strength of the theme of modernization in
the campaigning rhetoric of its left-wing parties (both the PCI and the
PSI) was the tell-tale sign that the country always considered itself
somewhat of a laggard with respect to the more advanced 'North'.
Furthermore, the two parties of the Italian Left have never been
together in power since the break-up of the post-war National Unity
government (1947). The French Left – which never considered itself
backward – exhibited another deviation from the 'southern paradigm'.
Yet it too did not really rule until the mid-1980s and – though France
was and is one of the richest countries in Europe – it too insisted that
its task was the modernization of a relatively backward form of capitalism. In all these 'southern' instances, politics exhibited a further special
feature: the existence of a culture of clienteles connected to faction
leaders (a strong feature of the Spanish and Greek Left, but far less
pronounced in the case of the PCI or the French socialists). Furthermore, though instances of political corruption and related financial
scandals have not spared the Nordic polities (especially Germany and
Austria and, to a lesser extent, Britain), they acquired a special significance in Greece and Spain and, above all, in Italy. Finally, we could
include among the characteristics of southern socialism the weakness of
employees' associations in terms of the percentage of workers belonging
to trade unions.

Like all taxonomies, this distinction between 'state socialism' in the
East, 'classic' social democracy in the North and a 'modernizing
socialism' in the South subsumes strong internal differences, from the
far greater importance of nationalism and populism in Greece compared
with Spain, to the hegemonic dominance of the social democrats in
post-war Sweden and Austria – almost always in power in the 45 years
from the end of the Second World War to the end of communism,
compared with the 17 years of the Labour Party and the 16 years of the

SPD. Nevertheless, these distinctions, though they have not entirely lost their validity, should now be contrasted to an unprecedented, Europe-wide convergence of the parties of the Left.

The state socialist parties of eastern Europe have disappeared. In their stead, post-communist parties, more or less well entrenched in their respective countries, have redefined themselves as social-democratic parties. As Peter Gowan amply and convincingly illustrates in his chapter, the post-communist parties of Poland, Hungary, Bulgaria and Slovakia have embraced the new market economics with varying degrees of enthusiasm while trying to regulate market forces, sustaining employment and defending the welfare state. In foreign policy they all seek admission into the European Union and NATO – with differing prospects. In so doing they have put behind them, again with varying degrees of credibility, their communist past and come closer to the western models of social democracy. In the space of a few years, under the accelerating impact of the break-up of the Soviet system, the erst-while intransigent upholders of central planning and of *de facto* one-party states have adopted the historical stance of the heirs of the Second International, once denounced by Lenin as renegades and revisionists.

In western Europe, the gap between southern and northern socialism has decreased in relevance, especially since Portugal, Spain and Greece entered the world of modern West European politics. This great drive towards convergence occurred in two stages. During the first stage – in the mid-1970s – the remaining right-wing authoritarian regimes of Europe vanished without leaving behind them well-organized and poten-tially destabilizing extremist parties. During the second, subsequent stage, the main socialist parties of these three countries became parties of government (in the 1970s in Portugal, in the 1980s in Greece and Spain). Concurrently, in France, the first left-wing government in the country's history was elected to power and stayed in office for an unprecedented length of time. The Mollet and Mendès-France govern-ments of the 1950s had been short-lived affairs while the bulk of the Left (the PCF) had remained in opposition. The National Unity governments of 1944–47 were led from the centre or the centre-right. The Popular Front of 1936 was in office for less than a year. It was Mitterrand's great achievement (all the more startling as his credentials as a socialist were so disputable) to have marginalized the PCF and established the Parti socialiste as the main party of the Left. The creditable performance of Lionel Jospin in the 1995 presidential election, his subsequent popularity and success in 1997 signalled that the Socialist Party is not an ephemeral 'flash-party', as some had hoped and others feared.

Italy was late in this race towards convergence. Craxi was no Mitterrand and preferred to support a Christian Democratic Party in the throes of a terminal crisis rather than courageously joining forces with a PCI rapidly proceeding towards social democracy. The end of the Italian anomaly required the demolition of the PSI. Once this had taken place (thanks to the unintended collaboration of magistrates and northern separatists), it became possible to spin the web which would produce for the first time in Italy, via a complicated system of deals and agreements, a government where the Left had the greatest weight.

The Nordic social democracies – so proud of their hegemonic positions and their undoubted achievements – likewise suffered a process of convergence. The jewel of their crown, full employment, was lost in the North too. In social-democratic Sweden, where, as late as 1990, unemployment levels of 3 per cent were considered scandalous and unbearable, there were, by the end of 1996, proportionately more jobless than in Conservative Britain. The continuing expansion of their welfare state came to a halt; the protection of existing positions became the watchword of the Left.

This reduced the welfare gap between North and South. Though the differences are still very significant, the improvements in welfare provisions in Spain under González and in Greece under PASOK are undeniable – as Paul Kennedy and Vassilis Fouskas show in their respective contributions.

Further convergence has been achieved under the rubric of 'Europeanization'. As recently as the early 1980s, Papandreou's Greece regarded itself as an anti-imperialist country on the margins of Europe; PASOK's socialist ideology was a blend of nationalism and populism profoundly hostile to European Union and NATO. Under Costas Simitis (but the changes had preceded him), PASOK has wholeheartedly accepted that Greece has no role outside Europe. More generally, the European Union has become the most visible instance of the ever-closer policies of the European Left. All the post-communist socialist parties of eastern and central Europe want to join the Union which they see as offering them security and the vision of a prosperous future. In the West, socialist parties which had been for so long reluctant to enlist in the European project changed their positions and applied to join, successfully in the case of the Austrians, Finns and Swedes, unsuccessfully in the case of the Norwegians. Parties which have for so long been lukewarm Europeanist, such as the British Labour Party, though still far from out-and-out euro-enthusiasts, have repositioned themselves — at least domestically — among the integrationists.

Wider continental convergence has been further facilitated by the decline in intra-left rivalries in countries where the mainstream socialist parties faced a more radical competitor to their Left — often but not always a communist party. Cooperation between the parties of the Left has become more frequent: social democrats frequently cooperate with the Socialist People's Parties in Denmark and Norway, with the post-communist parties in Sweden and Finland or with the Greens in Germany. In Spain, France and Greece, the less cooperative communist parties — so much weaker than the socialists — are often ignored. The most important change, however, has occurred in Italy. Until the explosion of the Tangentopoli scandals, some predicted that the Italian Socialist Party would eventually overtake the PCI/PDS and that the latter would simply become a small, less effective and ghettoized party. The end of communism provided Craxi's PSI with the terrain for a massive ideological victory. But, as Giulio Sapelli acutely demonstrates in his chapter, the PSI missed its chance well before the explosion of the scandals. By the time the grounds had been cleared of the un-lamented party of Bettino Craxi, the PDS took over what should have been the historical function of the PSI. It became the rallying point for a wider realignment of Italian politics, leading, eventually, to the formation of the centre-left government of Romano Prodi. The recalcitrant communists — those unwilling to accept a change in the party's name survived, as Rifondazione comunista, to become Italy's equivalent of the Nordic radical left: not a pristine anti-system party but a responsible, though not docile, organization offering critical support to the Prodi government. The dream of the leader of the PDS, Massimo D'Alema, namely the transformation of Italy into a 'normal country', is not far from being fulfilled — however unexciting this prospect may be to those who longed for a more ambitious transmutation.

In the early 1980s the British Labour Party had shifted well to the Left, adopting a policy of wide-ranging nationalization, while becoming neutralist and pacifist, and profoundly hostile to the European Community. Its strategic framework implied the isolation of the country from growing European and global interdependence. As Colin Leys reminds us in his chapter, the first phase of this departure from a British national road to socialism occurred under Neil Kinnock. It was, however, after the electoral defeat in 1992 (its fourth) and a momentary lull under John Smith's brief tenure, that the Labour Party underwent a radical change in policies and ethos. Under Tony Blair's neo-revisionist leadership, the British Labour Party repositioned itself as a centre-left party. Britain had long been the only country in Europe where the party of the Left was – in terms of organization and image – the political expression of the trade union movement. This ceased to be the case. The historical ties with the trade unions have been so redefined that Blair could declare – albeit in an interview with the *Financial Times* (16 January 1997) – that his party has become 'pro-business'. The British Labour Party had also been the only European party preserving, if only in rhetoric, the aim of collective ownership as the final goal of the party; this too came to an end.

Less than ten years after the end of the communist system, the European Left, across both East and West, speaks with a consistency of language and tone unrivalled in its history. The contrast with the period between the creation of communist parties and their collapse after 1989 are obvious enough. But even in the years before 1917, the differences between the organized parties of the Left were glaring: in Britain a powerful trade union movement was still torn between supporting a reformist Liberal Party and a nascent Labour Party taking its first faltering steps. In Germany a mighty, exceedingly well-organized Marxist social-democratic party had constructed a real state within a state while expecting the terminal crisis of capitalism. In much of the Balkans barely existing organizations of leaders without followers were struggling to emerge from what were still largely agrarian societies. In Spain and, to a lesser extent, in Italy the vestiges of anarchism still held sway over important sections of the working class. In France it was only in 1905 that a socialist party emerged, united in name yet deeply fractured between the Jacobin workerists of Jules Guesde (whose Marxism would have prompted Karl Marx to declare that he was not a Marxist) and the gradualism of Jean Jaurès.

The present convergence is due only in part to the break-up of the communist system. As some of the contributors point out, there is little evidence that the fall of the Berlin Wall directly affected the socialist parties, or contributed, significantly, to delegitimize their policies. Leaving aside, for obvious reasons, the former communist parties, the only social-democratic party which was seriously affected was the SPD – as Thomas Meyer explains. In Spain the momentous events of 1989 were welcomed by the PSOE, but they had little direct effect on the party which had dropped its Marxist label more than a decade earlier. Nor, as Paul Kennedy points out, did the PSOE became 'less socialist': it achieved more in the field of welfare provision during its final two terms in office than it did between 1982 and 1989. In Britain, Labour neo-revisionism had started in the mid-1980s. Greece has been affected profoundly, but for geo-political rather than ideological reasons. As Fouskas explains in his wide-ranging chapter, the fragmentation of Yugoslavia has unleashed a war on Greece's doorstep and led to the rise of a new Macedonian question, while the end of communism in Albania has led to an unprecedented flow of illegal immigration into Greece. The transformation of Balkan politics has forced Greece to review its position: it is no longer the only capitalist country in the Balkans and the influence of Turkey is likely to expand not only towards the Balkans but also towards the former southern republics of the USSR.

Thus the end of the Cold War – a complex and far-reaching turning-point in contemporary history – has had intricate and differentiated effects on the politics of the continent. Its contribution to convergence – especially the convergence between the Left in the East and the West – should not be under-estimated. Nevertheless, it would be one-sided to focus exclusively on this aspect. Globalization, real or perceived, has been the other great force towards convergence. It is undeniable that capitalist globalization has contributed significantly to a realignment of the European Left away from its traditional terrain: a 'national' social democracy based on a welfare state and full employment.

The new pan-European Left has accepted the constraints of the new global capitalism. How far these constraints are over-estimated – as Colin Leys suggests has been the case with the Labour Party – will be, no doubt, at the centre of future debates. In the meantime the perception of globalization has brought about momentous changes. As François Hincker explains, such a perception constituted a fundamental cultural break with the republican traditions of French socialism. Its Jacobinism – shared by the Gaullists – suggested that the French were really in charge of France. The realization that this may no longer be the case is reshaping the politics of the country.

In Britain, as Colin Leys argues, the perception of the importance of globalization led to an insistence that it was necessary to be 'realistic'. 'Keynesianism in one country' was now impossible. Corporate taxation and regulatory burdens should be no higher than elsewhere, and wage levels should be kept down to compensate for lower productivity. Thus the policy options open to the party became extremely narrow. Perhaps the Blair-led Labour government will develop a self-confidence enabling it to gauge with some accuracy the effective room for manoeuvre.

Nevertheless, there is no denying that the perception of globalization has brought convergence not only to the Left but also between Left and Right, and largely and unavoidably on the terms set by the Right. Such convergence, in reality, had existed before: for most of the 1950s and the 1960s, Left and Right (the democratic constitutional Right, not the extreme Right) shared common values – full employment and the welfare state. In the 1970s there was a widespread acceptance (across the political spectrum) that it was not possible to rule a country without the participation of the employees' organizations. In Greece (see Fouskas' chapter) New Democracy expanded the state and increased public spending. PASOK's apparent 'leftism' was facilitated by a 'Right' governing from the centre-left.

By the 1990s the situation had changed radically. The mood on the Left had become more pessimistic, a predicament vaguely reminiscent of the defensive strategies adopted in the 1930s. In the East, as Peter Gowan shows, the post-communists parties were seen to offer the best protection against unavoidable deregulation, market forces and globalism.

They may or may not succeed, but the point is that they face an agonizing dilemma, illustrated by Giulio Sapelli in his chapter on Italy. Will it be possible to pursue the financial restructuring required by the international community while defending the welfare state and promoting the renewal of industrial growth?

Europe may have become the great hope of the Left, but the Maastricht convergence criteria have imposed considerable difficulties which may rebound unfavourably on Europeanism and damage the Left in member countries. A resurgence of nationalism in the continent would favour the Right far more than the Left. In eastern Europe, the post-communists (as Peter Gowan explains) are increasingly identified with anti-nationalism. In Greece (see Fouskas), PASOK under Simitis has abandoned the nationalism of Papandreou. In Italy, where euro-enthusiasm is still high, it is the Right of Berlusconi and Fini which is the least Europeanist. In France, anti-EU sentiments are largely confined to the Right. In Britain, the stronghold of anti-Europeanism is in the Conservative Party. In Spain (as Kennedy points out), in the run-up to the 1996 election it was the conservative Partido Popular which adopted a cautious attitude towards European integration (promptly reversed after their electoral victory – the Right too can find itself constrained). Those on the Left who are still reluctant to sign up to fully fledged integration tend to be on the 'far' Left; these include the Socialist People's Parties in Norway and Denmark, the communists in Greece, Spain and France, and the Campaign Group of MPs inside the Labour Party.

Paradoxically, the Europeanism of the Left – though it cannot be taken for granted – appears to favour an unexpected reversal of traditional alliances. Those key sections of European and international capitalism which favour integrationist policies appear increasingly dismayed at the Right's nationalism and lack of enthusiasm for Europe. Nowhere is this more visible than in Italy where, with an almost audible sigh of relief, the 'markets' welcomed the 1996 victory of the Left in the way they knew best: the lira bounced back against the Deutsche Mark and the Milan Stock Exchange shot up. A cautious welcome to Simitis was expressed in Greece by bankers and employers. In Britain and Spain it can no longer be assumed that entrepreneurs will automatically line up against the Left. In Italy, as in the former communist states, it is the post-communists who are endeavouring to stabilize their countries; it is the Right which is volatile. As Gowan writes: 'Paradoxically, economic growth and the wide base of popular support for a gradual transformation towards a western-oriented national capitalism seems to offer the most secure prospects for the development of a

centre-left in a fairly stable political context.' Whether this signals a
new compromise between the Left and capitalism is too early to tell.

So convergence within the Left is paralleled by convergence between
the Left and the Right. To some extent this is the unavoidable effect of
wider interdependence. If national politics is increasingly constrained
by a globalized economy, it is hardly surprising if these constraints force
both sides towards similar policies. Widespread unemployment general-
izes fiscal crises. The expansion of money markets reduces control over
exchange rates for both Left and Right. Nevertheless, convergence is
also facilitated by the increasing homogeneity of the communication
systems and, above all, by the mass media. When radio and television
were less influential, the political parties of the Left relied on their own
organization and their own sub-culture to carry their messages. Even
during electoral campaigns a relatively sophisticated message could be
handed down from leaders to followers who would, in turn, carry the
message to their neighbourhoods and workplaces, adapting it to specific
audiences. In the 1950s socialist and communist leaders could address
directly large meetings of loyal followers in open squares or large halls,
and, at length, explain party policies using a relatively select language.
Now, most political messages are filtered through a communication
system. Leaders do not speak directly to their loyal followers, but to a
much larger and less attentive audience. They compete with sit-coms,
films, soap operas. The disadvantage is that the politicians' message
must be short and succinct; what has become known as the 'sound-bite'.
It acquires the pattern of a commercial advert: a slogan selling a political
product. As the political products are similar (prosperity, no inflation,
low taxes, good public services and so on), the politicians tend to sound
the same. As it is easier for top leaders to obtain access to the media,
there is a marked concentration of interest in personalities. In turn the
leaders are often selected on the basis of their ability to perform adequately on television. There is no time for democratic consultation of
the membership when decisions must be taken on the spot. Reactions
to the policies of one's opponent must be instantaneous. This leads to
an enormous concentration of decision-making power in the hands of
the leader. Major policies – once often discussed widely by the party's
senior leaders – are now announced on television by leaders thus able,
in practice, to coerce their parties into accepting the new line. Occhetto's

proposal to change the name of the party and Blair's decision to campaign for the effective removal of Clause 4 from the party programme, though technically announced to party activists, were in fact media events. Disagreement with the decision of the leader would now weaken the party as a whole and risk electoral catastrophe. It is in the Labour Party that this process has gone the farthest. As Colin Leys points out, in the months preceding the May 1997 general election, all that journalists wanted to know was what Blair thought. They took it for granted that if he disagreed with previous conference decisions, these could no longer be seriously considered as party policy. Even where some form of democratic centralism prevailed, it has now been substituted by a media-directed centralism. This has particularly affected political parties whose complex organization makes it difficult to provide the façade of unity required by the media – as is the case with the SPD. Thomas Meyer examines this problem thoroughly and persuasively. The SPD had spent several years preparing its new Basic Programme (Berlin, 1989) – the first since that of Bad Godesberg – aimed at providing the party with a framework for united action. The Berlin Programme was not the outcome of the victory of one section of the party over another, but the result of complex debates and discussions which involved the entire organization. The party, however, was handicapped by the existence of different centres of power: the party leader is usually not the candidate for Chancellor while the prime ministers of the SPD-led *Länder* are senior politicians who have to face the challenges of government, such as fiscal crises and the implementation of austerity policies. In this situation it is difficult to establish discipline and coordination. As leaders jostle for positions on television and engage in a war of soundbites, the complexities of the party programme go by the board. A similar problem was faced in Italy in 1994 when the Left did not have a candidate for office while the Right appeared united behind Berlusconi (and Berlusconi's fall from power was largely due to the fact that this unity did not extend to the Northern League). The chances of success of the centre-left increased when the Olive Tree appointed Romano Prodi as its leader. However, the situation will remain unstable because a conflict may well erupt within the coalition between Prodi and D'Alema (the leader of the largest party, the PDS) or between D'Alema and his rival within the PDS, the deputy prime minister Walter Veltroni.

The Labour Party had taken on board – far more than the other parties of the European Left – the lessons of how to manage the media. Colin Leys traces the Labour obsession with image-making to the period following the defeat of 1987. Since then, disagreements within the party have not emerged in spite of the rapid renewal of the party and the abandonment of many dearly held beliefs. The pay-off was a massive electoral victory for Tony Blair's 'New Labour'. The costs, if any, will not materialize for a while.

As the millennium approaches, the tocsin bell is far from tolling the death of the Left. The obituary of the French Left, prematurely composed after their massive defeat in 1993, has had to be scrapped after Lionel Jospin's decisive victory in the election of June 1997. Nowhere in western Europe are any of the main parties of the Left in danger of becoming permanently unelectable. In most of eastern and central Europe – with the significant exception of the Russian Federation and the other CIS countries – reconstructed socialist parties (the former communists) contend for power. As I write, socialist parties are in government, usually in coalition, in virtually all the countries of the European Union except for Spain, Ireland and Germany (where they are in power in a majority of *Länder*).

Of course, the policies of the parties of the Left are now dissociated from the radical perspective they once held – that of ending capitalism. But they are bereft of plans for social reorganization which could live up to the aspirations of their followers. Their aims are defensive: to protect the achievements of the past, to continue to improve social life under capitalism, to promote an ethos of cooperation and to enhance social and civil rights. At a time when capitalism appears triumphant, has no worldwide opponent and is poised to entangle 'all peoples in the net of the world-market' (Marx), such ambitions may not be as modest as they appear.

This convergence on the Left may provide an opportunity for unity of action which is unique in the history of the socialist movement. It is a convergence which is bound up, more than ever, with the future of European integration. Just as the rise of traditional social democracy could not be separated from the rise of the nation-state and the successes or failure of its national economy, the future of the Left will depend on the success or failure of the European Union.

I

The British Labour Party
since 1989

COLIN LEYS

By 1989 the British Labour Party was already far advanced in the most radical reconstruction it had undergone since its formation in 1900. In the general election of 1983, the party's vote had fallen to 27.6 per cent of the total cast, barely avoiding relegation to third place and the prospect of eventual elimination as a major political force. To avert this, its newly elected leader, Neil Kinnock, set in motion a dual process of transformation. First, he concentrated power in his own hands, at the expense of the party's grass-roots activists, whose pressure for a left-wing response to the crisis of the 1970s was seen as having been responsible for the 1983 defeat. Second, he used his enhanced power to jettison long-standing socialist policies seen as irretrievably unpopular with the voters. This process was overwhelmingly driven by the need for electoral recovery; it is not clear that the collapse of the east European and Soviet regimes, culminating in 1989–90, played any significant part in the process, except by reinforcing the general feeling that socialism everywhere had been discredited.

In 1989 the reform process reached one of its first defining moments, when the party's annual conference endorsed the recommendations of a major Policy Review, launched by Kinnock following the party's third successive election defeat in 1987, to abandon three of Labour's most emblematic former policies (the restoration of trade union rights and immunities removed by Mrs Thatcher during the 1980s, the renationalization of recently privatised industries, and unilateral nuclear disarmament). Even more significant in the long run, however, were the organizational changes that had made this possible. In his determination to remove power from the hands of left-wing party activists, Kinnock laid the foundations of a new kind of party. Hitherto the Labour Members of Parliament constituted a parliamentary 'wing' of the wider party (the Parliamentary Labour Party or PLP), which enjoyed *de facto* authority but always had to secure support in the much wider extra-parliamentary organization, and especially in the highly decentralized trade union movement on which the party depended for both funds and the core of its electoral support. Now, however, Kinnock was building a party run by a professional elite overseen and directed by the office of the leader. He was enabled to do this by the increasingly desperate desire – not least on the part of the trade union leadership – to see the party return to power.

The key element in the new party apparatus was a team of professional media and campaign managers, organized in a new Campaigns and Communications Directorate and a Shadow Communications Agency. Party policy was increasingly determined on the basis of their judgements (derived from opinion polling and 'focus group' research) of what voters wanted. Although the party constitution still provided for an elaborate democratic policy-forming process, culminating in decisions made by majority votes at annual conferences, most significant policy decisions and new initiatives were now made in the front bench's new professional 'teams', the rest of the party being expected to acquiesce for the sake of unity. What increasingly prevailed, then, was what Eric Shaw calls a new political 'paradigm', derived from the discourse of marketing: policies came to be treated as products, selected so as to 'position' the party as advantageously as possible in relation to the voters' known attitudes and preferences.[1]

Of the many other developments that accompanied this far-reaching change, only one – the most fundamental – can be mentioned here.[2] This was the drive, which eventually proved surprisingly successful, to expand party membership and enfranchise it. The number of individual members rose from 280,000 in the mid-1980s to over 400,000 by October 1996 and they were now to vote (by postal ballot) for the selection of parliamentary candidates, for the election of the party leader and, finally, for the endorsement of general policy packages proposed by the leadership. This development, known as OMOV ('One Member One Vote'), did not just disempower the activists who had previously dominated local party decision-making (since they were the people who did the work and took the trouble to attend the meetings where votes were taken); it also involved a formal reduction in the weight of the votes cast by trade union representatives at party conferences, initially down to 70 per cent of the total, and later (once the party's individual membership had recovered to more than 300,000) to 50 per cent; this became operational at the party's 1996 conference. By this time, 'sources close to the leadership' (that is, party spin-doctors) were speculating about the future abolition of the party–trade-union link, with state funding for parties – a measure known to have the support of the leader, Tony Blair – making up for the 50 per cent of party funding that the unions still provided. What was emerging was a mass party of largely inactive individual members having a plebiscitary, rather than any organic, relationship with a leadership cadre of professional politicians.

In 1992, however, notwithstanding all these changes, the party suffered its fourth consecutive election defeat. Kinnock resigned and was replaced by John Smith, who in effect called a halt in the 'moderniza-tion' process. Under his leadership, the only significant change was the final extension of OMOV to the choosing of parliamentary candidates and party leaders. In 1994 Smith died of a heart attack and was replaced by the leading modernizer, Tony Blair, and the trajectory of the Kinnock years was resumed.

Although the modernizers around Blair saw themselves as carrying forward Kinnock's organizational initiatives, in terms of ideology they represented something new. Kinnock had wanted to make the party electable, but with his background in the Welsh Labour movement he never wholly abandoned the idea that capitalism was an unjust *system*, which should some day – however distant – be replaced by socialism. Tony Blair, by contrast, coming from a Conservative family background and a public school, saw socialism only as a set of values to be applied *within* capitalism (a distinction Blair himself sometimes signalled by inserting a hyphen in the word 'social-ism'). In his thinking, capitalism was inevitable; and if Labour – now effectively renamed 'New Labour' by the modernizers – wanted to be the dominant party of government it had, as he told Japanese business leaders in Tokyo, to be seen as 'the party of business'.[3]

What serious meaning – if any – 'socialism' conceived in these terms may have, is the central question which this chapter must try to answer. But before examining the policies that have actually flowed from the modernizers' logic, three general factors that govern it need to be grasped: the way policy is now made, the tactical and strategic considerations that underlie it, and the intellectual context on which it draws.

The policy-making process

In the past, when a new leader assumed office, the attention of the media was automatically focused on how far his known policy preferences coincided with the positions recently adopted by the party's annual conferences. In Blair's case, all that journalists wanted to know was what he thought. They took it for granted that if he disagreed with previous conference decisions, these could no longer be seriously considered to be party policy. Thus when, for example, Blair expressed the view that Regional Assemblies should be established in England only if they were supported by a majority of the voters in each region, this effectively superseded Labour's former commitment to introduce them by a simple Act of Parliament. Similarly, the party's commitment to restore elected local government control over schools which had 'opted out' of it under the Conservatives' legislation was abandoned after internal discussions between the leader and the party's 'shadow' education minister; they were to keep their opted-out status, but with a change of name ('foundation schools'). Many other policy commitments – such as the introduction of a minimum wage, the abolition of General Practitioner 'fundholding' within the National Health Service, the creation of a Scottish Parliament with power to raise and spend taxes and the restoration of a 'publicly owned' railway system – were significantly diluted in speeches by Blair and his front-bench colleagues. Lists of policy commitments abandoned or significantly modified under Blair's leadership featured regularly in the press, and few of the changes resulted from debates at party conferences. They were often announced first in the media, which could then be relied upon to treat any critical reactions within the party as evidence of a 'split', making opposition difficult.

As a result, policy change was driven forward by Blair and his closest colleagues with only 'regular and ineffectual spasms of Old Labour discontent'.[4] For example, the unions complained strongly about Blair's refusal to set a specific figure for the minimum wage which the party was committed to introduce (as well they might, given that the party's commitment to a minimum wage had been a quid pro quo for their accepting the party's earlier decision not to restore the legal immunities that had been stripped from them during the 1980s). Roy Hattersley, the former deputy leader under Kinnock, complained bitterly about David Blunkett's decision, as shadow education minister, to leave the grant-maintained schools outside Local Education Authority control, and his failure to give unambiguous assurances that they would not be allowed to pick and choose pupils for admission. Alan Simpson, the secretary of the Socialist Campaign Group of left-wing Labour MPs, protested against the leadership's apparent willingness to entertain the possibility of Britain joining the planned European Monetary Union without a prior democratization of the EU's political structures. But in effect all these remained, or became, 'New Labour' policies.

Tactics and strategy

Four main strategic ideas have governed the policy thinking of 'New Labour.'

The first was that the next election had to be won, both to save the country from a fresh instalment of neo-liberalism, and to avert the real risk – after so long in opposition – of the collapse of Labour's far from cohesive coalition of social forces. This meant catering to the voters' existing ideas, rather than seeking to build support for new ones; moreover, the electorally crucial ideas were those of voters who had to be won back to Labour, not those of voters who had suffered most under Conservative rule, few of whom were likely to vote for any other party.

Second, voters' preferences have been shaped not only by 20 years of new Right propaganda, but also by profound changes in the real world. People no longer identify themselves primarily in terms of social classes or as producers, the workforce is no longer predominantly male, jobs are no longer permanent or secure at any level, the state is no longer regarded as a benign or reliable ally through life's vicissitudes. 'New Labour' policies must reflect these realities.

Third, today's media – even radio and television, which are supposed to be politically neutral – make it hard for new policies to be appropriately propounded and rationally debated; as Labour's leading media expert puts it, 'politicians' ability to make a persuasive case ... is much diminished because of the limitations of the thirty-second soundbite, repeated by a dozen or more different channels and news bulletins in a single day', while the overwhelmingly right-wing tabloid press systematically misrepresents everything Labour says.[5] Thus, giving all issues the best media 'spin' is an electoral necessity, and this means keeping tight control over all policy pronouncements.

Fourth, the aim must be to win at least two successive elections, so that long-term policies, such as those concerning education and training, have time to bear fruit. This means that Labour must win acceptance by capital as a suitable, and if possible even a preferred, governing party, so that investment will be forthcoming to support the growth on which everything else depends. And this in turn means being 'realistic' about the constraints imposed by globalization, such as the impossibility of 'Keynesianism in one country', the need to keep corporate taxation and regulatory burdens no higher than elsewhere, and the need to keep British wage levels down to compensate for lower productivity.

These electoral orientations clearly limited the policy options open to the party extremely narrowly; but it was a hallmark of the modernizers' thinking that they must, in the last analysis, be paramount. To think otherwise was dangerous self-indulgence.

The intellectual context

Although the evolution of Labour ideology and policy under Blair was begun under Kinnock's leadership, there are significant differences. There is a different rhetoric, symbolized by the 'New Labour' label adopted by the Blair leadership (in imitation of Bill Clinton's self-description as a 'New Democrat'), and it has different intellectual roots.

There were probably fewer significant intellectuals in the Blair leadership team than at any previous time in the party's history; people of the independent intellectual authority of Richard Crossman, Tony Crosland or Tony Benn were conspicuous by their absence. Nor were there any noticeably original or creative thinkers outside the ranks of the leadership to whom New Labour was obviously indebted. Instead, and symptomatically, there was a proliferation of new 'think tanks' of various kinds, pools of what might be called 'average' intellectual labour power, which aimed at bringing useful ideas from a wide variety of sources to the attention of the leadership, and doing 'policy relevant' research and reflection. By the late 1990s at least four such groups linked to New Labour were in business: the Institute of Public Policy Research (IPPR) and Charter 88 (both founded in 1988), Demos (established in 1993), and Nexus (formed in 1996).

Although it was formally a non-party institution, the IPPR's first chair (Tessa Blackstone) and first deputy director (Patricia Hewitt, fresh from supervising Labour's Policy Review) were both prominent Labour figures; its task was to provide Labour, following its purge of old policies, with a body of solidly researched policy documents. Its publications have a characteristic blend of 'realistic' (in the 'modernizers' sense) assumptions about the permanence of global capitalism, and well-documented analyses of economic and social problems and suggestions for their amelioration within the limits of the possible. David Miliband, the secretary to the IPPR's much publicized Borrie Commission on Social Justice, became head of research in the leader's office under Tony Blair, and was said to be an important link between the IPPR and New Labour; but if the fate of the Borrie Report is any guide (it was 'never seen again', in the words of an ironic song sung at Labour social gatherings), the IPPR should probably be seen more as a useful source of data (and of staff assistants to ministers in the Labour government) than of new ideas or principles likely to be adopted by New Labour.[6]

Even less central to New Labour's thinking, perhaps, is Charter 88, which focuses on issues of democratic rights and liberties. Its advocacy of proportional representation and a written constitution, both dear to the Liberal Democrats and both unpopular with Blair and his team, makes it a tainted source, although its substantial work on issues such as devolution and quangos has undoubtedly contributed both to New Labour thinking and to building public support for constitutional reform.[7]

The case is different with Demos, launched in early 1993. Geoff Mulgan, its founder-director, was formerly adviser to Gordon Brown, then Blair's shadow Chancellor of the Exchequer, and felt that 'public policy and political thinking' had 'become too short-term, partisan and out of touch'. Explaining the thinking behind the establishment of Demos, Mulgan wrote:

> In the past creative thinking often came from within the traditional institutions of parliament and parties, and from within the main political ideologies. But these are no longer able to keep up with the pace of change in society, the economy, technology and culture. Society has become more porous and complex, as old traditions and hierarchies have broken down. Demos is a response to this new situation. It draws on ideas from outside the political mainstream.[8]

Mulgan's work, reflected in the general output of Demos, has certain distinctive features. One is an almost complete lack of serious attention to political economy, which he regards as a 'weak' field.[9] The result is utopianism, though this is presented, paradoxically, as 'realism'. The question posed is predominantly one of what to do about various trends that are inexorably working themselves out through the dynamics of modern capitalism and the technological changes it brings – this is the 'realism' part. What is utopian is that no particular constraints accompany the options considered, and no agents of change are specified. Second, there is a constant stress on complexity, differentiation, pluralism and choice. Partly this is code for abandoning analysis in terms of classes; partly it seems to be a post-modern embrace of difference and particularity (which goes with a rejection of 'grand narratives', of which critical political economy is one). Whatever its sources, the result is a dramatic eclecticism. The topics, concepts, analyses and perceptions that Mulgan draws from so many diverse fields are not brought into any kind of unity, but simply reappear in kaleidoscopically changing rearrangements. A third characteristic of Mulgan's work is a fascination with the new. For him, what is wrong with past socialist thought is above all that it is 'out of touch' with the 'pace of change'; being 'in touch' is the supreme virtue, and it is mainly found in the younger generation – another recurring theme in New Labour rhetoric.

The precise relationship of Mulgan's and Demos's work to the thinking of Tony Blair is not known; although Mulgan enjoyed considerable access to Blair, it seems more likely that there is an affinity between their thinking than that Mulgan has been a significant influence. At all events these characteristics – utopianism, eclecticism (or what Henry Porter has called the 'cinemascopic' quality of Blair's rhetoric), and a constant stress on the 'new' – are very marked features of his speeches too.[10]

Nexus, the fourth potential source of New Labour thinking to be considered here, is in some ways the most characteristic. Founded early in 1996 following a seminar arranged by the New Labour journal, *Renewal*, at which Blair met with some eighty intellectual sympathizers, it consisted essentially of a register (or data base, in Nexus's terminology) of about 1,000 individuals who responded to a call to pool their expertise.[11] The idea was for them to work in groups, meeting from time to time in seminars or conferences, but especially exchanging ideas and working papers on the Internet.

It remained to be seen how far such 'networking' would yield useful answers to such questions as, 'What version of equality does the Left now espouse, if any?'; or, 'The centre-left stands urgently in need of a new organising ideal – a working model of the kind of society it aspires to create. Can the notion of a "stakeholder society" fill the gap?'[12] What was significant was that such crucial questions were seen as quite open (and as capable of being answered by such means). Nexus was perhaps most interesting as an index of the extent to which New Labour, having distanced itself from most of Labour's 'traditional intellectuals' (now dismissed as 'old Labour'), had few deep intellectual foundations of any kind.

New Labour's intellectual limitations were, however, treated with remarkable indulgence by most political commentators; whether because they were impressed by Blair's rhetoric, or because they tacitly yearned for a change of government, or even (in some cases) hoped to influence it, is impossible to say. They were perhaps also affected by New Labour's heavy investment in media management. Peter Mandelson, in his role as director of the party's Campaigns and Communications Directorate in the late 1980s, had been Labour's answer to Mrs Thatcher's Press Secretary Bernard Ingham, tirelessly 'managing' news and tempting, cajoling or bullying journalists and editors to give favourable treatment to the Labour leadership, and he resumed this role (though quasi-informally) when Blair replaced Smith as leader in 1994.

A distinctive aspect of Mandelson's thinking – and one that seems likely to have contributed significantly to his intense unpopularity within the Labour Party – was that he accepted the electoral logic of social democracy in the age of global capitalism with a consistency and whole-heartedness of which most Labour MPs, let alone rank and file members, were incapable. He took it as given that globalization imposes very severe limits on all social and economic policies, so that the only ones worth promoting are those that capital – 'the market' – will accept; and he included in this the power of the increasingly globally owned media, and was determined to do whatever it took – including getting Blair to make his highly symbolic visit to the 1995 annual meeting in Australia of Murdoch's worldwide media executives – to win whatever political leeway this situation afforded (such as a less venomously hostile treatment than was given to Kinnock by the 37 per cent of British national newspaper circulation controlled by Murdoch – a strategy that was richly rewarded when in March 1997 Rupert Murdoch instructed the editor of the *Sun* to switch its electoral support to Labour). In his view, to do otherwise was sentimental self-indulgence which the party could not afford; his notorious alleged remarks about the party conference or the unions being dispensable were deliberate provocations to those who resist this logic. It is a logic that Blair clearly accepted, however much more diplomatic his public pronouncements were.

Mandelson had a very close personal relationship with Blair, and hence came to play an exceptionally powerful role in policy-making, which makes his 1996 book (co-written with Roger Liddle), *The Blair Revolution: Can New Labour Deliver?*, deserving of some attention.[13] While not a work of path-breaking originality, the book's case for New Labour as the vehicle of a viable philosophy of government was the most ambitious yet attempted, and far from incoherent. Its central thesis was that a new kind of social solidarity was needed for success in global markets:

> What are we doing to prepare for inevitable change? Are we going to gain from it and create a sense of social order alongside it, as New Labour wants, or are we going to let change wash over us, with the result that we slip further backwards economically and disintegrate further socially? The Conservatives ... argue that their stress on deregulation and low labour costs is the only way to prepare Britain

for a competitive future. Their instinct is to accept the situation of increasing insecurity – even welcome it and further promote it – as the price of remaining competitive in the modern world. New Labour utterly rejects this counsel of despair. The more secure, more cohesive and, as a result, more equal our society, the better our chances of economic success. This is not to delude ourselves that wealth is some-how created by governments or society. Wealth comes from personal effort and entrepreneurial flair, exercised through companies that have found the right formula (which differs from business to business) ... But just as good companies can pull countries up, bad government policies can drag companies down.[13]

That is, by not educating and training the workforce adequately, main-taining employment levels and hence consumer demand, removing the causes of social alienation and crime, and so on. The relative coherence of the argument is evident in this passage; at the same time, so is its relative superficiality – for instance, the assertion that wealth comes only from 'personal effort and entrepreneurial flair', a formulation clearly aimed at signalling an unconditional renunciation of Labour's 'interventionist' past. Both features were reflected in the ideology of New Labour propounded by Blair and his front-bench team.

New Labour's ideology

Although Blair claimed in March 1995 that 'a clear reconstruction of a modern ideology' was 'near to completion', this was not evident from his speeches down to that time;[14] they showed the signs of having been 'developed' by speech-writers and 'souped up' by spin-doctors for pres-entation. His speech to the 1995 party conference was admittedly an extreme example (at least until his speech to the 1996 conference). Its peroration went like this:

I want us to be a young country again.
Young.
With a common purpose.
With ideals we cherish and live up to. Not resting on past glories.
Not fighting old battles.
Not sitting back, hand in mouth, concealing a yawn of cynicism, but
    ready for the day's challenge.
Ambitious.

Idealistic.
United.[15]

One of the key-words in Blair's emergent ideology would eventually
be 'stakeholder'.[16] Already in the speech cited above he had said: 'I
believe that you cannot create a responsible society unless everyone has
a stake in it', and went on to list a series of kinds of 'stake' which
people needed to have, such as housing security, education, a welfare
system that encourages independence. The concept of having a stake
was thus already present, but as a general prerequisite of people feeling
responsible for their role in society; in other words, it was an ethical
concept, though Blair did add that there were costs involved in not
giving people these stakes. It was not until January 1996, in a speech to
the business community in Singapore, that he began to link the idea of
having a 'stake in society' to the idea of economic efficiency, arguing
that the one is necessary for the other:

> We need to build a relationship of trust not just within the firm but
> within a society. By trust, I mean the recognition of a mutual purpose
> for which we work together and in which we all benefit. It is a
> Stakeholder Economy in which opportunity is available to all, ad-
> vancement is through merit and from which no group or class is set
> apart or excluded. This is the economic justification for social co-
> hesion, for a fair and strong society, a traditional commitment of left
> of centre politics but one with relevance today, if it is applied anew
> to the modern world.[17]

'One-nation politics', he said, was 'not some expression of sentiment,
or even a justifiable concern for the less well off'. In 'a global economy'
it was necessary to make everyone cooperatively productive: 'Working
as a team is an effective way of working; or playing a sport; or running
an organization. My point is that a successful country must be run the
same way. That cannot work unless everyone feels part of the team,
trusts it, and has a stake in its success and future.'
    Even in his Singapore speech, however, Blair's emphasis was still on
the immorality of social exclusion: 'an underclass of people, cut off
from society's mainstream, living often in poverty, the black economy,
crime and family instability, is a moral and economic evil ... wrong, and
unnecessary, and incidentally, very costly.' But the speech marked the

emergence of a distinctive New Labour argument. Instead of being concerned for the underclass as a matter of class interest (old Labourism) or moral obligation (Blair's 'socialist ethics'), concern for the poor (now reconceptualized as the 'excluded') was now presented as necessary for national competitiveness in the era of globalization.

This formulation also fitted well with Blair's recurring stress on the duties owed by the individual to the community – a moral theme he plainly found more congenial. In return for having a 'stake' in the community, individuals have obligations towards it – to take the jobs it offers (which, Blair maintained, justified the principle of 'workfare'); to ensure that one's children attend school (Blair supported penalties for parents of truant pupils); to be polite to one's neighbours (Blair strongly backed a Labour Party proposal to give local authorities powers to evict repeatedly abusive tenants); to be law-abiding (Blair's most famous slogan was 'tough on crime, and tough on the causes of crime'). He rejected what he called 'early Left thinking'. In his view this had focused on rights guaranteed to individuals by the state, to the exclusion of the responsibilities owed by individuals to the community. He also rejected the 'social individualism' of the 'libertarian Left', 'where you "did your own thing"'.[18] Whether there is any sense in which Blair's ethical stance can be considered 'Left' is questionable; but it undoubtedly corresponded quite well with the sentiments of many of the voters of 'middle England'.[19]

Blair's speeches as leader show a growing ideological adroitness, in which the new Right's opposition between collectivism and individual freedom is displaced by a new articulation between the two, but with the collectivity defined as a community of individuals whose economic life remains individualized. For example:

> Let us talk of rising living standards. And let's make that mean cash in the pocket. But let's make it mean more than cash too. Let's make it mean rising standards of behaviour, rising standards in schools and hospitals, rising standards of mutual respect. Those are the living standards that make us one nation – a nation bound together by what unites us, not pulled apart by what divides.[20]

As critics of all stripes have pointed out, the most characteristic *trope* in New Labour rhetoric is the rejection of what it holds to be false or irrelevant oppositions – between Left and Right, capitalism and social-ism, capitalists and workers, state and market, or good and bad *structures* – with, as a rule, little supporting argument. The result is a distinctive kind of idealism, coexisting with the insistence on 'realism' about the new globalized economy. The 'realism' consists essentially of the asser-tion that global capitalism is a permanent and irremovable fact of life, not an inhuman and ultimately self-destructive system; correspondingly, politics is the art of living with it, not a vocation to overcome it. The idealism consists in the assertion that socialist ethics offer an economic-ally superior basis – one more conducive to national competitiveness – for living with global capitalism.

The flavour was well summarized by Henry Porter in a very favour-able survey of Blair's first year as leader: 'Nothing seems the same as it was; even the old distinctions between left and right no longer matter as much as generational differences appear to.' And what is distinctive about the new generation? Porter quotes 'a close political ally' of Blair:

> Tony had been thinking along these lines long before he was made leader. In fact he was impatient under John Smith to reform the Labour Party. He understood that a whole new generation of people in their thirties and forties had arrived and that they had attitudes and a whole culture which are light years away from the old Labour Party. Intellectually *they accept the restrictions in responsible policy-making that now exist.*[21]

Blair, said Porter, had

> realised that things are not as clear as they appeared to be in the eighties and that many of the new home owners and new parents – in his words, 'the moderate middle-income majority' – are also con-sumers of Murdoch's various media products. They are ... concerned with social and economic issues ... but perhaps the emphasis is more on the good management of a society than on fairness or compassion. And this is exactly the direction Tony Blair has taken Labour, arguing that a compassionate society is firstly a competently run and prosper-ous society

and so on. Or as Blair put it, in the sound-bite language of modern-ization:

> What we are about is a partnership between the public and the private

sectors, rather than a battle between the two. We are about reforming the welfare state, making it a platform of opportunity. Tough on crime and tough on the causes of crime. Rolling back the quango state. It is extremely important to make sure before you start getting lost in the thicket of policy that the public has really got the big picture.[22]

The word 'socialism' now figured in party literature and the leader's speeches rather rarely, and always in carefully circumscribed language, usually emphasizing the degree to which it is *not* socialism as it used to be understood. Socialism, for Blair in particular, refers not to a social system (that is 'old' dogma) but to an ethical ideal: and modernising Labour policy means dropping all previous ideas about the *application* of that ideal; that is, not just 'old Labour' ideas about public ownership or the welfare state, but also, indeed even more categorically, all the thinking and practice pioneered by the 'new Left' in the 1970s about participative democracy.

Lest this leave an impression of purely opportunist adjustment to perceived electoral necessities, let us conclude this section with a quotation from one of Blair's speeches which paints the kind of broader picture that he favours (what Porter, perhaps unkindly, calls 'political Cinemascope'), and makes explicit the hegemonic ambitions of his ideological project. Celebrating the fiftieth anniversary of the 1945 Labour government, which he identified as having drawn its strength from a broad national consensus, Blair declared: 'I passionately want to lead a party which once again embodies and leads the national mood for change and renewal.' He concluded:

Socialists have to be both moralists and empiricists. Values are fundamental. But socialism has to be made real in the world as it is and not as we would like it to be. Our commitment to a different vision of society stands intact. But the ways of achieving it must change. Those should and will cross the old boundaries between left and right, progressive and conservative. They did in 1945. What marks us out are the objectives and the sense of unity and purpose by which we are driven. Our task now is nothing less than national renewal. Rebuilding our country as a strong and active civil society. We should gain confidence from the government of 1945; confidence in our values, in our insights and in our ability to deliver change. The generation of 1945 has set us an example which it is an honour to follow.[23]

What Blair did not acknowledge, but what his rhetoric could not conceal, was that New Labour lacked at least two crucial assets which the government of 1945 possessed: a coherent project for social reform, distilled by several generations of socialist thinkers, advocated by tireless propaganda and endorsed by a large majority of the public as a result of bitter experience; and a world trade and investment regime (laid down at Bretton Woods in 1944) which gave national governments the freedom to pursue such projects without the detailed approval of the financial markets.

New Labour's policies

This section reviews briefly the main elements of the policies which New Labour ideology sought to rationalize.

Economic policy Gordon Brown, Labour's prospective Chancellor of the Exchequer, explicitly accepted that the globalization of financial markets means that if inflation rises, or the ratio of public debt to GDP rises, the cost of borrowing will rise still further; therefore he 'will take no risks with inflation': 'the war on inflation is a Labour war ... Brown's law is that the government will only borrow to invest, public debt will remain stable and the cost effectiveness of public spending must be proved ... nobody should doubt my iron resolve for stability and fiscal prudence'.[24]

On the other hand, he pointed out that the risk of inflation was higher in Britain than elsewhere because under-investment restricts capacity. Therefore a medium-term growth strategy must accompany anti-inflationary monetary and fiscal policies. This should consist of a range of measures to raise investment levels, such as tax incentives for savers to save and for companies to invest, making pension fund managers more responsible for the long-term investment strategies of the companies in which their ever more dominant funds are invested, and putting the onus on take-over bidders to prove that the effect will be to increase efficiency and serve the public interest.

Almost all such measures were, however, suggested rather than promised: New Labour said they were 'possible options', that there was 'a strong case' for them, that it would 'consider' them. This caution was due to fear of adverse market reactions to almost any measure that might limit market freedoms; and there was the further constraint of the Maastricht convergence criteria for joining the EMU, which limit inflation to no more than 1.5 per cent higher than the best-performing member state's, and public borrowing to 3 per cent of GDP.[25]

New Labour was also obsessed with the electoral need to shed the party's former 'high taxes' image. Both Brown and Blair had repeatedly declared that the aim must be 'fair taxes, not high taxes'; 'the days of reflex tax and spend politics are over'.[26] People 'do not want nor will they get a Labour Government that will add to the burden of taxes on ordinary tax payers';[27] on the contrary, New Labour would like to cut the lowest rate of income tax to 15 or even 10 per cent.[28] At the same time there would be 'no return to ... penal rates of high personal taxation' for the rich;[29] while corporate tax rates must also remain internationally competitive.

If taxes cannot rise, and borrowing is limited to investment spending, current public spending cannot expand except through growth leading to more buoyant revenues, which may well take a long time to appear; and, consistently enough, Blair indicated that virtually no new spending commitments would be made by the next Labour government unless they were matched by corresponding savings or cuts:

> I have asked the Shadow Cabinet to submit to me written bids spelling out their priorities and their legislative demands. And I tell them ... some of them will be disappointed. We will not be able to do everything overnight but we will make a start and make a difference ... I have asked colleagues to submit proposals that will make such a difference at little or no cost. And I have asked them to look for savings in their own departmental areas. Government is about hard choices.[30]

One casualty of this policy stance was New Labour's only remaining commitment to public ownership. At the party's 1995 conference, Blair promised that 'there will be a publicly owned and publicly accountable railway system under a Labour government'.[31] Six weeks later the party's shadow transport spokesman rephrased this as a 'publicly controlled and publicly accountable' system, 'and in due course publicly owned also';[32] six months later renationalization even of part of the system was made conditional 'on the availability of resources, and as priorities allow'.[33]

In seeking policies that will 'make a difference at little or no cost' New Labour assigned special priority to measures to reduce unemployment, which would not only reduce suffering and wasted lives but also cut social assistance spending and raise tax revenues. Included among such measures are shifts in the welfare budget aimed at ending the 'poverty trap'. The principle of universal payments has been abandoned; the aim is to 'target' public spending on the long-term unemployed, offering subsidies to employers who take them on, and changing the incentive structure of benefits and taxes to make it worthwhile for unemployed people to take jobs.

As one continues down the list of ideas, what emerges most strikingly is how severe are the limitations which the exponents of New Labour's thinking are convinced they must accept. Mandelson and Liddle acknowledge that New Labour policy contains 'no single big idea, no clever policy wheeze, which is going to transform Britain's prospects overnight', but they assert, with an optimism it is not easy to share, that 'small step-by-step changes in a consistent direction will produce gradually more impressive long term results'.[34] No wonder that Blair is concerned to emulate Mrs Thatcher's success in winning a long spell in office: 'My ambition is not to win an election but to transform a country. To win one term and then be rejected would be the biggest failure and betrayal of all.'[35] Yet it is difficult to imagine that such a pinched and tentative series of marginal adjustments to the Thatcherite economic legacy can make a significant impact, let alone transform a country, even over two parliaments.

In a systematic review of New Labour's 'supply-side socialism', the economic historian Noel Thompson identifies four defining elements: first, abundance and choice become the ends, and equality, community and other socialist values the means; second, these ends and these means are held never to be in conflict (what we have called New Labour's characteristic *trope*); third, because of this, the power of private capital is not seen as a problem against which the state must be able to deploy countervailing power (hence New Labour's assertion that *regulation* of markets can achieve all that public ownership – now 'discredited' and in any case no longer affordable – could do); and fourth, that wherever New Labour economic thinking does, even if inadvertently, assign priorities, it is the 'traditional City–Treasury goal of stability' that comes first.

Fair is efficient, cooperative is competitive, deflation means growth
... Of course ... low inflation, currency stability and the expectations
they will engender may lay the basis for a sustained rise in (mainly)
private investment and that, in turn, will engender a supply-side
miracle and a strong economic performance. But what if, in the short
run, deflation means a rise in unemployment? What if objectives
conflict? ... in the real world, when the crunch comes, as it so often
does soon after a Labour government takes office, it will, like its
forebears, have to confront the problem of how best to deploy scarce
resources among competing ends ... In such circumstances and with
no clearly articulated priorities and with the crucial levers of power
in the hands of others, the danger is that ... it will move along the
line of least resistance ... the deflationary line which provokes least
resistance from the City, the IMF, the US Federal Reserve and the
US Treasury.[36]

Or in the less restrained language of the journalist Iain Macwhirter:

A decade and a half of free-market Thatcherism has reproduced
levels of social inequality unseen since Victorian times, and the social
fabric is being destroyed by mass unemployment. New Labour has
no particular remedy other than to ask businesspeople to be more
responsible. Yet the reality of the market is that it lacks a social
conscience. The interests of the wider society always have to be
imposed from without by democratic control ... Two Conservative
parties is one too many.[37]

Education Tony Blair repeatedly stated that education would be his
'passion' in government. Together with technical training it is a key
'supply-side' policy area, as well as an issue of social justice – equality
of opportunity; and one that, in New Labour thinking, offers scope for
improvement at little or no expense (Blair several times cited a speech
by the former Permanent Secretary at the Department of Education,
who 'argued that there was room for a thirty per cent improvement in
the education system within existing budgets').[38]

For example, one idea was to switch educational spending to improve
the employability of the least-favoured category of unemployed young
people: for instance by abolishing the 'assisted places scheme', under
which £120 million per annum have hitherto been spent on fees for
children from lower-income – but still mostly middle-class – families to

attend private schools, and spending part of the savings on reducing class sizes for five- and six-year-olds to a maximum of 30; and by abolishing the 'child benefit' received by the families of all children aged 17 and 18 who presently continue in full-time education – a predominantly middle-class group – and using the savings to finance schemes aimed at encouraging more young people to continue in education after age 16 than presently do so. And the one new tax that Gordon Brown was willing to countenance, a one-time 'windfall' tax on the profits of the privatized utilities, was to be spent on a new set of options for long-term unemployed young people.[39]

In spite of the fact (which New Labour spokespeople emphasized) that the education system had been seriously under-funded under the Thatcher and Major governments, no significant expansion of spending on education was envisaged (unless we count Gordon Brown's suggestion that the country's estimated £3.2 billion backlog of school building and equipment repairs should be tackled by a government partnership with merchant banks).[40] Improvements in schooling are to be made, in the last analysis, by more and better efforts by teachers, head teachers and parents (who, for example, would become formally responsible for ensuring that their children do specified amounts of homework), policed by more inspections and 'league tables', and involving the removal of 'failing' teachers and the closing of 'failing' schools.[41]

Health A similar logic underlay New Labour's approach to the National Health Service. It was seen as an area where Labour enjoyed an electoral advantage (people overwhelmingly supported the NHS and wanted it 'rescued' from the financial strangulation and the threat of 'creeping privatization' implicit in the Conservatives' post-1989 market-oriented restructuring). But partly responding to the wish of the NHS staff not to have to undergo any more reorganization, Labour policy-makers proposed to retain the 'purchaser–provider split' of the so-called 'internal market', but to abolish its financial logic. In place of actual purchasing, there would be 'commissioning'; the resulting savings in bureaucracy would be used to reverse the run-down of resources for 'front-line' health-care provision.[42] Hospital ownership would revert from the independent hospital trusts to the National Health Service, but hospital management would remain in the hands of the Trusts' managers. 'Fundholding' by general practitioners – the allocation of funds directly to family doctors with which to purchase routine specialist treatment for their patients – was also to be replaced by 'commissioning', through which GPs would in theory retain the enhanced power to get prompt and appropriate treatment for their patients that fundholding had given them.

Apart from the administrative savings that were expected from ending the internal market (about which it was possible to be somewhat sceptical), however, further improvements in health care would, as in education, have to come from the more efficient use of existing funds, not from higher spending. Both health authority and hospital trust boards would be made more representative of the communities they served (that is, no longer composed predominantly of Conservative businessmen, as hitherto); Labour's proposals also asserted that these boards would as a result be 'genuinely accountable', though since they would still be appointed, not elected, this claim seems questionable.[43]

Social security The overall commitment of New Labour was to reduce the share of GDP spent on the welfare state; to the extent that unemployment could not be drastically cut (the youth employment scheme mentioned earlier was an effort in this direction), this meant that any improvement in welfare provision would have to come from improved 'targeting' (that is, shifting away from universal provision). The chief focus of debate here was state-provided old age pensions, which successive Conservative cuts had rendered so inadequate that several million retired people were reduced to living on means-tested public assistance. New Labour policy-makers resisted all proposals for re-establishing state pensions at a more realistic level, and re-indexing them to the growth of average earnings, on the grounds – hotly contested by 'old Labour' critics – that this would mean intolerable new spending commitments; instead they proposed to improve the lot of the poorest 700,000 old people through targeted special assistance, and to look to occupational and private sector pension schemes to make up the growing shortfall in state pension levels.[44]

Constitutional change Rather than pursue New Labour thinking in a dozen other policy fields, from the environment to crime – virtually all of them evincing a similar blend of sensible, if limited, low – (or zero-) cost modifications to the Thatcherite institutional legacy – it is more useful to focus attention on one final area that illustrates particularly clearly the nature and limitations of the project: the constitution. A speech by Tony Blair in February 1996 pulled the various threads together: local government 'renewal', including a qualified end to 'rate-capping' (that is, central government-imposed ceilings on local taxation powers), elections of a third of council members every year, and encouragement for referenda, citizens' juries and other innovations; re-establishing a strategic authority for London; elected mayors for London and other major cities; elected regional authorities in England, subject to approval in regional referenda, for strategic planning and to oversee regional quangos; a parliament for Scotland elected by proportional representation, and an assembly (not necessarily so elected, and without tax powers) for Wales, both to take over the functions currently performed by the Scottish and Welsh Offices and their related quangos; a Freedom of Information Act; the incorporation of the European Convention on Human Rights into British law, permitting British courts to adjudicate cases under it; abolition of the voting powers of hereditary members of the House of Lords, with a view to the subsequent creation of an elected upper house; and a referendum on whether the electoral system should be changed to proportional representation (a pledge inherited from John Smith's days as leader).[45]

Most commentators saw this as a radical and far-reaching programme which would tend to crowd the parliamentary timetable; and some of its elements were the subject of a pre-election agreement between Labour and the Liberal Democrats early in 1997, covering the House of Lords, devolution for Scotland and Wales, the European Convention on Human Rights, a Freedom of Information Act and a referendum on the electoral system – making it harder for Labour subsequently to renege on any of these. Yet even this aspect of New Labour's project, which had relatively modest cost implications, had significant limitations. For example, there was no proposal to restore significant *powers* to local government, even for London. The party's former commitment to reform the judiciary, beginning with the creation of a new Ministry of Justice, separate from the anachronistic office of the Lord Chancellor, was abandoned. There was also an ambiguity in Blair's commitment to a Freedom of Information Act; would it give citizens a general right to all state-held information, or only to information held by the state about themselves?[46] The commitment to an elected upper house was moved to the relatively distant future, and increasingly overlaid by hints that it would not be purely elected.[47]

There were also significant silences. For instance, no undertaking was made to reconstruct the state to make it capable of mastering the market, rather than serving it; there was no promise to reverse the Thatcherite transfer of authority from the central civil service to commercially oriented and substantially unaccountable 'executive agencies'. And although in Scotland and Wales unelected quangos would be largely replaced by a parliament and an assembly, in England there were no plans to abolish them, or to substitute election for appointment of their members: it was not clear that Blair's call for 'rolling back the quango state' meant more than making quangos less purely Conservative in composition, and somewhat less secret. In general, the proposed reforms would at most make modest adjustments to Britain's uniquely central-ized, elite-managed and undemocratic state.

Conclusion

In spite of all these reservations, New Labour's policies in October 1996 were perhaps somewhat more extensive, more coherent and more concerned with the fate of the country's worst-educated and poorest members – 'the excluded', in the language of 'post-socialism' – than media coverage suggested. The contrary impression was partly due to the fact that a complex set of policies cannot be presented in sound-bites, and partly to the journalists' obsession with 'splits', so that what is seen as newsworthy is not whether newly announced policies make sense, but whether they betray inner-party divisions. The 'New Labour' government which took office in May 1997 would clearly not make changes as radical or far-reaching as those of 1945–50, but it would none the less make a significant change of direction and tone from the previous 18 years.

Yet there was something about the policies themselves that justified the impression of insubstantiality. It is difficult to appear weighty and forceful if what you propose is essentially to do better with less. The magnitude of the goal envisaged in Blair's rhetoric ('national renewal') and the scale of the means proposed – from a more representative group of advisers for the Bank of England, to compulsory school homework – were just too disproportionate. Staying within the constraints that Labour's modernizers accept rules out radical proposals; but without radical measures, there could hardly be a radical improvement in the performance of Britain's economy. The results of a 101 modifications to existing supply-side policies would be neither massive nor swift; and it was a telling symptom of Labour's failure to offer a convincing alternative to the Conservatives' overall legacy that in the autumn of 1996 the leadership allowed itself to be drawn into a 'Dutch auction' with their opponents on the issue of who were the strongest champions of 'moral values'. As Tariq Ali commented: 'Incapable of promoting policies to alleviate the suffering of the two million unemployed and millions of underprivileged citizens and thus help bring about a society more at ease with itself, our politicians instead have clambered onto the morality bandwagon.'[48]

Moreover, on many issues, the hope of achieving even modest success presupposed that all the relevant players would be interested in collaborating with a Labour government. In reality, innumerable vested interests would bitterly resist, and Conservative efforts to reduce Labour's massive electoral lead would not be confined to rational debate on the merits of New Labour's policies. An intemperate far-right campaign in the shape of a national-populist attack on 'Europe' was launched already in 1995, to be halted – how far and for how long remained to be seen – only by Labour's resounding election victory in May 1997. And the Conservative press could be relied on sooner or later to resume its habitual hostility towards Labour on many other fronts.

Yet the economic constraints faced by New Labour should be honestly acknowledged. Some commentators argue that the fact that the proportion of GDP taken in taxes by different OECD governments varies from 33 per cent in the USA to 68 per cent in Sweden shows that globalization is not a serious constraint on national policy-making.[49] But this misses the point. The Swedish government could take 68 per cent of Sweden's national income in taxes for two reasons: they had a highly productive industrial sector, and a population accustomed to enjoying comprehensive and high quality social security and services which were expensive, but which they could afford. Britain has none of these advantages, and the Labour Party, even if it thought there was a sure way to raise productivity by spending tax revenues (which it no longer does), is not seen by either business or the wider electorate as competent to do so. Moreover, multinational corporations have already built Britain's lower wages and corporate tax levels into their investment plans, as offsets to the lower productivity they can expect to achieve in Britain. A significant increase in either wages or company taxation, *prior* to a rise in productivity, would be a significant deterrent, and would be energetically denounced by the financial press and punished by the financial markets.

A logical response would be for the Labour Party to see globalization as a problem that must be overcome by seeking alliances with other progressive parties, especially in the EU, to work towards a new international trade and investment regime – a replacement for the Bretton Woods system; including, in particular, a new set of controls over capital flows that would allow governments rather than multinationals to have the decisive say in each country's economic and social development. But without having campaigned long and hard from this position – without a powerful groundswell of popular support for it – it could be electorally very dangerous for the Labour Party to adopt it. Not only have the Conservatives taught the electorate to expect low income taxes (partly by using £200 billion of receipts from North Sea oil and the sale of state assets for current spending); more generally, voters, even those who are out of work, have become quite deeply imbued with consumerism. If the Labour Party belatedly adopted a position critical of the market it would immediately be accused of wanting to return to a high-tax, inefficient, state-controlled economy. It was to pre-empt exactly this charge – which was seen as having fatally injured the party in the 1992 election – that Blair pushed through the rewriting of the party constitution in 1995, to drop all reference to public ownership and make a categorical commitment to the market.

Of course, this logic can become an end in itself, and self-proving: the absence of any criticism of the market reinforces its ideological hegemony. But short of an economic cataclysm severe enough to shatter conclusively the dream of unending growth in real personal disposable incomes, the constraints which globalization does impose on policy are real enough, at least in the medium term. Meantime the organization of the party, and the mind-set of its elected leaders and their professional staffs, are being systematically and thoroughly refashioned in line with this 'new reality'. Achieving office and doing some good within the bounds set by 'global market forces' increasingly become the real limit of their aspirations.

The vulnerability of New Labour to the harsh realities of capitalist politics is nowhere better illustrated by the faith exhibited by both Brown and Blair in economic 'honesty'. Their pledge not to 'play politics' with public finances seems to be based on the hope that such good behaviour will be rewarded by the approbation of non-partisan 'markets' (the Conservatives feel no such need, having played politics with the public finances, when in office, at every election since the 1950s, without ever losing the support of either the City or the CBI). It is possible that Brown's promise to follow the 'golden rule' of borrowing only for investment is necessary to reduce business opposition. It is doubtful, though, that actually following the rule will secure business support for Labour and against the Conservatives in the first election of the new millennium.

Closely related to this is New Labour's lack of a strong emotional and ideological bond with their newly enlarged membership. Blair's stakeholder rhetoric has hegemonic aspirations and maybe – though less certainly – some hegemonic potential, but it was still far from having a strong hold on the feelings and dreams of a mass public. This seemed likely to be due in part to the inherently elitist character of the modernizers' project. Drawing all power to set policy into the hands of an increasingly tightly coordinated circle of senior politicians and their 'staffs' made it possible to redirect party policy sharply away from many of its long-standing commitments, and in ways that appealed to mainstream media commentators and reassured the floating voters of 'middle England'; but it did so at the expense of no longer having a potent force of engaged and committed opinion-leaders in the party rank and file. Yet this is important, so long as Labour's presence in the institutions of the state and the economy remains relatively weak. When in office, the only effective weapon a Labour government can deploy against opposition to its policies is public opinion. It is doubtful if the reasonable,

circle-squaring arguments advanced by New Labour have the capacity
to mobilize the sort of resolute, hard-edged public opinion that would
be needed to overcome bitter and well-funded opposition – of the kind,
for example, that was mobilized by business against further nationalization in the 1950s.

In the 'honeymoon' period immediately after Labour's unprecedented electoral victory on 1 May 1997, however – with 419 seats
out of the total of 655 – doubts and reservations of this kind were at
a discount. The scale of the Conservatives' defeat – reduced to 165
MPs, and eliminated completely from Scotland and Wales – exposed
dire weaknesses in their grass-roots membership and national organization; and this, combined with the electorate's apparent rejection of the
'Euro-scepticism' espoused by a majority of Conservative candidates,
made an early come-back seem unlikely.[50] The tables had been dramatically turned. Barring accidents, it was now the Conservatives who must
try to adjust their policies, and their party organization, to the dictates
of electoral centrism. New Labour's 'radicalism of the centre' would be
constrained only by socio-economic realities and the will of the Labour
leadership, not the threat of being outflanked further to the Right by
the opposition. In the course of the coming parliament, therefore, the
real significance of the modernizers' politics would be fully revealed.

2

The Italian Left after 1989: Continuity and transformation

GIULIO SAPELLI

The paradox of the Italian 'anomaly'

The Italian 'anomaly' (the lack of alternance, the role of the Communist Party, and so on) was a leitmotif of much intellectual debate, including journalistic diatribes, in the 1970s and 1980s.

The different positions, in both theory and practice, among communist and socialist 'revisionists' and neo-Marxists were connected to another debate. There were those who held that the renewal of, and struggle for, Italian socialism should proceed by accentuating the Italian anomaly not only from European and non-European forms of capitalism but from party politics and party systems in general.[1] And there were those who believed that, to be successful, any policy of 'progress' had to start by reducing and even abolishing this anomaly, above all by drastically reducing the influence of the PCI to the advantage of the PSI.[2]

Whichever position one wants to assume – no small matter – one of the crucial aspects of that debate was the need to justify or deprecate, with more or less intelligence and elegance, the relation of forces between the political parties of the Italian Left whether electoral, political or cultural.[3]

It was evident that Italy was a case of deviancy in Europe and even

44

(apart from certain Asian situations) in the rest of the world where the hegemony of the Left was held by socialist and/or social-democratic parties rather than communist parties.[4]

The 1990s signalled the end of the Stalinist communist era; and this, inevitably, had implications for what was left of the international workers' movement and the issues still left unresolved from the Cold War. With respect to these historical events, the inheritance of the Italian Communist Party, though now divided between two new parties, the Democratic Party of the Left (the PDS, the name the PCI took after 1991) and Rifondazione Comunista (the name taken by those who opposed the change of name), continues to exist in spite of all the intervening ideological and political changes. In fact, the heirs of the PCI have even strengthened their supremacy over the historical inheritance of socialism in party terms; little is left, after all, of the Italian Socialist Party (PSI).

As has been acutely remarked by Mastropaolo, Italian communism changed in a way different from that envisaged by Kirchheimer in his well-known essay.[5] The PCI became a 'catch-all' party (at least in its inspiration and collective image) well before becoming a party with large electoral influence and before renewing itself ideologically. Historically, parties characterized by mass integration reach the threshold of governmental power when they have already lost their sub-cultural identities and militancy. Then, they rapidly become opinion parties able to satisfy different political demands. This was never the case with the PCI which had transformed itself into a party with a wide social base and with a strong influence among the agrarian and urban middle classes – especially in central Italy – well before it had reached the threshold of government, while keeping its remarkable organizational structure based on the militancy and activism of its members.

It is equally true that the PCI (and even the PDS) never totally settled its accounts with Stalinism and Brezhnevism officially and clearly, for instance in a congress declaration, or in important books written by its leading intellectuals or major political leaders.[6] Nevertheless, there is no doubt that its emancipation from the international communist movement, though protracted, had been accomplished. It had started from the diffusion of Gramsci's thought and Togliatti's elaboration of an 'Italian way to socialism'.[7] It continued in conflict with the USSR over the invasion of Czechoslovakia in 1968, and in direct polemic with the bureaucracy of the Soviet dictatorship during the 'democratic Polish revolution'. It did all this without ever turning back. The voyage was finally concluded when Enrico Berlinguer declared in 1981 that 'the forward drive of the October revolution has been exhausted'.[8]

The pragmatic (rather than ideological) process of the political disengagement of the PCI from the USSR, helped by the tragedies of Stalinism and post-Stalinism, matched its electoral growth and did not hinder its expansion in the 1970s. In that period the PCI remained a communist party with strong ties to the Comecon and the Warsaw Pact countries, but it had a social-democratic practice and heterodox cultural roots in comparison to the Soviet 'vulgata'.[9]

Thus, in spite of what all the theories of political modernization have told us, belonging to the 'international communist movement' did not impede the party's great development during the 1970s.[10] Kirchheimer's theory should therefore be reversed. In the second half of the 1970s, the PCI became a large non-class-based party with significant electoral influence and great national prestige, yet it did not lose its roots in its sub-cultures nor its potential for collective mobilization.

The problem with the PSI was different. The PSI confirmed Kirchheimer's theory but only in part, despite what was claimed by its apologists, including even first-class contemporary historians.[11] It confirmed the theory only in the sense that it transformed itself in theory and in practice only when it became a party of government completely immersed in electoral expansion. But this changed occurred rather late: not when the party first entered government in the 1960s, but when Bettino Craxi was its leader, from the mid-1970s to the early 1990s.

This 'socialist neo-revisionism', to use Donald Sassoon's brilliant definition, had in the PSI of the 1960s and 1970s one of its most interesting exponents in ideological and programmatic terms.[12] However, in the 1980s and 1990s this revisionism coexisted with – and was finally suffocated by – what can be defined as the 'neo-caciquismo' typical of socialist parties in southern Europe. These parties are steadfastly dedicated to a practice of familist Caesarism profoundly intertwined with economic and political corruption. The leader of the political party becomes the leader of the party's 'political economy' – in the sense that he controls its financial resources – and, like a grotesque reincarnation of Michels' metaphor, exercises his power in an autocratic and familist manner, following a well-established Mediterranean practice.

The socialist clientelism of southern Europe is characterized by the rapid transition from the clientele of the 'party machine' to that of an autocratic and personal patronage system, which gradually destroys the party itself as a more or less centralized organizational machine. This is replaced by a *cliques* of local notables dominated in turn by the *leader maximo* in control of the political economic machine.[13]

Here lies the other paradox of the Italian anomaly: the inability of Craxi to exploit the crisis of communism.

This irreversible crisis exploded under the double impact of revolutionary pressures from below in Poland and in the German Democratic Republic, and of the increasing fragmentation at the top of the bureaucracies of Stalinist origin in dictatorial regimes in Czechoslovakia, the Balkan states and, naturally, in the USSR. It might be thought that this would signal a victory for the so-called 'autonomous' faction of the PSI, traditionally the most distant from the PCI and the most active in defence of dissenting voices in Stalinist countries.[14] This faction, over the years, established almost complete control over the party which, in turn, came under the domination of Bettino Craxi. But the indisputable 'ideological victory' gained by the PSI when communism collapsed did not produce a political victory. On the contrary, the PSI entered into so deep a crisis that the centenary of the foundation of the party was not even celebrated. The oldest and most innovative Italian party since its foundation and, historically speaking, the most important ideologically for the renewal of the Left, foundered in turmoil and splits.[15]

The vicissitudes of the PSI are the most relevant manifestation of a typical phenomenon of Mediterranean Europe first dealt with by Meynaud and, later, by Legg in his study on Greece.[16] This phenomenon consists in the direct connection between the 'weakness' of parties ('weak' because they are centred round personalities and unable to select elites which are not exclusively based on patronage) and their overwhelmingly clientelist behaviour.

Against the formalist exponents of the self-referential school of Italian academic political science (who share this infirmity with the current neo-classical rhetoric of many economists), I have tried to 'demonstrate' that the weakness of Italian and southern European parties as systems of solidarity and identity is due to the strength and, even more, to the extension of their clientelistic network. In turn, clientelism grows because the parties are weak and buy support which they cannot find in other ways.[17]

Contrary to the political science consensus which insists on 'partito-cracy' these parties are 'weak' not 'strong'.[18]

The fragmentation of the PSI – and, for other reasons, of the DC – can be explained precisely in relation to its intrinsic weakness: its power rests on a fragile network of interests bordering on criminality and illegality, dominated by the necessity of establishing consent around individual leaders and not supported by values and a sense of solidarity which might have silenced these interests.[19] This explains why the party was so rapidly destroyed by the investigation of the magistrature, the *Mani Pulite* (Clean Hands) team. Otherwise its sudden disappearance would seem to be arcane and mysterious.

It is important to stress this not so much for pedagogical reasons but, rather, to underline the futility of analytical attempts to explain the transformation of the Left, especially the communist Left, simply in terms of international influences and interdependence. This has recently been attempted with great ingenuity.[20]

The PDS resisted pressures towards disintegration even though they surfaced – albeit to a lesser degree than in other parties – when the full extent of political corruption (a system I called 'kleptocracy') was fully revealed.[21] The PDS survived because it was the heir, historically speak-ing, of the PCI, the only Italian example of the 'institutionalization' of politics and of parties.[22] And this in a nation characterized by a prevalently low institutionalization of politics – the original cause of the weakness of parties and of all instruments typical of polyarchies.[23]

Between 1989 and the first half of the 1990s, the lengthy process of the transformation of the Italian Left came to an end and so did its political 'anomaly'. The 'anomaly' was resolved partly because the PCI was transformed, as other communist parties, into a party oscillating between liberal democracy, social democracy and socialism (but this we shall discuss later), and partly because the PSI disappeared into a diaspora of small party-like fragments held together by a strong per-sonalistic cement, consistent with its past (which we shall also discuss).

The decision of the Socialist International to appoint the current

Table 2.1 Chamber of Deputies: share of the vote 1987–96

	1976	1979	1983	1987	1992	1994	1996
PCI/PDS	34.4	30.4	29.9	26.6	16.1	20.4	21.1
Rifondazione Comunista					5.6	6.0	8.6
Socialists	9.6	9.8	11.4	14.3	13.6	2.0	–
Green				2.5	2.8	2.9	2.5
DC	38.7	38.3	32.9	34.3	29.7	–	–
PPI				–	–	11.1	6.8
Dini List				–	–	–	4.3
Lega Nord				–	8.7	8.4	10.1
Forza Italia				–	–	21.0	20.6
CCD/CdU				–	–	–	5.8
MSI/AN				5.9	5.4	13.5	15.7

Notes: AN (Alleanza nazionale) is the new name (1994) of the former neo-fascists of the MSI. The PPI (Italian Popular Party) included the CdU in 1994. CCD/CdU are Catholics allied with Berlusconi's Forza Italia.

Table 2.2 Seats obtained by party coalitions in the Chamber of Deputies (single-member constituencies only)

	1994	1996
Olive Tree		246
Progressive Coalition	164	
Freedom Bloc	164	169
Clean Government Bloc	137	
Progressive Pact		20

Notes: 75 per cent of seats in the Chamber are fought in single-member constituencies under the first-past-the-post system (as in the UK and the USA); consequently, allied parties need to agree on a common candidate. In 1994 the Progressive Coalition included the PDS and Rifondazione Comunista but not the Popular Party. Forza Italia formed in the north a common list with the Northern League (the Freedom Bloc) and, in the south, a joint list with Alleanza nazionale (Clean Government). In 1996 the Olive Tree included the PDS and the Popular Party. In some constituencies the Olive Tree fought the election jointly with Rifondazione Comunista under the name of Progressisti. In 1996 the Freedom Bloc consisted of Forza Italia and AN only (the Northern League stood on its own).

leader of the PDS, Massimo D'Alema, to be one of its vice-presidents (in September 1996 in New York) sealed symbolically the end of the 'anomaly'. This concluded the long-haul strategy of gradual rapprochement towards the International the PCI had started in the 1970s, at the time of Ostpolitik. Bettino Craxi had always tried to use his veto power against extending membership first to the PCI and, later, to the PDS, knowing that his consent was required. This illustrates how the end of the anomaly required a change in the relations between the forces of the Italian Left: the PCI/PDS was able to overcome Craxi's vetoes thanks to 20 years of political work with other European socialist parties.

The resolution of the anomaly required the quasi-concurrent transformation in the political support achieved by both the PCI and the PSI. The electoral figures illustrate this transformation (see Tables 2.1 and 2.2). After the severe losses of 1987 and 1992 – the latter due to the split with the uncompromising and neo-Marxist group of Rifondazione Comunista – the PDS began to recover while the PSI disappeared altogether.

Faced with this, sections of the old Socialist Party parliamentary group found a place in new political alliances. Some joined, in 1994, the Progressive Coalition (when the centre-right won the elections) and, in 1996, the Olive Tree Coalition (when the centre-left won). But the majority of the leading cadres and voters of the PSI went the other way, joining the post-fascists of Gianfranco Fini or Silvio Berlusconi's Forza Italia.[24] A group of socialist leaders still devoted to the Craxian legacy and ready to resurrect his leadership were immediately attracted to the Right. In the Sicilian regional elections of 1996, these groups or 'quasi-groups' sided with Berlusconi and Fini and obtained 3 per cent of the votes.[25]

The contradictions of the struggle against political parties

As we have seen, one of the most important transformations of the Italian Left after 1989 was the disappearance of Bettino Craxi's PSI as a political force of any significance. The PSI had defined its identity throughout the 1980s as the party which had defeated the attempt of Enrico Berlinguer and Aldo Moro to bring about the conditions for alternation between political parties within the international constraints of the Cold War (what was known as 'the historic compromise'). According to the two statesmen, the transition from 'polarized pluralism' (as theorized by Sartori) to 'centripetal pluralism' (theorized by Farneti) could have been realized avoiding both an internationally backed reactionary counterattack (Berlinguer's fear) and the transformation of the DC into a purely conservative party at the mercy of international interests (Moro's fear). Extremely powerful interest groups manoeuvred against this plan. The assassination of Aldo Moro in 1978 by obscure powers in defence of these interests led to a defensive version of the project of a 'historic compromise', depriving it of most of its radical potential. The project failed in the face of a terrorist offensive which forced the PCI to support in parliament the Andreotti government. The PCI was caught in a web of contradictions: a party of change supporting a government unwilling to change. This led to an unavoidable crisis with its traditional supporters. The transformation of the PCI into a social-democratic party, free of ideological ties with its Stalinist past, could have occurred only through a more thorough ideological revision, leading to a break with the USSR and active government participation on the basis of a specific political programme of reform.

This did not happen and, in 1979, the party returned to opposition, having failed to understand the deep social and cultural transformations occurring in Italian and world capitalism. Instead, these transformations were the starting-point for Craxi's 'modernization' programme. The latter appeared therefore destined to fill the void left by the PCI (whose capacity for political innovation had sharply declined) and resisted for over a decade all communist attempts to spread their influence towards the centre.

It was precisely when this plan appeared to be achieving success that it began to break down.

In 1989, the long Italian political cycle, which had started in 1943 with the fall of fascism, and continued with the Resistance and the Republican Constitution, came to an end as international conditions changed. The lasting achievement of a democratic political system founded on political parties was questioned for the first time in Italian history by a variety of forces held together by the industrial and financial bourgeoisie.[26] This attack had considerable popular support because of the contradictions and the injustices resulting from the domination of political parties. Nevertheless, there is no denying that what was also targeted to the point of destruction was a parliamentary democracy governed by political parties.[27]

Intensified by the collapse of the USSR, a contradiction which had appeared in the 1980s developed irreversibly: the contradiction between a national welfare state based on political parties and the requirements of an international economic system entering the era of financial liberal globalization at great speed. The main features were the abnormal expansion of public expenditure, with its apex during the 1980s, escalating and widespread corruption, and the proliferation of oligarchies and clienteles of industrialists and parties. Those in charge of the destiny of the Italian economy were 'internationalists' whose express purpose was to find a new role for Italy in the international division of labour. Through endless contradictions and prevarications they moved towards the destruction of a system which had been developing during 40 years of republican life. The target was, above all, a democracy organized by the political parties.

It was here that the Socialist Party of Bettino Craxi missed its historic chance.[28] For instance, on the issue of privatization, it hesitated and wavered, unable to develop a proper 'meso-governmental' strategy, relying instead on putting up obstacles against privatization or multiplying patronage.[29] The PSI thought of privatization purely as a means for further expanding personal and *clique* power. To preserve its clienteles, the PSI let its neo-revisionist programme fade away, even though it had strong intellectual liberal-socialist roots on the question of welfare and was tenaciously distinct from the ideology of the PCI. The party became increasingly 'southern' – a trend which started in the early 1980s.[30] The PSI forfeited its traditional social base to become a party of the 'new middle classes' – often people who uphold a rhetoric of market competition while being protected from the market by public spending and corruption. All of this was achieved through a propaganda machine which provided Craxi and his retinue with a large following among the intellectual bourgeoisie. This was the PSI's new core of active supporters along with public-sector managers – 'shared', however, with the DC according to a complex and solid agreement. It was not by chance, then, that when the PSI foundered, much of its electorate, particularly the political speculators among them, joined the post-fascists or Silvio Berlusconi's party.[31]

The contradiction between the ideology of neo-liberal modernity and a clientelist practice became clear in 1989 (the tragic irony of history!) when an organic alliance was formed between Craxi and the DC – now merely the pure instrument of clienteles. Such an alliance damaged the prospects of the smaller parties of the centre. It led the Republican Party to distance itself from the government while depriving the liberal and the social-democratic parties of any ideals they might have had. Aldo Moro's prophecy, namely, that if the DC did not facilitate the alternance of parties in power, it would become a mere government front for sectoral interests, was fulfilled – though he could not have imagined the international context within which this would happen, one in which the USSR no longer existed. Nevertheless, the substance of his fear came true at the political and cultural levels. His followers, after his murder, were unable to stop the DC – plagued by internal division – from self-destructing.

The PSI chose to become the ally of Giulio Andreotti and the other DC leaders; that is, those who, after 1979–80, controlled the party. In so doing it sealed its fate: the DC was destined to be destroyed by decisions taken by cabals in secret rooms where power is invisible. From here it was a short step to the crisis.

The political significance of this alliance was that it symbolized to mass public opinion the end of the modernizing project of the PSI. Craxi was unable to see that what was developing was a virtual plebiscite against the old politics of the ruling parties. He mistakenly invited the electorate to desert the polls on the occasion of the 1991 referendum for the modification of electoral law. The electorate utterly ignored him. It is true that this referendum was seen by much of the Italian bourgeoisie as a dress-rehearsal for the destruction of mass parties and the foundation of a Caesarist regime. Nevertheless, the arguments against it are not convincing because the PDS itself also supported the referendum. Craxi's appeal turned out to be a total failure and the image of the PSI as a ground-breaker of modernization was destroyed once and for all.

This was the context in which Achille Occhetto, the last secretary of the PCI and the first of the PDS, proposed to change the name of the party and to break decisively with its communist past. He appealed directly to the mass media without consulting the PCI leadership.[32] Though the arguments he used were weak, the break with the USSR was clear-cut – all the more so as the system was collapsing. The motivation for political activism was now no longer to be found in the communist or socialist tradition, but rather in a modernized version of radical-liberal and liberal-socialist thought.[33]

This initiative, as Giuseppe Vacca has pointed out in a masterly essay, 'liberalises the political market'. It contributed to the wider process of the disintegration of the party system independently of the judiciary.[34]

The consequences for the PCI were profound. Divisions which had hitherto remained underground, thus hiding the deep changes that had occurred within the party, now arose. The protagonists of this change included most of the old leaders who had not been previously consulted and who opposed it in varying degrees; the party apparatus which overwhelmingly supported Occhetto and accepted the new liberal-socialist ideology; and the rank and file militants who, though divided, on the whole followed Occhetto while still holding on to the fundamental values of Italian communism.[35]

A split was inevitable. It was engineered by Armando Cossuta, the historical leader of the pro-Soviet wing who traditionally took a moderate 'rightist' stance. Cossuta had been the reference point for the Soviet Union within the PCI ever since the PCI began dissenting from Moscow, well before 1981. When a similar split occurred in the Spanish Communist Party, the Soviet Union was routed because its 'man', General Lister (a hero of the Civil War), had no followers. In the Italian case, things went quite differently. After all, the USSR was no more when the PCI finally became the PDS. What should have been the 'pro-Soviet' party (Rifondazione Comunista) rapidly became a focus for rank and file militants, some workers' groups in large industries and some members of the 'red' sub-culture in central Italy who wanted to preserve an intransigent class politics and a 'proletarian internationalism' (of which Cuba was the rallying point). The new party also attracted the extra-parliamentary Left, including Trotskyist groups, and, above all, the old socialist Left of the ex-PSIUP – the party which, in 1964, had split from the PSI in protest against socialist participation in government and which had joined the PCI in the 1970s after disastrous electoral results. Indeed, Fausto Bertinotti, who belongs to the PSIUP tradition, became the secretary and *de facto* leader of Rifondazione Comunista, while Cossuta became President.

Occhetto's political strategy was straightforward, though his frequent tactical twists and turns led to crisis and electoral defeat. The idea that the relation between socialism and democracy (socialism as the expansion of democracy) was the terrain where political battles had to be fought was now abandoned. This had been what distinguished the PCI throughout its post-Second World World War history. The new goal was a society characterized by individual rights protected and enhanced by formal institutional mechanisms which had their optimal paradigms in the existing liberal democracies of modern industrialized societies. 'Changing Italian society' meant changing its political system not its capitalism. To contribute to this 'revolution', the PDS led the campaign to change the electoral system from a proportional one to a so-called 'majoritarian' one – which is what actually happened in the referenda of 1991 and 1993.

The 'institutional' tactic was not pursued with sufficient consistency, however. The electorate and the militants of the PDS were baffled when, after the crisis of Giulio Amato's government in 1993, the two PDS ministers chosen by the new PM, Carlo Azeglio Ciampi, resigned.[36] The refusal of a majority of MPs to lift Craxi's parliamentary immunity – thus allowing him to escape abroad – was the direct cause of these resignations. The request of the magistrates had been more than legitimate and the procedures used by a majority of the magistrates against political leaders always had ample legal grounds. But this does not justify the decision of the PDS to vacate the political struggle in favour of seeking a purely legal resolution – via the judiciary – of problems which should have been solved politically. In this sense a political vacuum was created. It was filled by Silvio Berlusconi and Gianfranco Fini who could derive great advantage from an agenda centred on the dichotomies 'old' versus 'new' and 'honest' versus 'dishonest', thus obscuring any confrontations about social issues.[37] Although the PDS had never directly participated in national government, it none the less had considerable experience in local government with the PSI and also, less frequently, with the DC; moreover, it was involved, although in a limited way, with allegations of economic and political corruption.

Having chosen a rhetoric supportive of the judiciary, rather than a clear
and uncompromising analysis of the past and a project for the future,
the PDS found these factors being turned against itself; it was, after all,
simple for the media and the party's political opponents to depict the
PDS as heir to an old party somewhat tainted by the old system.[38]

The PDS found itself disarmed and incapable of asserting its
political autonomy. It used uncritically themes of 'modernity' pioneered
by the PSI. This loss of ideological distinction favoured those who
wanted to settle the account with the Craxian PSI not through a political
struggle, but by supporting uncritically all the activities of the magistrates involved in the battle against corruption. This strengthened the
position adopted by the majority of Italians – and intensified by a
massive media campaign – which identified the entire political class
with corruption. It shifted the political confrontation away from the
terrain of programmes and interests to a confrontation between the
'old' (that is, the 'partitocracy', a largely discredited political class) and
the 'new'. This was far more advantageous to the new parties: Berlusconi's Forza Italia, the Northern League and Fini's Alleanza nazionale
(AN) – the ex neo-fascist Italian Social Movement which had rapidly
reconstructed itself as a democratic party whose main political platform
was the reform of the constitution in a presidential sense.

The extraordinary transformations of politico-economic relations
taking place in the international arena were not understood, not even
when the PDS accepted that it was necessary to support emergency
governments run by technocrats (though, even here, as we have seen, it
stepped back from fully participating in the Ciampi government) or to
approve electoral reform. And this at a time when the central role played
by international financial capital enhanced the importance of supra-
national monetary institutions and prevented national Keynesian
economic policies.

All parties found themselves constrained to adopt policies aimed at
decreasing the public-sector deficit and had to abandon the uncontrolled
expansion of expenditure of the past.[39] The diminution of the public-
sector deficit and the recovery of financial credibility had become the
necessary conditions for remaining in an international financial circuit
dominated by great regional powers such as Germany in Europe and
Japan in Asia, or by the USA on a world level.

It is no accident that between 1993 and 1996, until the victory in April 1996 of the Olive Tree Coalition (and excluding the short-lived and fractious Berlusconi government of 1994), Italy experienced governments led by senior officials of the Bank of Italy (such as Ciampi and Dini) or by personalities from the financial world and the civil service.

The defeat of the PDS in 1994 was in a sense, inevitable. An electoral alliance (the Progressisti) had been formed with various forces of liberal-socialist non-Craxian inspiration (such as Alleanza democratica) and Rifondazione Comunista.[40] However, this alliance was unable to attract the moderates of the centre who instead turned towards the centrist Catholic PPI, the post-fascist AN and Forza Italia. Moreover, the Progressisti had not been able to prevent the reconstruction of an anti-communist front championed by Berlusconi who turned out to be the true winner of the elections. The fact that anti-communism was the dominant leitmotif of the campaign of the centre-right, despite the break with the past achieved by Achille Occhetto, has not yet been analysed in appropriate depth.

The crisis of the leading left-wing force must therefore be understood within the context of the reconstitution of a centre-right alignment able to fill the vacuum left by the political demise of the DC and of the PSI.

Towards an irreversible transformation

The defeat of 1994 caused the PDS to rethink its ideological and political line. Achille Occhetto resigned; Massimo D'Alema became leader and introduced a radical change in policy.

First, he divided his opponents' front which was already in crisis after the defection of Umberto Bossi's Lega Nord from the Berlusconi government. When the government of Lamberto Dini (a former senior official of the Bank of Italy and previously a minister in the Berlusconi government) was formed, the PDS committed itself to support the government policy of financial recovery as long as the welfare state was not dismantled. Thus, social security was reformed after negotiations with the trade unions. Berlusconi's attempt to do the same without the unions' consent had caused a storm of protests leading to the largest demonstrations since 1945.[41]

Second, D'Alema tried to construct a political rather than a social system of alliances ranging from the moderate centre to the Rifondazione Comunista. With RC, D'Alema made an electoral rather than a government pact, in order to maximize the chances of returning left-wing candidates in first-past-the-post constituencies.[42]

The anti-communist front of Berlusconi and Fini was thus weakened thanks to the presence of a strong centrist component (the PPI and Dini's own list) in the new electoral alignment which now defined itself as 'centre-left'. Romano Prodi became the leader of the new Olive Tree alignment. Prodi was a former Christian democrat, a technocrat, a university professor and former chairman president of IRI (with ENI, one of the most important Italian state companies). He was linked to the moderate Catholic Left and represented a wide range array of political, cultural and economic interests.

The Olive Tree Coalition won the elections largely thanks to D'Alema's shrewd strategy, particularly the alliance with the PPI, but also because the new electoral law penalized the splits which arose in the centre-right alliance – an example is the split of the AN when Pino Rauti formed his own far-right group. Moreover, the Lega Nord was no longer in alliance with Berlusconi and Fini. Its decision to stand alone in the elections favoured the centre-left.

Italy experienced a considerable political transformation. For the first time since 1947 former communists have entered the government. Giorgio Napolitano, the veteran leader of 'communist revisionism', was given the politically sensitive post of Minister of the Interior at a time when the country was faced by the Northern League's 'secessionist' threat and the investigations on economic and political corruption were resumed. For the first time, strategic ministries such as Finance, Education and Scientific Research were assigned to leading personalities of the PDS, including Walter Veltroni who became Romano Prodi's deputy prime minister.

The government's composition reflected the constraints which had led to the PDS's new policy. The key offices in the economic departments (except for Finance) were assigned to reliable men representing the big interest groups of the new globalized financial capitalism. Former Christian democrats who had joined the Olive Tree Coalition through the PPI label were allowed to restore their links with a substantial sector of the middle classes through a renewal of clienteles and patronage more extensive than those of the past when Italy could be defined a 'republic of political parties'.[43]

In fact, until the 1980s, those in charge of forming these clienteles, whether openly or secretly, were the parties themselves. Now they are no longer able to perform this task directly. Consequently, the proliferation of secret power-centres occurs at a much more rapid rate than in the past. This involves not only the middle classes but also the high echelons of the prosperous bourgeoisie. Internecine conflicts began to break out. They are likely to escalate in the future. Particularly involved in this struggle for power are groups around Lamberto Dini and the former socialists who have opted for the centre-left, as well as groups supporting the centre-right. All are involved in a bitter conflict aimed at enlarging their electoral base.

Inevitably, this will leave the Left untouched.

Inside the area of government, former socialists who support the Prodi government – smaller in number than those who have joined, less visibly and openly, Berlusconi and Fini – continue to resent the hegemony of the PDS even though they were elected in 'red' constituencies thanks to the PDS. As they had done in the past, they continuously threaten to change sides. In the wider socialist electorate things have changed considerably since the days of Craxi. The overwhelming majority of this electorate now supports Fini and Berlusconi and no longer follows its former socialist leaders. There is also a new centre-left electorate with no ties to the old Socialist Party but who vote for ex-socialists simply because – under the first-past-the-post system – they have no choice. It is therefore difficult to measure how serious, in reality, is the electoral strength of the former socialist area.

Little else has changed inside the Left. The smaller and weaker groups fight for their survival and in order to have more independence and influence. Distinguishing themselves from the PDS is a good way of achieving this objective.

The real novelty on the Left, apart from the PDS, is the small group of 'Social Christians'. They are not very significant electorally but carry considerable intellectual weight.[44] They are, largely, former trade unionists, leaders of voluntary organizations, intellectuals and members of the 'lower clergy'. They waver between the PDS and the Left of the

PPI where they have considerable influence. Their role is to provide sustenance to those Catholics locked in bitter conflict with a resurgent conservative Catholicism. However, a Catholic 'Left' has never been able in Italy or in the rest of Europe (and unlike in Latin America) to become electorally and politically powerful.[45]

The PDS has seen its traditional electoral strength confirmed, though this is threatened by industrial change, by the transformation in the class structure of the country, by the neo-populism of the Northern League and the Right, and by the split with Rifondazione Comunista – a party which enjoys significant support among the workers in central Italy and wherever the old communist sub-culture still prevails.[46]

The situation, therefore, is fluid and uncertain. No new 'social block' has been consolidated. In the short term it is impossible for this to happen given the situation which characterizes Italian and international capitalism. A worldwide hegemony of a new finance capitalism built on monetary flows has asserted itself over industrial capitalism and traditional financial capitalism (which linked banks and industry). With the full deployment of financial markets we have a situation where capital flows become independent of industrial production, driving them towards constant restructuring and, in effect, constantly weakening them. Hence the social and political instability experienced throughout the world, from France to Japan and South Korea.

Paradoxically enough, this structural instability, far from weakening, is likely to strengthen the Olive Tree government in the long run. After the failure of the Right to form a strong and stable coalition, the Olive Tree government is the remaining point of reference for all those economic groups calling for the financial restructuring of a strategically important country.

It is necessary to bear in mind, however, that, in the context described above, the tasks facing the Olive Tree government are difficult. In a country with a high public deficit, as is the case with Italy, the international power of the new capitalism, where money and finance are independent of industrial growth, exerts an even heavier weight. International and domestic constraints strengthen each other mutually to make it difficult to pursue a non-monetarist economic policy. This is evidenced by the basic continuity in economic policy since the Amato government of 1992–93 until today. The economic policies of the governments of Ciampi, Berlusconi (the latter lacking the support of the leading organs of international financial capitalism), Dini and Prodi do not differ significantly. Policy is carried out according to the constraints of international financial oligarchies. The Prodi government has tried to resist international pressures aimed at dismantling the welfare state by using fiscal policy. In order not to penalize the lower income groups, this policy has targeted mainly the upper middle classes. This could have substantial political electoral repercussions. But all attempts to contain the constant de-industrialization of the country have been ambivalent and inefficient. This process continues very rapidly, affecting above all those large firms which are involved in international competition and which are affected by the growing financialization of the world economy.[47]

This is the challenge facing both the new government and the PDS. Will it be possible to pursue the financial restructuring required by the international community while defending the welfare state and promoting the renewal of industrial growth? Basically, the dilemma appears to be a return to the classic dichotomy between the long and the short term. Between protecting jobs and wages in the short term while, through the European Monetary System, containing inflation, stabilizing purchasing power and also reforming the state machine and eliminating unproductive earnings.[48]

Inevitably, the PDS will raise again those themes and problems originally advanced by 'socialist revisionism', and will try to do so without irreversibly detaching itself from the neo-Marxists of Rifondazione Comunista who are indispensable allies of the government.

Does not this process of ideological transformation lead to the formation of a large US-style 'Democratic Party' where all the components of the Olive Tree Coalition can find a common political home? This project is supported by many in the present coalition, including many inside the PDS itself.

D'Alema is opposed to this, preferring instead to move decisively towards modern 'socialist neo-revisionism'.[49] He wants to do so from a relatively 'Left' position and is encouraged by Rifondazione Comunista (which looks more and more like a party poised halfway between the Second and Third International) and by the (Italian) communist tradition towards which D'Alema feels a certain pride tempered by a critical attitude. Unlike Occhetto, he has no wish to denounce it like a repented sinner. In other words, D'Alema, while firmly condemning Soviet communism, is ready to defend the merits of the Italian variety. This contrasts with the attitude of Occhetto whose 'repentance' was in effect a cause of the electoral defeat. It enabled the opposition to launch an 'anti-communist' campaign against an opponent who, by repudiating his own past, appeared to deny his independence from Stalinism and the contribution the communists had made to the construction of Italian democracy.

While the general situation is in turmoil, that characterizing the world of the trade unions appears singularly static. Its historical divisions remain unchanged. Indeed, they are occasionally accentuated when they compete against each other in negotiations with the government and the entrepreneurs. There are attempts to return to traditional neo-corporate or 'triangular' intermediation by making the unions joint partners with the government and the employers' association in the business of 'economic restructuring'.[50]

Elements of continuity with the past are also present in the political parties. The PDS witnessed a pattern of generational clashes similar to that which occurred in Craxi's PDS. In both instances, a generation of 'forty-year-olds' (i quarantenni) was backed by an older leader (Craxi in the PSI and Occhetto in the PCI/PDS) under the banner of change and modernization, though the historical context was quite different. In both instances, the older generation of leaders was eliminated and activists were silenced by autocratic methods.

In reality, this pattern is a further reflection of the limited institutionalization of the Italian political system. This process was intensified after the collapse of the DC and the PSI. The mafias, fraternities, networks of friends and lobbies have grown in strength and have become more visible and influential in every sector of Italian society. This occurred also in the PCI, and therefore later on in the PDS, although less so than in other Italian parties.[51]

For the 'socialist diaspora' this simply intensifies what had occurred in the past, because the political class which had emerged under Craxi had already transformed the PSI into a business network of clienteles and individuals on the make.

The case of the PDS is different. It was shaken at its roots by the trend towards constructing personal power networks and clienteles. On the one hand, the personal power of some old and new leaders grows on the basis of familist and clientelist ties. On the other hand, the will to resist a trend which would de-institutionalize the party and make it the same as all the others remains strong, especially among those activists and cadres which rely on a strong party machine rather than on personal favours. Inevitably, they fight back, trying to revive the organizational tradition of Italian communism in the new context.

Though no clear ideological or political differences yet distinguish these internal differences, it appears that the liberal-socialist and radical-liberal themes of Occhetto's have been adopted by the new forces promoting the de-institutionalization of the party – in effect its Americanization – while the democratic-socialist themes seem to be advanced by those who, like Massimo D'Alema, have tried to promote a renewed socialist tradition while preserving a politics not based on personalities and clienteles. But here, too, the scenario is unstable, and the circulation of elites proceeds rapidly while their transformation is now irreversible.

3

The Left and the crisis of the Third Hellenic Republic, 1989–97[1]

VASSILIS FOUSKAS

Thus, the [Greek] economy contains in its very existence these two, historically inextricable, unbridled trends: that of the capitalist East, on the one hand, and of the capitalist West, on the other. A double 'barbarism': the former is 'uncivilized', the latter is too much 'civilized'. In this context, what seems to be a dawn from the one side, comes as twilight from the other ...

Pantelis Pouliopoulos, 1934[2]

It has been recognized for some time now that the Republic founded by Konstantinos Karamanlis in 1974 and further consolidated under the socialist rule of Andreas Papandreou in the 1980s, is drawing to an end. The account always comes down to the following: Greece was comfortably secure during the Cold War period. It was the only capitalist country in the Balkan peninsula and was far more economically developed than Turkey; whereas now, after the dissolution of the Warsaw Pact, the geo-political and geo-economic weight of Turkey is bound to grow and hegemonize the wider zone of the Balkans and the Near East.[3] This fact, the account goes, dovetails with the poor economic performance of the country which constantly fails to reach western European standards. Even if overtaken by countries that joined the European Union later, such as Portugal and Spain, Greece succeeded in becoming a cog in the European wheel. The blame is always attributed to the Panhellenic

Socialist Movement (hereafter: PASOK) which, instead of modernizing the country by keeping pace with European developments and neo-liberal trends in the 1980s, developed populist, clientelist, corporatist and, in a word, anti-modernizing policies.

Fairly coherent and easily understandable as an argument, although – as I shall show – debatable in real political terms, this account becomes the source of an authentic conflict which deepens the Greek political crisis. The whole story has divided the political spectrum, cutting across its constituting elites both of the Left and Right: those advocating priority for national, security and defence issues and a strong presence of the state in strategic economic sectors (for example, the defence industry, telecommunications) are considered as populists; those according primacy to the modernization of the Greek economy on the basis of the European integration process, are assessed as modernizers. As early as 1989, Costas Simitis himself – the modernizer Prime Minister since January 1996 and a long-serving economics minister in socialist cabinets – put the question as openly as follows:

> The state can no longer satisfy various social demands. Its weakness leads to frustration and to fears that vested interests will be undermined. Social groups intensify their struggle in order to defend their position. Political parties, to retain their clientele, are under pressure to resort to populism. But populism creates new hopes, new demands and the crisis deepens. *This vicious circle must be smashed. The answer to the crisis cannot come only through party antagonism. It will also be the result of the antagonism between populists and modernizers within the parties themselves.*[4]

My attempt to theorize this real division of modern Greek polity has led me to a certain schematization of the political and social conflicts, although I do not accept all the criticisms of the negative aspects of PASOK's populism.[5] Nevertheless, what remains to be seen is not merely the extent of convergence between the Left and the Right on modernizing or populist grounds, but the degree of differentiation, if any, between them. To put it another way, is there any difference between the modernizing social-democratic factions of PASOK and the neo-liberals of the New Democracy (hereafter: ND) after 1989? To what extent, moreover, can the 'populist–modernization' divide, as practised by the governing elites, be a false political conception? In this context, a number of new questions can be posed: What is the party reaction to the post-1989 Balkan settlement? How do parties – and the Left in particular – deal with the crisis of national Keynesianism as well as their own crisis?

Unfortunately, recent contributions avoid such questions. Apart from a few indigenous contributions, there are hardly any concrete analyses of the post-1989 political and socio-economic landscape of Greece. PASOK will not monopolize my analysis, not only because a comparison between the Left and the Right would provide a convincing argument, but also because a part of the period in question saw the ND in office. Therefore, the analysis will be balanced by alternately concentrating both on the Left and the Right, although the main focus will be PASOK itself. The communist and ex-communist Left will receive attention only when examining the 1989–91 period, where it played a significant role.

I shall begin with some background information with regard to the evolution of the Greek social formation and the transition to democracy. Then I shall outline PASOK's administration in the 1980s. Next I shall move on to analyse the 1989–90 special conjuncture, and the role played by the communist Left. Then I shall deal with the government policies of ND and the Macedonian question. In opting for this, I took into consideration the fact that the collapse of 'really existing socialism' had hardly, if at all, influenced the political performance of PASOK. Rather, the impact it had over the Greek political system as a whole came through the re-emergence of nationalism in the Balkans. Finally, the new administration of PASOK from 1993 to the present, as well as the new premiership of Simitis will be assessed.

By providing an overall account of the Left and examining the major features of the crisis of the post-1974 regime, it may be possible to reach some conclusions on the notion of the 'populism–modernization' dilemma in the Greek polity.

Late modernity and the advent of
the Third Republic

The Greek social formation underwent three historically distinct phases of modernization. The first phase mirrors the political bipolarism between Charilaos Trikoupis and Theodoros Diligiannis during the second half of the nineteenth century and manifests the will of modernizer Trikoupis to promote both institutional reform and public works (for example, railways). The second phase corresponds to the era of the liberal statesman Eleftherios Venizelos, when the bourgeois breakthrough and agrarian reform were accomplished. Skilfully expanding the influence of Greece in the Balkans by employing a homogeneous nationalist discourse, Venizelos expressed the interests of the Greek bourgeoisie – a class extended across the arc Near East–Constantinople–Macedonia – modernized the country, mobilized wide popular strata in politics and led the battle against the King and the old political class of *tzakia*.

The third phase of modernization concerns the post-war economic boom of the 1950s and 1960s and corresponds to the international cycle of the so-called 'golden capitalist age'. Mass foreign direct investment, chiefly American, strengthened Greece's economic performance and a significant part of the population started to migrate from agricultural zones into urban centres as well as abroad. As early as 1963, the masses claimed political participation, an opening up of the existing limited democracy and forcefully expressed their opposition to the Crown. This reformist democratic movement was successfully represented by the party of the Centre under the leadership of George Papandreou against the then politically conservative bloc of Karamanlis and the King. Both the events and the hopes came to a close with the military coup of 1967.[6] It should also be noted that all three phases corresponded to international cycles of growth and advanced the socio-economic and institutional performance of the country without ever 'catching up' with leading western capitalist countries.

The year 1974 signalled the transition from authoritarianism to democracy, the establishment of a republic with a new constitution. The Communist Party of Greece (hereafter: KKE) and the Eurocommunist Communist Party of Greece-interior (hereafter: KKEes) were legitimized.[7] Konstantinos Karamanlis and Andreas Papandreou founded ND and PASOK respectively. The leader of ND withdrew Greece from the military structures of NATO; a tactical move to appease popular discontent over the Cyprus issue. His greatest success in foreign policy was the gradual abandonment of the dogma that 'the war danger for Greece comes from the North', inspired by the anti-communist propaganda of the Cold War. Karamanlis, after the Turkish invasion of Cyprus, considered Turkey to be the principal rival of Greece in the south-east Mediterranean, thus changing the country's political and defence priorities. At the same time he started negotiations for Greece's entry into the European Economic Community (EEC). Skilfully separating Greece from the increasingly complex Iberian entry negotiations, Karamanlis successfully reached an accession agreement with the Community in April 1979. The Treaty of Accession came into effect on 1 January 1981.[8] These are the major achievements of the Right under Karamanlis.

PASOK's welfarism and 'crisis of crisis management' in the 1980s

Meanwhile, some structural limits to further economic advance appeared. In point of fact, the crisis of the Bretton Woods system (1971) and the subsequent oil shocks (1973, 1979) coincided with the rise of the post-junta mass movement and affected the profitability of the economy. ND responded by expanding state interventionism and boosting aggregate demand. A number of nationalizations took place in the banking sector, transport (including air transport) and shipyards. Welfare measures were introduced, thus preparing the ground for PASOK's generous welfare policies throughout the 1980s. However, one fact which needs to be stressed is the very specific role the state had to play in order to stave off crises. The governor of the Bank of Greece in 1978, Angelos Angelopoulos, argued:

> There are some private enterprises which are very important for the overall performance of the national economy. Nevertheless, due to internal and external factors, they encounter financial difficulties which are bound to increase as Greece approaches the European Common Market. It would be wise, therefore, to increase the spending to them ... In essence, a new state organization, helped by commercial Banks, should be set up, in order to subsidise or take over the management of those enterprises facing economic problems.[9]

Thus, in the wake of the state's expansionary policies, a genuinely specialized economic apparatus began to take shape at the core of public managerial activities, thus directly affecting its fiscal performance. Accordingly, a new political class, essentially Keynesian and deeply statist, began to emerge under the directives of the ND under Karamanlis.

Throughout the 1980s, the state, under PASOK, continued to expand this form of intervention, despite a worsening of public finance. In point of fact, PASOK's populist leading group expanded the public sector, while keeping wage rises in industry around 30 per cent, a real increase close to 6 per cent yearly. PASOK did very little to reform public administration, while the setting up of an efficient tax machine was delayed, thus encouraging an underground economy and various illegal economic activities.[10] Papandreou did not hesitate to dismiss Costas Simitis – then Minister of National Economy – in 1987, when the latter attempted to apply a package of austerity policies, as had been projected by the pro-monetarist economic assessor of the Bank of Greece, Nicos Garganas, in 1984–85 (the so-called stabilization programme). Simitis aimed at the realization of a feasible modernizing policy which, among other things, would have to reform the backward tax system, modernize the cumbersome state administration and, with great care, launch the privatization of 'lame ducks' as well as progressively liberalize the financial market. The final targets were the curbing of inflation and public deficit in order to facilitate the synchronization of Greece with European developments vis-à-vis the Single European Act (1986) and the Maastricht deadline (1992).

The above facts are of paramount importance and should receive attention because, contrary to international neo-liberal trends spearheaded by Margaret Thatcher and Ronald Reagan, the ruling political parties in Greece showed an unprecedented pro-Keynesian resistance to change. PASOK, in particular, concretely protected the labour market, substantially increased the size of the public sector,[11] exploited internal and external borrowing in order to finance the deficit, advanced political democracy and significantly expanded welfare measures.[12] Thus, despite the stagnation in private capital performance and growth ratio, people's income potential and purchasing power increased drastically. The 'hidden sector', various multi-professional structures (small businesses, self-employed people in tourism and elsewhere, occasional employment and so on), all of which were unassailable by the inefficient tax machine of the state, could operate freely. Despite the 26 per cent growth in real

personal incomes during the 1980s, personal income tax receipts were
still at the low level of 4.5 per cent of GDP, which is less than half the
OECD and EC averages.[13] Moreover, strong family ties and a widespread
sense of community backed the creation of a prosperous, although
highly unproductive, societal structure.[14] Compared to its northern
European partners, one could argue that Greece was a poor country
with rich people. Only the Italy of the 1970s and 1980s, perhaps, could
also belong to this bizarre category. There was no major drift towards
neo-liberal policies as was the case in François Mitterrand's France (the
famous U-turn, 1982–83) and in Felipe González's Spain (especially
from the second half of the 1980s onwards).

Nevertheless, national Keynesianism could no longer be the solution.
Double-digit inflation, a high public debt and remarkably low rates of
GDP growth eroded both the country's economic potential and European confidence. Allegations of corruption, 'raw' clientelism and misuse
of government power, could all fit the perceptive term 'crisis of crisis
management', coined by Claus Offe in his analyses on the crisis of the
Keynesian state.[15] PASOK was at the heart of this form of crisis. In this
context, if we cannot talk about the beginning of a fourth phase of
growth in Greece in the 1980s – something which is likely to be said for
the western economies as well as for Spain and Italy – we cannot equally
talk about a neo-liberal PASOK at the time, let alone the pro-Marxist
PASOK of the first post-junta period (1974–81).

To sum up: broadly speaking, while Greece's economy, institutions,
socio-political movements and periodic crises did historically correspond
to those in the rest of Europe, Greece failed to achieve those rates of
industrial and technological growth that would have permitted the
country to compete equally with other capitalist countries in international and European markets. In this context, the three distinct phases
of economic growth, outlined above, pertained to a historically uneven
type of development, typical of capitalist modernity. The full application of political democracy after 1974 coincided with the international
crisis and the pause in the rates of growth. The ND implemented pro-
Keynesian policies in order to stave off the crisis. PASOK, once in
office, continued the expansion of political democracy and used the
state's interventionist capacity powerfully, especially its welfare dimension. Thus, the ruling political class of the third Republic – inclusive

of highly paid civil servants and diplomatic bodies – is transversely enmeshed within the national state, namely, its 'Keynesian' apparatus and functioning. By the end of the 1980s the PASOK, not being able to control inflation and public deficit, was led to what could be called 'crisis of the crisis management'. On the other hand, its policies contributed to the creation of such a 'welfare society' which even the most prosperous advanced economies of the West would admire.

The 1989–90 conjuncture and the failure of the communist Left

In 1989 PASOK seemed to be exhausted. It had already presented signs of electoral decline in the 1985 general election, while many from within its ranks started openly to criticize Papandreou's authoritarian behaviour. In essence, PASOK's leading group around Papandreou were subjected to criticism from both the Left and Right of the party: from the left wing because the traditional socialist positions of the movement had been tacitly discarded (for example, anti-NATO and anti-Europe); from right-wingers because fundamental inner-party democratic principles as well as efforts to modernize the country had been abandoned. In addition, after allegations that prominent cadres of PASOK and Papandreou himself were involved in a number of financial scandals, both the communist Left and the ND advanced a concerted attack against the socialists.

As a major opposition force, the ND party, under the new leadership of Constantine Mitsotakis, attempted to seize the opportunity and take the lead in the situation. For their part, the two main forces on the left of PASOK, the KKE and the Hellenic Left (hereafter: EAR), had their own reasons for opposing the socialists: in fact, they examined ways of collaborating with each other not only in order to avoid the perverse effects upon them caused by the crisis of 'really existing socialism', but also to capitalize on the crisis of PASOK.[16] As early as February 1989 the coalition of the Left and Progress (hereafter: SYN) was set up. Its organization was very loose, something which was favoured by the KKE, who were afraid of being absorbed in the SYN, thus mirroring the negative experience of the pre-junta United Democratic Left (EDA) within which the KKE had risked dissolving.

Papandreou lost the election of June 1989, but, to the bitter dis-
appointment of SYN, PASOK retained about 40 per cent of the vote
(see Appendix, Table 3.1). As no parliamentary majority could be
formed, a three-month government coalition between ND and SYN
ensued. Tzannis Tzannetakis, a moderate ND conservative, was appointed Prime Minister. The main purpose of the government was to
investigate the scandals allegedly committed by the socialists. According
to a specific judicial regulation drafted by the pre-war cabinet of the
dictator Ioannis Metaxas, if no government was to be formed, the
scandals could not have been examined by the parliament resulting from
an ensuing election, therefore they would have been repealed and, finally,
cancelled. Accusations were made against Papandreou too, because of
some evidence that he was involved in the so-called 'Koskotas affair' –
named after a rich businessman and banker accused of illegalities at the
Bank of Crete.

The aim of this Hellenic 'historic compromise' – once very much
hated by the KKE but beloved by the 'revisionists' of the ex-KKEes –
proved to be a poor caricature of the original Italian. SYN failed to
become a credible alternative force both *vis-à-vis* PASOK (in opposition)
and ND (co-government). It offered no realistic opposition to the Right.
Public opinion, understandably, thought that the Right–communist coalition was just a deliberate effort to bring PASOK and Papandreou to
trial; in other words, that their common aim for both was PASOK's
dissolution and a sharing out of the booty.

No doubt, SYN was totally unprepared to face this challenge. In
point of fact, such an alignment summing up post-Eurocommunists
and pro-Stalinists could only produce a politically incoherent and
ideologically confused organism. Then, a more careful examination for
alternatives, in order to avoid a pact with the Right, had to be found in
June 1989. As prominent jurists argued at the time, a convenient constitutional solution for the SYN had to be found so as to avoid an
alliance with the Right or accusations that 'SYN leaves the country
ungoverned'; at the same time, institutional guarantees for the non-
repeal of the scandals could have been given.[17] SYN's major political
mistake was committed none the less when, by the end of the Tzannetakis government, PASOK called for a new parliamentary majority by
proposing proportional representation – a reform which would have

been to the advantage of SYN. SYN, with its front-bench spokesman Leonidas Kyrkos, leader of EAR and for years a historic moderate figure of KKEes, refused to approve the proposal on the grounds that the formation of a new PASOK–SYN majority would be a 'parliamentary and institutional coup'.[18]

Between autumn 1989 and spring 1990, a three-party coalition government (PASOK–ND–SYN) replaced that of Tzannetakis, since the November 1989 polls had once again given no single party an overall parliamentary majority. The new provisional Prime Minister, the elderly Xenophon Zolotas, a widely known professor of economics and a long-standing governor of the Bank of Greece, now had to deal with major economic policy matters, such as inflation and the public debt. Zolotas hoped that cross-party responsibility for an austerity programme could be achieved, and on this basis he appointed three chief economists, each of whom was from one of the three different parties supporting his premiership: George Gennimatas (PASOK) and Iannis Dragassakis (SYN) were respectively appointed as Minister and Deputy Minister of Economic Affairs, while Andreas Andrianopoulos, an extreme neo-liberal cadre of ND, became Minister of Finance. This hope proved a chimera and the consensual approach to economic and social problems failed, since both PASOK and KKE – the former with its dominant populist faction, the latter through the SYN – vetoed any major anti-popular decision proposed. This began to assume extreme proportions. The most farcical episode was when the government subsidized flour producers in order to keep the price of bread stable, since the trend in the rise of the price of flour was irreversible. Zolotas' operation failed, while Mitsotakis and ND argued that the Left was not a responsible governing partner and forced a new election.

The economy could no longer afford cabinets without policies. Clear-cut reforms were required. In the two coalition governments, SYN was the major loser. It proved unable to capitalize on a number of political opportunities raised in the 1989–90 conjuncture and play a major role in the shaping of modern Greek polity. It lacked political strategy and organizational cohesion, being a hotch-potch of old-fashioned Stalinists and liberal socialists. On these shaky grounds, SYN proved unable to aggregate either populist or modernizing forces from ND and PASOK. It split again in 1990–91. The basic reason for this was the divisions within the KKE, the backbone of SYN. Its thirteenth Congress (autumn 1990) proved to be a struggle between 'renovators' and 'conservatives'.[19] The former tendency, being explicitly in favour of European integration and the notion of a Euro-Left, saw the SYN as the new political umbrella which could accommodate a respectable post-communist Left after the end of the Cold War. The latter firmly insisted on the party's rigid Leninist principles and put forward pure anti-European stances. The KKE, for the second time since 1968, was really split in two: pro-Europeans and anti-Europeans, 'modernizers' and 'populists'.[20] Finally, despite enjoying a marginal majority, the latter faction won the overall battle due basically to the control it had over the party apparatus. Iannis Dragassakis (a former deputy minister), Mimis Androulakis (the charismatic modernizer spokesman of KKE) and Maria Damanaki (a prominent parliamentary cadre), and many more, predominantly young, members, all decided to leave the KKE, a party which, for more than two decades, had inspired their political ambitions, strategic projections and communist dreams. The KKE proved 'unreformable': a sort of George Marchais' Parti communiste and Alvaro Cunhal's Partido Comunista.

The right-wing management of power, 1990–93

Social and economic policies   Prime Minister Mitsotakis found himself in a predicament when he was forced to barter with the two Muslim deputies in order to form a government. Finally, he shaped a cabinet on a slender parliamentary majority, counting on the sole vote of Democratic Renewal's deputy (hereafter: DIANA), a splinter group of ND headed by today's President of the Republic, Costis Stephanopoulos. This fact counted both in terms of inner-government stability and intra-party balance of force and, perhaps more crucially, in terms of political determination. Thus, when crucial decisions in line with the party's neo-liberal programme were to be taken, the dispute between the populist–statist faction and the modernizers became apparent. Under such conditions, the ND centrist leading group around Mitsotakis attempted to 'straddle' the two extremes in order to avoid organic crises which would have led to the toppling of his government. As we shall see, this proved unfeasible.

ND applied a wide range of supply-side policies, in line with its neo-liberal inspired economic programme.[21] In an attempt to free suppressed market forces, ND concentrated its effort on four economic fronts: (1) financial deregulation; (2) ending labour market rigidities endorsed under the PASOK government; (3) deregulation in goods/services markets and public sector consolidation through fiscal retrenchment and privatization of ailing state firms; (4) curb inflation and decrease the balance of payments deficit.

All the four targets should, *ceteris paribus*, leave room for direct private investment, increase the respectability of the country in the eyes of the world markets and improve Greece's credibility in Europe. While a considerable improvement occurred in several economic indicators, the overall result was not as satisfactory as initially hoped.

In the banking sector, consumer credit was liberalized and a law incorporating EC banking directives was introduced in 1992. Nevertheless, neither the growing sophistication of financial operators nor some crucial institutional obstacles – such as the lack of a clearing channel for inter-bank transfers – were lifted. Inflation was brought down to 11 per cent – it was running at 21 per cent in 1990 – but it was still far behind the OECD average. Privatization policies brought no spectacular results, either because of the opposition of the trade unions which made the implementation process slow, or because they had been partial, or because of the lack of clearly established rules. As far as the labour market was concerned, free collective bargaining with no state intervention became the rule and impediments to part-time work were considerably reduced. All private-sector wage settlements since 1991 were concluded without government interference. In addition, wages were frozen and a new pension law passed in September 1992 aimed at limiting the government subsidy to one-third of pension expenditure. With regard to the reform in public administration, overall achievements were the poorest: the proclaimed neo-liberal goal of reducing employment in the wider public sector by 10 per cent failed to materialize, while the reform of the tax-collecting system was very slow. Lack of expertise, coordination and over-running proved highly costly.[22]

PASOK, KKE and SYN apart, opposition to these policies came from ultra-monetarist ND politicians gathered around Andreas

Andrianopoulos, for a short time Minister of Finance. Andrianopoulos argued that no tolerance should be shown to the demands of PASOK, the KKE and the trade unions. He proposed the full privatization of the Hellenic Telecommunications Organization and disagreed over the privatization of AGET, one of the biggest cement-exporting companies in Europe, because a considerable part of its shares had been bought by the National Bank of Greece. All the ten biggest state manufacturing loss-makers were to be sold, no matter what the social or even political costs.[23] Andrianopoulos' other major concern was the reform of the public sector, its over-staffing and inefficiency. 'Reforms on this front', he said, 'are running with the speed of a hedgehog.'[24]

With a view to meeting the Maastricht convergence criteria and easing inner-party conflicts, the Mitsotakis government presented a rather ambitious Convergence Programme 1993–98 in December 1992, the principal goals of which were the reduction in inflation and the public sector borrowing requirement, tax reform, the boosting of direct investment, the offsetting of the public sector's inefficiency via drastic privatizations, moderate real wages and reduction in general public spending (pensions, various benefits and welfare contributions); in other words, a fully fledged supply-side monetarist project. Once again, despite verbal determination, the centrist leading group of ND proved incapable of convincing the populist inner-party opposition, while equally failing to meet the radical demands of neo-liberals. The statist Keynesian apparatus created by Karamanlis and reinvigorated by Papandreou, an apparatus at the core of which lies the entire power of the ruling class of the Third Republic, proved to be very durable, hence difficult to dismantle so quickly.

GDP growth in 1993 was significantly less than 2 per cent and inflation remained in double-digit figures. And while unemployment rates increased further,[25] no real fiscal improvement was made. The public sector borrowing requirement continued to exceed 10 per cent of GDP and this resulted in an increase in the debt/GDP ratio.[26] This was a *de facto* failure to modernize the public administration and improve tax-collecting. The whole picture would be incomplete if a new dimension, which tended to worsen the crisis, is not added: the opening of the central and East European markets provided low labour costs and that increased competition with Greece. At the same time, the flow of considerable numbers of illegal immigrants – mainly Albanians and other eastern European nationalities – tended to increase unemployment, under-employment and job precariousness, since farmers were showing a clear preference for the low-wage eastern European labour. This was to increase social tensions and the general nationalist climate in the Balkans which, in Greece, was connected to the old Macedonian question. Mitsotakis' cabinet proved particularly impotent in dealing with this issue, his nationalist Minister of Foreign Affairs causing the breakdown of the government.

Foreign policy and the 'Macedonian question' As we have seen, Karamanlis had reversed the prevailing defence dogma that Greece's main danger came from the USSR, claiming that the real problem was Turkey and its overt or covert claims over the Aegean Sea. The historic leader of the Greek Right proved correct, although he failed to foresee the crisis of 'really existing socialism' and its effects on Greece. Had this been done, more confidence and less embarrassment would have prevailed today in dealing with the FYROM's[27] claim to be recognized under the name of Macedonia, the name of a northern province of Greece.

The Macedonian question, involving almost all the Balkan forces in the past, was bound to re-emerge when FYROM – in Greece known as the Republic of Skopje, after its capital – followed other constituent parts of former Yugoslavia and became independent. At the heart of the dispute between Greece and FYROM were the following issues: the question of name; some irredentist claims traced back to the Anti-Fascist Assembly of the National Liberation of Macedonia and embedded in the preamble to the constitution of FYROM;[28] the use of the Star of Vergina in the flag of the new state, which was found in the tomb of Philip II of Macedonia near Salonica; the printing, by extreme nationalist organizations in FYROM, of maps and banknotes, the former depicting a unified Macedonia encompassing the Greek province and the white tower of Salonica.

For a variety of reasons, Mitsotakis initially adopted an intransigent position. First of all, he wanted to avoid harsh conflicts with his nationalist fellows and, especially, with the Minister of Foreign Affairs, Antonis Samaras, who had succeeded in reaching a favourable agreement for Greece in December 1991, in a meeting with the EC foreign ministers.[29] Secondly, he recognized and took into account a strong nationalist sentiment in the Greek society which, *per se*, was but the result of a national identity crisis after the loss of secure political and ideological identities prevailing in the 1970s and 1980s.[30] Mitsotakis acted unsuccessfully as inner-party mediator between nationalists and pro-Europeans.

After the failure of the so-called 'Pinheiro package'(1992), Mitsotakis toned down nationalist demands.[31] This embittered Samaras who, in the late summer of 1993, decided to break from the ND and, together with other deputies, to create his own party, Political Spring (hereafter: POLA). Despite the fact that the moderation of nationalism in foreign policy was profoundly realistic, Mitsotakis acted rather perfunctorily and inconsistently, while Samaras gave the impression of a competent and coherent nationalist politician.

Consequently, the government of ND was on the verge of the collapse and lost the election in October 1993.[32] On the one hand, its economic policies, although improving somewhat the economic performance of the country, had paid lip-service to the institutional and fiscal reform, while failing to deal adequately with unemployment, inflation and the balance of payments deficit. Ultra neo-liberals constituted a permanent threat to the centrist leading group of Mitsotakis while PASOK's and KKE's opposition blocked any anti-popular measure. On the other hand, Mitsotakis failed equally in shaping a working inner-government majority on the Macedonia issue. The intransigent nationalist–populist wing of Samaras split, causing the fall of the government. A soft nationalist faction gathered around the Minister of Defence, Ioannis Varvitsiotis, and extreme neo-liberals, for the time being, decided to stay in. Thus, ND's 'radiography' can be read, *mutatis mutandis*, alongside PASOK's one: a populist faction composed of pro-Keynesians and pro-nationalists, and a modernizing current composed of neo-liberals.

PASOK's return to power, 1993–97

The 1993 'Regeneration Programme' of PASOK Once again in power in October 1993, PASOK could no longer play the populist card. Although Papandreou capitalized much on the 'Macedonian question' by adopting a nationalist stance similar to that of Samaras,[33] no 'third road to socialism' or anti-European slogans could really find support among the Greeks. The pro-popular/social, as against the technocratic/ neo-liberal, modernization it promoted in the 1980s, had amalgamated the party's electoral clientele against neo-liberal economics, though a new generation of highly politicized intellectuals was distancing itself from populist slogans. The problem for PASOK was how to abandon rhetoric and shape a convincing and pragmatic social-democratic policy which, while preserving the old clientele, would improve the country's economic indicators.

PASOK presented a 136-page programme for the 1993 election. In the main, it encompassed a pro-Keynesian philosophy similar to that adopted by the French socialists after the 1983 U-turn, or the British Labour Party in 1987.[34] It had three fundamental aims: (1) to advance the defence and security system of the country; (2) to modernize its social and economic structures; (3) to modernize and reform public administration also via decentralization of powers and various incentives, including an increase in wages. Though the post-war model of development was exhausted, the state still had a strategic national role to play, namely, to rehabilitate the social cohesion which the Right, via its neo-liberal policies, has severely damaged since 1989. The tripartite social contract remained fundamental and plans for the privatization of strategic national industries (for example, shipyards, electricity, war industries, telecommunications), and welfare institutions (the health system, education), had to be abandoned. The two-thirds society of deprivation and urban decay was the result of neo-liberal economics (here the PASOK document mentions the case of American society). The fundamental socialist goal was led to reverse this reality. For Greece this meant overcoming the Athens-based model of distorted growth. In the final instance, what counted for PASOK was the human being, not technocratic logic.[35]

I would argue, therefore, that PASOK remained in a Keynesian framework, although now much more sophisticated and, certainly, with pronounced elements of self-criticism: 'We must admit that, despite our efforts [in the 1980s], we failed to reverse the traditional archetypes of development and realise the great change [*allaghi*] ... *There is a need to fight populism, corporatism and clientelism.*'[36]

The notion PASOK held about the role of the nation-state in its programme assured that the 'populism–modernization' divide could be bridged. As we saw earlier, the PASOK document presented its three pillars as an organic whole, thus avoiding the risk of giving priority to one or the other. The intra-party conflict between 'populists' and 'modernizers' had become more sophisticated. By institutionalising its components at the heart of the state, the struggle was not only about policies but also about the succession to Papandreou, as his health had been progressively worsening after 1989.[37] What was at stake was which party faction would lead the party after Papandreou, whether it would succeed in doing so and how the party could be kept united afterwards. All these questions notwithstanding, PASOK had changed since 1989. First and simply, it could not easily return to the state what ND had already given to the market. Secondly, although it looked at the economy through Keynesian eyes, it tried to present itself as a competent, pragmatic, non-populist political force. In fact, the beginning of the post-Papandreou era had, although tentatively, begun.

Governmental policies and the qualification of intra-party/state conflict   Papandreou appointed an experienced cabinet. Simitis (a potential modernizer) accepted the Ministry of Trade and Industry, while Gherassimos Arsenis and Akis Tzochatzopoulos (both populists) were appointed as Defence and Interior ministers respectively. Vasso Papandreou (no relation), a highly respected former European Commissioner, was excluded. George Gennimatas, despite fighting cancer, became Finance Minister because of his popularity and strong ties with the unions. Thus, any major anti-popular measure could potentially soften labour opposition. This allocation of ministerial positions reflects precisely the degree of sophistication and institutionalization of the intra-party conflict and the way the entire cabinet structure was hemmed in by the 'populists–modernizers' divide, thus preparing the ground for what was to come.

PASOK took over while the rate of growth was very low (around 1 per cent) and with inflation running around 11 per cent (four times the EC average). The liberalization of the financial market – a reform process which began in the mid-1980s – had proceeded satisfactorily, but the public sector borrowing requirement was excessive and the public debt was over 115 per cent of the GDP. Low rates of growth, high inflation and no fiscal consolidation were the three crucial problems that the ND had failed to resolve. PASOK, for its part, was to provide a halfway solution somewhere between the programme announced and the actual policies implemented.

In line with the programme approved at its third Congress (1994), PASOK attempted to protect public utilities by following a policy of a limited opening of the share capital to the private sector. Thus, either they have again been set under state control (for example, the Athens Bus Company whose privatization from the ND caused 8000 lay-offs and enormous labour protest) or delayed.[38] The intended privatization of 50 per cent of OTE (telecommunications) was cancelled at the end of 1993, to be replaced in 1994 by a less ambitious flotation plan (25 per cent). Nevertheless, even this was postponed, as PASOK alleged weakness of the stock markets.[39] From a large cumulative decline under the 1990–93 ND government, a small increase in wages occurred. This was roughly in line with expected inflation and applied to government employees.[40] Encouraged by EU financial help,[41] the government budgeted a sharp rise in public investment. As announced in the 'regeneration programme', efforts intensified to improve the tax-collection system and modernize the public administration, but all the while keeping almost intact over-running in the public sector. In addition, the restructuring and/or privatization of 'ailing firms' was very slow.

In all, and despite pro-monetarist European requirements, PASOK in government attempted to keep pace with its declared pro-Keynesianism, boost aggregate demand through public investment and 'roll back' privatization of public utilities, while protecting wages and welfare institutions, the national health system in particular. Needless to say, this policy contrasts sharply with that pursued by ND monetarists.

Improvement in the main economic indicators was minimal, while there was renewed speculation against the drachma in May–June 1994. Consequently, PASOK was forced to draw up a new Convergence Programme, 1994–99. This programme, less ambitious than that of ND, consisted of reasonable growth projection and a moderate public debt target. PASOK continued to grant particular importance to state-financed investment, a fact which still points to a strong pro-Keynesianism. However, few of the pre-election promises were accomplished. Indirect taxes were raised, farm income was taxed, the protective status of the Greek steel industry was removed and currency markets were largely deregulated. Some privatization took place in the largest of the companies in the state-controlled Industrial Development Bank (ETVA); the Skaramangas shipyards were to be sold in 1995. This caused a bitter disagreement between Papandreou and his Industry Minister Costas Simitis.[42] The dispute went on for some time, until Simitis was forced to resign once again. The ensuing cabinet crisis was further aggravated when Papandreou, on 21 November 1995, was taken seriously ill. Two months later, still under intensive care, Papandreou agreed that a successor should be found.

New inner-party alignments were formed. Simitis tried to impart a sort of 'collective leadership' among PASOK members and assumed responsibility on the grounds of a concrete modernizing platform. On 18 January 1996, Simitis defeated the populist factions though he did not remove any of his defeated rivals from their ministerial posts.[43]

Simitis' new revisionism   Soon after the election of Simitis, the Turkish Prime Minister Tansu Ciller, in an attempt to reinforce her position after inconclusive elections in December 1995, appealed to nationalist instincts, provoking the new Greek cabinet. Turkish commandos disembarked on the Greek islets of Imia and took down the Greek flag. The crisis, the worst between Greece and Turkey since 1987, was a troubling reminder of Turkey's internal problems, rather than a mere test of the new Greek premier who, although he could avoid extreme anti-patriotism, acted calmly.[44] Both populist factions were less temperate.[45] The government of Ankara had to resolve unique awkward problems, from the Kurdish and Armenian questions and the powerful rise of Islamic fundamentalism to the country's poor human rights record and still backward economic performance.[46] Turkey often resorts to a 'display of power and determination' *vis-à-vis* Greece by way of appealing to the nationalist and anti-western feelings of the masses. On the other hand, Greece still enjoys a remarkable degree of capitalist stability and prosperity and, unlike its Balkan neighbours, has a highly homogeneous ethnic population.

The way Simitis had been elected to the premiership and won the September 1996 national election,[47] the lingering influence of Papandreou, still strong after his death,[48] the Turkish challenge in the

Aegean Sea as well as the appalling events in Cyprus in the summer and autumn of 1996, have clearly shown that the modernizers' future course will not be a royal road, smooth and free of risk. The fourth Congress of the party in June 1996 confirmed this trend.

PASOK's Congressional Theses signalled an important break with the past.[49] In contrast to its 1993 and 1994 positions, the document recognized that the degree of globalization deprives the state from acting as a major organizer of social allocation of resources. Therefore:

> The modern conception of the welfare state cannot be identified with the post-War keynesian model. It cannot be an opportunistic charity state delivering according to the economic conjuncture. On the contrary, its institutions should be incorporated in the whole process of development and restructuring of productive activities. Its institutions should be able to guarantee new jobs ... new insurance policy.[50]

Nevertheless, the welfare state is not going to be abolished. It needs a profound restructuring and modernization so as to collect resources effectively and allocate them rationally: 'The main contradiction is between the forces of production and a healthy economy on the one hand, and the forces of mediation and underground economy, on the other.'[51] The new state could therefore draw resources by curbing the 'hidden sector' and achieving a fair distribution of income and wealth.

The new division of labour, technological innovations, information systems and bio-technologies, in a word, the entirely new socio-economic landscape offers possibilities for new social and political alliances. In an important passage, the new leading group of PASOK declared its position on the populism–modernization split as follows:

> The youth, an important fraction of the middle class ... the majority of educated people, a number of big and small entrepreneurs belong to the strategy of modernization and restructuring. All these strata promote creatively technocratic-scientific advances, and encourage development and production ... On the other hand, there is that perennial confrontation with the inner-circles of rentiers and retailers, of speculators and 'black economy' which circumvent the national income and hamper any real process of development.[52]

PASOK realises that the very *locus* of populism–modernization split lies in the social/technical division of labour which, in turn, reshapes itself under the aegis of the political cycle and the restructuring of the relations of production. Furthermore, as populists are embedded within the party and state machine *ad hoc* arguing against any idea of separation between the state and the party,[53] any reformist attempt should start from the reform of the linkage between economy, society and the state. Political personalities apart, the whole problem in this respect should be closely seen alongside the institutional materiality of the party and state machine in which the entire transversal populist–corporatist body of the Third Republic is encompassed. Consequently, the problem of the Greek polity according to the new leading group is institutional reform: this, among other things, includes constitutional revision, modernization of the state machine, autonomy of the judiciary, reinforcement of the State of Law, creation of adequate mechanisms to dictate rules to the market overseeing the process of privatization, radical reform of the parliament and so forth.[54] In this context, changes in the party and its ideological premises are required.

Simitis' administration argues that the organizational form needs to change in order to face the new challenges successfully, such as the fragmentation of the social fabric and the speed with which knowledge and information are moving. Hence the need for PASOK to open up to society.[55] Accordingly, 'democratic socialism' assumes a new content, amply democratic, libertarian and solidaristic. PASOK itself no longer represents the democratic and socialist alignment, but the Greek centre-left. In conclusion, this is entirely the agenda of new revisionism,[56] adopted by all major forces of the European Left in the 1980s.

PASOK does not fail to underline Greece's commitment to the Balkans. The country's geo-political and geo-economic position, its economic potential and European identity point to an active policy in this area. As far as the Cyprus issue is concerned, the Congress endorsed a qualified version of the 'united defence doctrine'.[57]

To sum up: under Simitis' leadership PASOK has begun a real break with its populist past. It conceives the dynamics of contemporary capitalism in a modernizing, developmental and strictly pro-European framework, without under-estimating Greece's potential in the Balkans. Institutional changes are fundamental not only for the success of modernization and Greece's European commitment, but also for the survival of the welfare state in an attempt to protect it from crude neo-liberalism. By adopting the new revisionist projection, PASOK's modernizers present themselves in a fashion which is distinguishable both from the PASOK's populist faction and ND's monetarists.

Conclusion

PASOK in the 1980s resisted neo-liberalism in a way that, on the one hand, damaged state finance while, on the other, improved people's living standards. This could no longer be the case in the 1990s either under PASOK's or ND's rule. The exhaustion of the Republic in the era of Papandreou concerns the inability of the Greek state to institutionalize the aggregate demand management and, therefore, to act as a Keynesian state. In point of fact, today's crisis is strictly linked to the process of European integration along neo-liberal lines. In this respect, PASOK has little room for manoeuvre. It can only adjust itself to the transformation of capitalism and advance institutional and political reforms. PASOK is forced to implement part of supply-side policies in order to mitigate the fiscal crisis of the state and reach European requirements. Nevertheless, PASOK's pro-welfare conception, and the socialist culture performance of its cabinet members which often undermines market extremism, point to significant policy divergences between the two parties.[58]

The populists–modernizers cleft within PASOK has assumed a new qualified dimension. The antithesis is adjusted to the new phase of modernization and the post-Papandreou era. Populists, however, still concentrate their efforts on national defence and security issues, while arguing for generous redistribution policies. In point of fact, these are the issues on which ND populists, the POLA party of Samaras, the KKE, some fractions of SYN, as well as the newly formed party of Dimitris Tsovolas which split from PASOK, are focused. This all reflects the specific degree of the crisis of the Greek polity. New political fragments and splinter groups are appearing, composing and decomposing themselves on the political stage, the splitting matrixes being both major parties. The recent national election confirmed this trend as well as the need for a total renewal of the political system. However, the amalgamated antithesis between populists and modernizers within the two major parties of the Third Republic is reflected and conceived by their politicians through a falsified notion: by prioritizing either national issues or economic modernization, they forget the historical fact that no linear articulation exists between the two variables. There can very well be a strong military power under pre- or semi-modern socio-economic conditions and vice versa. The example of Greek–Turkish relations speaks for itself. The fact is that Greece still remains a major Balkan force with far fewer internal problems than Turkey or any other country in the region.

PASOK has stressed and will go on stressing Greece's potential in the peninsula. Greece is not only a European country, it is a Balkan country too. It is therefore historically linked both with the West and the East, with the 'dawn and the twilight' of the communist Pouli-opoulos, though he did not seem to know – nor do we today – which side represents the dawn and which the twilight. Nevertheless, we all are aware of barbarism and how to avoid it.

Appendix

Table 3.1 Electoral results 1989–96

Parties	June 1989		Nov 1989		April 1990		Oct 1993		Sept 1996	
	Seats	(%)	Seats	(%)	Seats	(%)	Seats	(%)	Seats	(%)
ND	44.28	145	46.19	148	46.89	150	39.30	110	38.12	108
PASOK	39.13	125	40.68	128	38.61	123	46.88	170	41.49	162
SYN	13.13	28	10.97	21	10.28	19	2.94		5.12	10
KKE							4.54	9	5.61	11
POLA							4.87	11		
DIKI									4.43	9
Others	1.40	2	1.12	2	1.47	3				

Notes: SYN was founded in 1989 by KKE, EAR and other minor Left forces; the KKE left the coalition after the 1990 election. POLA (Political Spring) is the right-wing nationalist party founded in 1993 by Samaras. DIKI: Tsovolas' national populists. PASOK and SYN presented joint candidates in single-member constituencies; they won one seat in November 1989 and four in April 1990.

Table 3.2 State aid to manufacturing

	Per cent of value added		ECU per person employed	
	1986–88	1988–90	1986–88	1988–90
Belgium	4.3	4.1	1.606	1.665
Germany	2.7	2.5	994	984
Greece	24.3	14.6	2.983	1.502
Spain	6.8	3.6	1.749	936
France	3.8	3.5	1.437	1.380
Ireland	6.2	6.0	2.139	2.175
Portugal	2.2	5.3	302	758
UK	2.6	2.0	770	582

Source: OECD Economic Surveys, *Greece* (Paris: OECD 1993), p. 16.

4

The PSOE: Modernization and the welfare state in Spain

PAUL KENNEDY

In 1989 the Spanish Socialist Workers' Party had good reason to feel satisfied with itself. In the general election held in October that year, the dominance of the PSOE was confirmed by its capture of exactly half of the seats in Congress. The election had taken place against the background of an exceptional economic boom as the country enjoyed the highest investment-led growth in Europe. In June, Spain had rounded off its successful EC Presidency by taking the peseta into the Exchange Rate Mechanism, further proof, if it were needed, of the Spanish socialists' commitment to European integration. A vibrant Spain had at last 'arrived'.

In reality, 1989 marked a turning-point in the fortunes of the PSOE. The 1990s proved to be far more problematic for a party which appeared to lose its touch as its much-vaunted organizational dominance and strict party discipline gave way to internal feuding. As the PSOE became mired in an apparently never-ending series of corruption scandals, it emerged that Spain was experiencing its deepest economic recession in over thirty years. Nevertheless, the party gained an unprecedented fourth consecutive election victory in 1993, albeit with the loss of its overall majority, remaining in power with the parliamentary support of the Catalan nationalist group, Convergència i Unió (Convergence and Unity – CiU). The PSOE was finally defeated by the right-wing Partido Popular in the March 1996 general election although, to the surprise of

most commentators, the gap between the two main parties was a mere
1.4 per cent. The PSOE had been in power for over thirteen years – a
quite outstanding record for a social-democratic party at a time when
social democracy was generally acknowledged to be in retreat before the
dynamism of the New Right. Moreover, an early return to power for
the PSOE did not appear unrealistic.

Of course, 1989 also marked the collapse of communism throughout
eastern and central Europe. The momentous events of that year were
welcomed by the PSOE, but had little direct effect on the party, which
had dropped its Marxist label a decade before the fall of the Berlin
Wall. The communist-led Izquierda Unida (United Left) found the
implications of 1989 far more challenging.[1] The PSOE was indirectly
affected by the collapse to the extent that the demise of 'real socialism'
further undermined the capacity of the state to intervene in the economy. Yet, as we shall see, the PSOE was able to achieve far more in the
field of welfare provision during its final two terms in office than it did
between 1982 and 1989.

This chapter will examine the Spanish socialist government's record
in office from 1989 to 1996 and will seek to provide a rigorous analysis
of the policies which it implemented. Many commentators have sought
to disparage the policies carried out over the years as being generally in
line with neo-liberal prescriptions. Although this argument is not without justification, as will be shown in the section on the PSOE's economic
policy, it overlooks several aspects of socialist policy which deserve
greater attention. Significant areas of the PSOE's policies in the economic field and beyond hardly bear out the charge that PSOE strategy
has been indistinguishable from that which would have been followed
by liberal/conservative parties.

We shall begin by examining the economic policy pursued by the
PSOE during the period and highlight the importance of the imperatives of European integration in the party's strategy. We shall then
explore the PSOE's record on the welfare state and public infrastructure
provision. After an examination of the party's role in the introduction
of social legislation, we shall conclude by examining areas in which the
socialists have been clearly interventionist. In this section, particular
attention will be given to the PSOE's role in the banking and energy
sectors and the party's distinctive record on privatization.

The PSOE and the economy: a case of the emperor's new clothes?

Any attempt to understand the PSOE's political and economic strategy must recognize the importance of the European project which underpins it. In order to grasp the PSOE's embrace of the neo-classical economics of the European project and the gearing of government economic policy towards meeting the convergence criteria for Economic and Monetary Union established at Maastricht, it is necessary to pause in order to examine the ideological crisis of social democracy. As John Gray argues, the declining class base of social-democratic parties, economic globalization and the consequent decline in the power of national governments have all weakened the foundations of social democracy; traditional policy levers are now obsolete.[2] Perhaps more than most European social-democratic parties, the PSOE acknowledged these realities and the party adopted a tough stance on economic policy from the beginning.

Analysis of a political party must pay due attention to the wider socio-economic and political circumstances in which the party acts. Exploring the recent phenomenon of European socialist governments' readiness to apply deregulatory, market-driven policies, Víctor Pérez Díaz argues: 'the adoption of fragments of neo-liberal policies and institutions was the result less of emulation and ideological conversion than of these governments' pragmatic disposition to adjust to the consequences of systematic pressures they were not in a position to resist, much less control.'[3] The collapse of communism in 1989 only reinforced this situation, providing further justification for the revision of traditional social-democratic economic policies. In essence, the PSOE acknowledged the obsolescence of many elements of the social-democratic model in the 1980s and 1990s and made a pragmatic judgment that the country's interests could best be served by being at the forefront of the European project. We shall examine the PSOE's stewardship of the Spanish economy and seek to explain the central role played by European integration throughout the PSOE's entire period in office.

In order to explore the PSOE's economic policies between 1989 and 1996, it is important to sketch out the main features of its handling of the economy in the preceding period.[4] When the PSOE came to power in 1982 it had been bequeathed an economy at its worst point since the start of the political transition. Unemployment stood at over 16 per cent, the highest of any member of the OECD, inflation had reached 14 per cent, GDP had grown by only 1.2 per cent in the previous year, while the public deficit had trebled since 1978. Anxious to secure membership of the EC by the end of its first term in office, the PSOE's response was to carry out a wide-ranging liberalization of the economy via the introduction of tight monetary, fiscal and wage policies. These measures were complemented by a massive restructuring of industry, aimed at improving the competitiveness of those sectors in crisis, including the steel industry, shipbuilding, electrical goods and textiles.

By 1986, the year Spain became a member of the EC, the PSOE's stewardship of the economy had been successful in several areas. Inflation was under control, GDP was growing at around the EC average for this period, while the balance of payments had been returned to surplus. Indeed, the International Monetary Fund was sufficiently impressed with the PSOE's streamlining of the economy to argue that, 'As Spain entered the EC, the fundamental macroeconomic imbalances that had plagued the economy during the previous fifteen years had been eliminated and market mechanisms had largely replaced previously pervasive government interventions'.[5] This endorsement by the IMF was hardly surprising; the austerity programme introduced by the PSOE during its first term in office was not dissimilar to the policies being implemented by conservative governments. The climate for domestic and foreign investment had markedly improved since 1982 and the economy was set to enter a period of growth which outstripped that of the European Community. Nevertheless, the unemployment rate had risen to 22 per cent, making a nonsense of the PSOE's 1982 election manifesto pledge to create 800,000 jobs during its first term.

The economic upturn in the western world, the abrupt fall in the price of oil during 1986 (Spain was particularly dependent on energy imports) and the vast amount of foreign investment which flooded into Spain following the country's entry into the EC all favoured the spectacular recovery which took place in the Spanish economy during the second half of the decade. From 1986 to 1990 Spain's GDP grew at an average rate of nearly 5 per cent per year – easily the highest increase in the EC. Domestic demand soared, increasing at an annual rate of around 7 per cent in the five years to 1990. However, Spanish industry was in no position to satisfy such a vertiginous rate of growth and foreign investments and imports flooded the country, attracted by the government's pursuit of an economic policy centred round a strong peseta and high interest rates. Spanish industry could expect little help from government, whose attitude was encapsulated by Industry Minister Aranzadi's quip that 'the best industrial policy is no industrial policy'. In a nutshell, the requirements of indigenous industry were sacrificed in the quest for foreign capital, which became increasingly important as a means of servicing a spiralling trade deficit. Between 1985 and 1989 the trade deficit soared from 2.5 per cent of GDP in 1985 to 6.4 per cent, giving Spain the highest deficit in terms of percentage GDP in the world. In addition, foreign penetration of the Spanish economy as a whole rose throughout the period. By the end of the decade 29.2 per cent of firms were owned by foreigners, 'one of the highest levels of overseas penetration of any developed country'.[6]

By 1989, the economy was starting to overheat. Between 1988 and 1989 inflation rose by a full two percentage points to 6.8 per cent, provoked by still buoyant domestic demand. The buoyant growth rates enjoyed by the Spanish economy in the late 1980s were unsustainable and the government's priority was now to pilot a soft landing by dampening demand and injecting a greater degree of discipline into the economy. The administration's response was, first, to adopt a more restrictive monetary stance from late 1988 onwards (interest rates rose from 10.5 per cent in September 1988 to 14.5 per cent in July 1989) and second, and more unexpectedly, to place the peseta within the Exchange Rate Mechanism (ERM) of the European Monetary System (EMS).

The decision to enter the ERM in June 1989 was an indication of the government's determination to bring the rate of inflation down to the average of ERM members and to tackle the current account deficit.[7] An exchange rate of 65 pesetas to the Deutsche Mark was fixed, with a fluctuation rate of 6 per cent. Expert opinion considered the parity to be excessively high given that at the time of joining the forecast deficit on current account was more than $11 billion, around 3 per cent of GDP.[8]

The peseta's entry into the ERM was not the only significant development at the Madrid European Council meeting which rounded off Spain's Presidency of the EC. The European Council also approved a three-stage plan aimed at Economic and Monetary Union, which obtained the unqualified support of the Spanish government. As long as the boom continued, the government's policy of attuning economic strategy to the imperatives of the financial markets in an effort to converge with the economies of the leading EC member states appeared to make sense, at least in purely financial terms. However, the end of the boom in 1991 brought to the surface the Spanish economy's macro-economic and structural disequilibria, which were of sufficient gravity to exacerbate the downturn.[9] When international economic conditions took a sharp turn for the worse in the 1990s and the full implications of the European Single Market and the Maastricht Treaty began to sink in, concerns grew about the magnitude of the economic challenges posed by Europe. At the very time that boom was turning to bust within the Spanish economy, the EC was making its heaviest demands upon the Spanish government in the form of convergence criteria which required a drastic reduction of the spiralling public deficit.

With monetary policy severely curtailed by the peseta's entry into the ERM, tight fiscal measures became the chief tool of government economic management and in the summer of 1992 a series of major fiscal revisions was introduced in an effort to tackle the public sector deficit. Shortly afterwards, the crisis within the ERM forced the government into a major reappraisal of monetary policy, including a devaluation of the peseta by 5 per cent on 16 September 1992. This action was followed by two further devaluations of 6 per cent on 22 November and 8 per cent on 13 May 1993, only weeks before the general election. According to the Economist Intelligence Unit, the abandonment of a restrictive monetary policy, 'which had converted a strong currency into an article of faith', and the narrowing of interest rate differentials with other European economies marked the return of a more realistic economic policy.[10] Nevertheless, the government's immediate reaction to the devaluations was one of dismay. As Torrero argues: 'the best proof of the lack of realism of economic policy is that the authorities responded to the devaluations with a feeling of resentment, if not anger.'[11]

Successive devaluations of the peseta after September 1992 led to a sharp fall in the balance of the capital account thereafter. The devaluations had a positive effect on Spanish exports, which at last became more competitive and their impact, allied to a sharp drop in domestic demand, helped cut the deficit on the current account to just 1 per cent of GDP, a vast improvement on the unsustainable levels of previous years.

A welcome result of the ERM crisis was that it led to a reappraisal of underlying economic realities throughout the European Union. Certainly, the shortcomings of the Spanish economy were laid bare. Five months before the ERM crisis, the government had drawn up a Convergence Plan, which outlined how it intended to fulfil the conditions necessary for participation in Economic and Monetary Union (EMU). The government's optimism was such that it not only expected the economy to fulfil the convergence criteria adopted at Maastricht, but to actually *exceed* them. This goal would be achieved by carrying out structural reforms aimed at promoting greater flexibility and deregulation within the economy, particularly throughout the public sector. In this way one million jobs would be created between 1992 and 1996.[12] However, the plan was made obsolete by the deterioration in the economic situation, culminating in the three devaluations following the ERM crisis of September 1992. For example, the plan's macroeconomic projections predicted that GDP would grow by 3 per cent in 1992 and 3.3 per cent in 1993, when in fact growth in 1992 moderated to a mere 0.8 per cent, before contracting by 1.2 per cent in 1993. Similarly, the plan's prediction for total public debt as a percentage of GDP in 1994 (45.3 per cent) was well below the actual figure, which exceeded the 60 per cent limit set at Maastricht. In short, the Convergence Plan as drawn up in 1992 was excessively optimistic and became even more so in the context of recession. The government had no option other than to acknowledge this fact and the projections were revised in July 1994. The credibility of the government in its handling of the economy suffered accordingly.

Aware of the magnitude of the challenges posed by EMU, Felipe González adopted a tough stance at the Edinburgh Summit in December 1992 when he successfully forced his EU partners into implementing the Maastricht protocol on the setting up of a cohesion fund which would provide aid to the poorer member countries to improve their competitiveness in the run-up to EMU. The resulting fund disposed of 15 billion ecus over seven years, with the bulk going to Spain. Yet, as

Heywood argues, 'even with a cohesion fund ... the convergence plans remain immensely ambitious'.[13]

In 1994 the government drew up a three-year deficit reduction plan aimed at reducing the deficit to 4 per cent of GDP by the end of 1997, the first official acknowledgement that it no longer believed it could fulfil the Maastricht criteria by 1997.[14] The government was no doubt encouraged by the postponement of the third stage of EMU to 1999. However, since a decision will be taken in spring 1998 on which countries fulfil the criteria to join EMU, Spanish participation appeared (at the beginning of 1997) unlikely, in spite of the efforts of the government of José María Aznar formed in 1996.

Nineteen ninety-four also witnessed two other significant developments. In May the government pushed through key changes in labour market regulations in a reform of the 1980 Workers' Statute. Aimed at a further deregulation and liberalization of the labour market, the move was bitterly opposed by the trade unions. With some justification, they claimed that the Spanish labour market was already suffering from more than enough 'flexibility' – 35 per cent of employees on fixed-term contracts as against an EU average of around 9 per cent, and Spain close to the bottom of the European league table for labour costs. The government remained unmoved.

The second landmark reform was the passage of legislation in June 1994 granting autonomy to the central bank, the Bank of Spain. Introduced in line with Article 107 of the 1992 Maastricht Treaty, the reform awarded the bank responsibility for the elaboration and implementation of monetary policy. With price stability as its lodestar, the Bank of Spain promptly tightened monetary policy in the form of higher short-term interest rates, provoking criticism from government circles.[15] The government's unease illustrated the dilemma in which the Spanish socialists found themselves. Keen advocates of further European integration, they were nevertheless uneasy about the practical results of surrendering such a vital economic policy lever, particularly fearing the possible effects on growth and employment.

The weak foundations upon which the economic boom of the late 1980s was based have been highlighted in recent years. The high levels of foreign penetration of industry and dependence on foreign investment characteristic of the period coincided with a further erosion in the country's already weak indigenous manufacturing base. The economic problems arising from the government's commitment to converge did little to boost the government's popularity, thereby contributing towards its defeat in the March 1996 general election. Moreover, the austerity measures which had been introduced by the government in order to fulfil the Maastricht criteria contributed to a far more sceptical attitude towards European integration in Spanish public opinion, traditionally one of the most pro-European in the EU. A Eurobarometer poll in May 1995 indicated that only 20 per cent of Spaniards believed Spain had benefited from membership of the European Union. The percentage of those who believed membership had not been beneficial – 60 per cent – was the highest in the EU.[16] As the economic implications of the Maastricht Treaty finally sank in, it was clear that, by 1996, Spain had woken up to the harsh realities of European integration.

Yet, more than any other single factor, European integration provided the PSOE with the framework for its economic policy. By the time the PSOE entered office in 1982, the European project was itself already beginning to reflect the dominance of New Right economic prescriptions over those of social democracy. Spain's entry into the European Community coincided with the EC's advocacy of more market-driven, deregulatory norms, as reflected in the Single European Act and the 1992 Maastricht Treaty, which indicated the path towards Economic and Monetary Union via price stability, fiscal orthodoxy and reliance on market forces. The PSOE's application of neo-liberal economic policies was legitimized by the fact that those very policies had now been incorporated into the European project. 'Europeanization/Modernization' became the party's leitmotif and was cherished as being the sole means by which Spain could achieve membership of the continent's leading group of states. The PSOE was able to make skilful use of European integration as a catalyst for a rapid socio-economic and political process aimed at consolidating Spanish democracy and 'catching up' with Europe. The Spanish socialists were therefore able to make much political capital throughout the 1980s from their identification with ever-closer European integration. This stance retained its validity as long as the European project could credibly be projected as the *deus ex machina* which contributed towards the PSOE's avoidance of the electoral failure suffered by most of its European counterparts during the period.

Table 4.1 The Spanish general election results 1989–96

	Votes (%)			Seats		
	1989	1993	1996	1989	1993	1996
PSOE	39.60	38.79	37.48	175	159	141
PP	25.80	34.77	38.85	107	141	156
IU	9.13	9.60	10.58	17	18	21
CDS	7.95	1.76	–	14	0	–
CiU	5.07	4.94	4.61	18	17	16
PNV	1.25	1.24	1.28	5	5	5
Others	11.2	8.9	7.2	14	10	11

Key: PSOE: Partido Socialista Obrero Español (Socialist Party); PP: Partido Popular (Popular Party); IU: Izquierda Unida (United Left); CDS: Centro Democrático y Social (Social and Democratic Centre); CiU: Convergència i Unió (Convergence and Union); PNV: Partido Nacionalista Vasco (Basque Nationalist Party).
Source: El País, 5 March 1996.

In this sense, European integration provided the PSOE with a progressive 'post-social-democratic' vehicle which obtained the party's full support. However, this scenario was dramatically altered after Maastricht when, in the context of recession, the Spanish people began to realize that European integration also necessitated sacrifices. Ironically, perhaps, it was the PSOE's commitment to the accelerated convergence outlined at Maastricht which was a contributory factor in the fall in popular support for the government during the 1990s and its eventual defeat at the polls in 1996.

In this respect, it is interesting to note that in the run-up to the 1996 election the Partido Popular adopted a cautious attitude towards European integration, which contrasted with the PSOE's traditional pro European stance. A statement on Economic and Monetary Union by Abel Matutes, shortly after his appointment as the Partido Popular's Foreign Minister, also cast doubt on the new government's commitment to the Maastricht timetable, when he called for 'the clock to be stopped', allowing countries like Spain to qualify. Finance Minister Rodrigo Rato initially supported Matutes, only to backtrack when the markets plummeted.[17] Despite this early equivocation, Aznar's party has since given its full support to Economic and Monetary Union as set down at Maastricht.

The social dimension: the PSOE and welfare

While commentators on both the left and right have highlighted the neo-liberal elements of the PSOE's economic policies, less emphasis has been placed on the socialists' record of social spending. While it is easy to accuse the PSOE of not having gone far enough, the Socialist government's achievements in health, education, pensions, unemployment benefits and other social provision were considerable. This omission is serious since no rigorous explanation of the PSOE's electoral strength over the years can ignore the party's record on welfare.

Spain's entry into the European Community and the PSOE's second general election victory in 1986 coincided with an economic upturn which encouraged hopes that more would be spent by the government on social programmes. Therefore, the government's refusal to spend significantly more on such programmes, even though the Spanish economy was growing faster than any other in Europe, led to a degree of public dissatisfaction which found its expression in the massive support given to the one-day general strike of 14 December 1988. During the PSOE's first term in office, the trade unions had generally accepted that the government's austerity policy had been necessary to prepare the Spanish for the competitive rigours consequent upon the country's entry into the EC. However, angered by an unemployment rate which stubbornly remained the highest in Europe and the steep rise in the number of short-term contracts following the introduction of legislation in 1984, trade union and public patience had been wearing thin. Described by Camiller as 'the most effective strike action in Europe in the eighties', the twenty-four-hour-long paralysis of the country was followed by a significant rise in public spending.[18]

Shaken out of its complacency, the government set to work on some quite historic achievements. In 1982 6 million Spaniards had no access to public health care. By the early 1990s spending on health care had more than tripled to 5.6 per cent of GDP and coverage had been extended to the entire population, while Spain boasted the highest proportion of doctors in the OECD. A measure of the success of the government's health policy is the Economist Intelligence Unit's claim that, 'During the 1980s and 1990s the private health care sector began to suffer a serious loss of clients to the public sector, due to the vast improvements in quality of the latter.'[19] Pension rights were similarly universalized and indexed to inflation regardless of whether or not people had paid social security contributions. By 1991 there were 2 million more pensioners than when the PSOE entered office and spending on pensions had increased three-fold. By 1995 pension payments amounted to 9.1 per cent of GDP, accounting for 23 per cent of total public sector expenditure. The popularity of the PSOE's pension legislation has left the Partido Popular government elected in 1996 with the difficult challenge of pension reform, a sensitive issue which cannot be avoided if the Aznar administration is serious about meeting the Maastricht convergence criteria. Yet Aznar has claimed that pensioners would not be adversely affected by budget cuts.[20] Spending on education had also increased five-fold during the decade 1982–92. While 1.4 million new school places were created, the school leaving-age was raised to 16 and the number of university students doubled. Between 1983 and 1995 the amount spent by the state on unemployment benefits more than doubled in terms of percentage GDP. Total public sector spending accounted for about 50 per cent of GDP in 1995, around half of which was accounted for by outlays on the welfare state, in line with the EU average.[21]

Despite these achievements, Spain still has the third lowest per capita welfare spending in the EU after Greece and Portugal. Although the number of beneficiaries of unemployment benefit increased from 633,537 in 1983 to 1,452,746 in 1995 it is important to note that half of Spain's jobless receive no unemployment pay. Given the disproportionate impact of unemployment on the young, the role still played by the extended family in Spanish society clearly remains significant.

Nor can it be claimed that the PSOE has contributed towards significant changes in welfare distribution. The late 1980s economic boom mainly benefited the middle classes, who were the main beneficiary of PSOE policies throughout the party's period in office.

The conclusion we can draw from the above would appear to be that while the PSOE's achievements in welfare provision have been considerable, the country still has some catching up to do. The Spanish socialists nevertheless support Sassoon's contention that late-twentieth-century socialists 'were forced to turn away from Keynesian state interventionism, but could not and would not become anti-welfare parties'.[22] These policies necessitated substantial increases in taxation. Indeed, during the 1980s, Spain's tax burden rose more than that of any other OECD country. It increased from 27.9 per cent in 1982 to 36.1 per cent in 1994 – although it is important to stress that the overall tax burden in Spain remains below the European Union average, which rose from 38.9 per cent to 42.2 per cent during the same period.[23] Furthermore, 50 per cent of the total tax revenues was paid by the richest 10 per cent, and 20 per cent of the revenues by the top 1 per cent of incomes.[24] For all the criticism of the PSOE's performance, including well-founded charges that the PSOE neglected the quality of welfare provision in favour of quantity, it remains to be seen whether the welfare state remains as safe in the hands of the party's conservative successors in government, particularly given their determination to meet the Maastricht convergence criteria for Economic and Monetary Union.

Infrastructure: the great leap forward

Another area of PSOE policy which ill fits the charge of neo-liberalism is the government's willingness to commit vast sums of public funds to infrastructure projects. Indeed, during the late 1980s the increases in social spending were dwarfed by those on infrastructural investment. The basic premise behind the government's policy was that large-scale public investment in infrastructure was vital if the country was to make good the gap with the EU's leading member states. The government's 1992 Convergence Plan formalized this commitment by pledging to maintain public investment at 5 per cent of GDP over the next five years.

Described as 'one of the most ambitious social capital investment programmes in Spain's modern economic history',[25] the PSOE's record on public works programmes is considerable. Between 1986 and 1991 public investment in roads, railways, ports and airports, oil and gas pipelines, communications and hydraulic projects almost tripled. Investment was particularly marked in the years leading up to Spain's *annus mirabilis* of 1992, when the country played lavish host to the Olympic

Games in Barcelona and the World Expo in Seville. Indeed, Catalonia and Andalusia gained the lion's share of infrastructural modernization during the four-year period 1988–91, obtaining 13.6 per cent and 20.6 per cent respectively of total spending on infrastructure. The government's decision to link Madrid with Seville via the high-speed AVE train on the occasion of the Expo was particularly controversial. Government approval of the scheme was viewed by many as being a political rather than an economic decision (Andalusia is a PSOE stronghold) and the scheme swallowed over half of total rail investment during its construction. Initially viewed as being something of a white elephant, the project has since proved successful. The government's use of the Olympic Games as a springboard for the transformation of Barcelona into one of Europe's great cities must also be considered a success.[26] The state bankrolled 70 per cent of the $6 billion investment in urban development, sports installations and infrastructural works considered an integral part of the Olympic project. Under the Olympic urban strategy, Barcelona increased its green areas by 50 per cent and placed public parks in 150 neighbourhoods. A sea-view promenade replaced the run-down dock area and 19 miles of coastline were cleaned up and turned into beaches. A ring-road was also built around the city, relieving Barcelona's chronic traffic congestion. The impact of the public works was about $21 billion between 1987 and 1992, 0.9 per cent of Spanish GDP. The city's socialist council has argued that the Olympic Games mitigated the effects of the 1993 recession. The PSOE was rewarded by seeing its vote in Barcelona increase at the 1996 general election despite being heavily defeated in all the other big Spanish cities. The success of the largely publicly funded Barcelona Olympics contrasted sharply with the chaotic organization in evidence at the commercially oriented Games held in Atlanta in 1996.

Other major projects included the building of 3500 km of highway between 1984 and 1993, and the completion of a 5400-km motorway network. Prior to its defeat in the 1996 general election, the socialist government had also announced plans to build a further 3500 km of motorway by 2007. Plans to update Madrid's Barajas airport also rounded off a significant programme of airport modernization.

By 1992, the deteriorating economic situation led to the first year-on-year decrease in the amount spent on public works programmes since 1984, and in 1995 the government formally dropped its commitment to maintain public works expenditure at 5 per cent of GDP. With gaps opening up in the public finances, the government chose to cut back on public works programmes rather than tackle the even more sensitive issue of social security reform.

Speaking at his party's 33rd Congress in March 1994, Felipe González reminded his audience that Spain was 'the country with the highest public investment in Europe, investment largely directed towards public works'.[27] It was a boast which could hardly come from the lips of a neo-liberal. Spain's infrastructure remains well short of the European average, but there can be little doubt that the progress achieved by the PSOE over such a comparatively short period of time has been little short of spectacular.

The PSOE and civil liberties

Discussing the progress made by the French socialists during the 1980s in the field of civil liberties, Sassoon draws attention to the lack of public and media interest in an area which contained several of the government's greatest achievements. 'Politics had increasingly become a matter of "getting the economy right".'[28] Similar reductionism applies in many studies of the PSOE. When it left office in 1996, the PSOE left on the statute book considerable advances in the field of civil liberties which its conservative successors will alter at their peril. This section will highlight several areas in which the PSOE has played a progressive role.

The PSOE and women's issues This section will provide an overview of the main achievements of the Spanish socialists in the area of women's rights. First, we shall examine the significance of the Instituto de la Mujer (Institute for Women's Affairs). We will then consider the PSOE's decision to introduce a quota system for women within the party and round off by exploring the PSOE's record on divorce, abortion and birth control.

A year after gaining office, the socialists founded the Instituto de la Mujer, which was given the task of promoting women's rights in Spain. The socialist government ensured that the Instituto was well-funded and its 1988–90 Plan of Action for Equal Opportunities for Women was a significant development in the field of sexual equality. The plan focused on five areas: legal equality, education and culture, work and labour relations, health, international co-operation and political participation. The Minister of Social Affairs claimed that when the Plan expired at the end of 1990, over 90 per cent of its objectives had been achieved.[29] By the start of the academic year 1987–88, Spanish universities had more female than male students, while in 1990, a wide-ranging Education Act was introduced which viewed sexual equality as one of its main aims.

At its 31st Congress in 1988, the PSOE also took the significant step of ensuring that at least 25 per cent of party posts would be held by women; women would also account for the same proportion in the party's lists at general, autonomous and local elections.[30] The PSOE's initiative was taken up by Izquierda Unida, which adopted a 30 per cent quota. The percentage of women entering parliament rose appreciably over the next few years. Following the 1989 general election, women accounted for just 6 per cent of diputados. This figure almost tripled to 17.6 per cent in 1993, before reaching 22 per cent in the 1996 general election (76 out of 350 diputados). Unable to ignore this trend, the Partido Popular had more women heading its party lists than the PSOE in the 1996 general election.

Divorce, abortion and birth control Before the socialists gained power, the UCD government had introduced a divorce law which provoked much controversy within the government. Indeed, disputes over the divorce law were a major contributory factor in the disintegration of the UCD administration. Once in power, the socialists opted not to alter significantly this fairly liberal piece of legislation. Despite the relative ease with which a divorce can be obtained, Spain's divorce rate remains low in comparison with other European countries (0.5 divorces per 1000 inhabitants in 1994).

Given the controversy surrounding the introduction of divorce it is not surprising that the UCD refused to tackle the question of abortion. Once in power, the PSOE grasped the nettle by introducing an Abortion Act which, despite a challenge from the Constitutional Court, became law in 1985. The legislation has nevertheless been criticized as being inadequate and despite repeated promises in party electoral pro- grammes, the PSOE had not broadened the terms of the Act before leaving office in 1996. In an interview during the 1996 general election campaign, the Social Affairs Minister, Cristina Alberdi, nevertheless claimed that in the event of a PSOE victory, a further liberalization of the Act would be a priority of the new government.[31]

The socialists also provided Spain with progressive legislation in the field of infertility treatment with its 1988 Ley de Reproducción Asistida (Assisted Reproduction Law). The Law provided for the setting up of a Comisión Nacional de Reproducción Asistida (National Commission for Assisted Reproduction), made up of representatives from government, specialists in the field, and a council with members from a broad social spectrum. Another PSOE initiative in this area was its 1990 birth-control campaign which sought to promote the use of contraception among the young. The campaign marked a nadir in relations between the Church and the socialist government and elements within the Partido Popular also bitterly opposed the government's scheme.[32] Since Spain has one of the highest rates of AIDS in Europe, the government felt that its campaign was more than justified.

To conclude this section on civil rights, it is important to stress that legislation in the field of education, divorce and abortion consistently met with the opposition of the Partido Popular. Although the PSOE's achievements in these areas may be criticized for being excessively timid, the position of women undoubtedly improved during the socialists' period in office. The PSOE government also passed new legislation on conscientious objection, habeas corpus and legal assistance, and attempted to overhaul the judiciary by devoting additional economic resources, which multiplied by two and a half times between 1982 and 1989.[33] The PSOE's initiatives have met with such a degree of popular support that should the present Partido Popular government seek to unravel these achievements, it will need to display even greater political courage than that required by the PSOE when it introduced the legislation.

The PSOE and interventionism: banking, energy and privatization

Heywood has rightly criticized attempts to caricature the economic policy of the PSOE as neo-liberal and has highlighted the banking and

energy sectors as areas in which the PSOE has been consistently interventionist.[34] In banking the socialists supported bank mergers so as to
create organizations better able to compete within the EU. Between 1987
and 1992 mergers and acquisitions affected 4 banks and 31 savings
banks.[35] The merger process was viewed by the government as being the
best means of protecting such a strategically important sector from
foreign take-overs.[36] A similar policy was pursued in the energy sector
as the socialists sought to limit the entry of foreign multinationals. The
Economist Intelligence Unit highlights the protection which the government has afforded the electricity utilities from external competition and
argues that despite the fact that most of them have been transferred to
the private sector, 'virtually all aspects of policy are determined by the
government'.[37] In a nutshell, the PSOE's policy in both banking and
energy was geared towards the preservation in national hands of large,
internationally competitive groups. Once again, the PSOE's actions
hardly bear out the charge of neo-liberal free marketeers. Indeed, given
the party's record on banking, the energy utilities and infrastructural
investment, it is difficult not to agree with the *Financial Times* when it
claimed in 1991 that, 'the Socialists have become more and not less
interventionist'.[38]

Paradoxically, the PSOE has even retained its interventionist credentials in its policy on privatization. The PSOE's privatization strategy
has stemmed more from its efforts to improve the performance of the
public sector rather than from any ideological predisposition to pursue
a deliberate privatization policy. Nevertheless, since the end of the 1980s
pressures imposed by the creation of the European Single Market and
the need to cut the budget deficit in an effort to meet the convergence
requirements of the Maastricht Treaty have accelerated the pace of
privatization. During its last term in office, 1993–96, the PSOE obtained
1120 billion pesetas from the privatization of public companies, compared to around 591 billion pesetas obtained from the sale of over thirty
public companies during the entire period 1982–93.[39] What has been
notable about the privatizations carried out by the PSOE has been the
socialists' determination to safeguard the public sector's retention of
management control and ultimately ensure national control of companies
regarded as strategic.[40] Using its policy of partial privatizations, the
socialist government was able to retain its presence via a comparatively

small stake, thereby maintaining the public nature of the companies concerned.

To conclude this section, the PSOE fiercely retained its capacity to intervene in sectors of the economy regarded as being of critical importance. Indeed, as Heywood argues: 'Far from rolling back the state, the PSOE government consistently used it as a leading player in its attempt to "make Spain work".'[41] Whether the post-Maastricht environment allows such a scale of intervention in the future is a moot point. In January 1996, the European Commission, after some hesitation, allowed the Spanish government to pump £440 million into the loss-making national airline, Iberia, only four years after a £600 million injection had been sanctioned. It is unlikely that such indulgence will be shown in future.

Conclusion

As Sassoon has argued: 'Modern social democracy cannot accomplish its tasks without a thriving economic base.'[42] The boom years of the late 1980s provided Spain with such a foundation and public expenditure grew accordingly as the socialist government introduced significant social reforms and established Spain's welfare state. These achievements were not inconsiderable in the context of an international political environment largely hostile to social democracy. The hegemonic political force throughout most of the 1980s, the PSOE found the 1990s a far more challenging decade as Spain's exceptional period of economic upturn came to an end. Not the least among the many challenges faced by the PSOE in the 1990s were the exigencies consequent upon the socialist government's identification with accelerated European integration. The dilemma for a social-democratic party such as the PSOE was particularly acute: how to fend off international competition and qualify for Economic and Monetary Union without destroying a system of social solidarity which was still well below the EU average. In the heady years which immediately followed Spain's entry into the EC, European integration appeared to bring little but good news for Spain and the PSOE. Integration offered the PSOE the ideal means of fashioning for itself a hybrid identity drawing on both neo-liberal and social-democratic elements. In essence the market could be embraced without totally restricting the party's capacity to lay the foundations of a modern welfare state. Support for the project remained solid, both within the party and within the country as a whole.

Given the PSOE's outstanding electoral success, it is perhaps not surprising that there was little internal party debate on the more controversial aspects of government policy, particularly in the economic field. Debate on economic policy was hardly encouraged by the fact that Felipe González himself considered Spain's European integration to be of such importance that any discussion was condemned as being a luxury which neither the PSOE nor Spain in general could afford. González's unquestioned leadership of the PSOE and the party's recognition that he had been (until his resignation in June 1997) its chief electoral asset meant that he was never seriously challenged on policy. This contention is particularly true with regard to European integration, which González has almost come to personify both within Spain and throughout the EU. This situation became less tenable when the Spanish economy entered recession in 1992 and the previous certainties of European integration were replaced by doubts. As one highly placed economist within the party informed me shortly after the PSOE's general election defeat in March 1996:

> Within the PSOE there has existed, to an extent, the view that there is only one possible economic policy, and that is the one dictated by the government ... Debates which should have taken place, did not take place. Why not? I believe that basically there was no debate because the PSOE is not prepared to permit debate within the party on economic policy.

In any case, as Sassoon has argued, the governments headed by Felipe González 'had pursued economic policies indistinguishable from those that enlightened Spanish conservatives – had they existed – would have pursued'.[43] Of course, crucially, the latter had not existed and it fell to the PSOE to implement progressive policies which had long since been introduced throughout much of western Europe – a feat whose difficulty should not be under-estimated. In the general election of 3 March 1996 the PSOE suffered its first defeat in 17 years at the hands of José María Aznar's Partido Popular – a party which, during the long years of opposition to the socialists, had finally managed to shake off its authoritarian image. It is perhaps one of the PSOE's main achievements that its period in office provided the political environment for the development of the 'enlightened Spanish conservatives' who have been so conspicuously absent throughout the nation's history.

5

The French socialists: Towards post-republican values?[1]

FRANÇOIS HINCKER

While there is no reason to suppose that the French Left remained unaffected by the historic rupture of 1989 symbolized by the fall of the Berlin Wall, it is impossible – so soon after the events – to offer evidence of any specific link between this pivotal event of global importance and the profound crisis of the French Left since the legislative elections in 1993, its convalescence since the presidential election in 1995 and its unexpected recovery in 1997.

Logic dictates that, after the disappearance of the terrestrial incarnation of the communist ideal, the Communist Party (PCF) should have suffered the same fate but, in fact, it had already collapsed. Since 1984 the share of the vote of the PCF had levelled to around 7–10 per cent. Its current state of affairs gives us no reason to assume a significantly greater rise or fall in the future as its 1997 results confirm. The PCF did not benefit in 1993 and 1995 from the crisis of the Socialist Party and it would be entirely gratuitous to think that this would have been any different if the Berlin Wall had not fallen. The causes for the communist decline were structural: the disappearance of the industrial sectors which used to be the bastions of communism; the erosion of the features of a communist 'alternative society', so typical of France, by the evolution of a more global society with more flexible working practices, increasingly democratized secondary education and a more homogeneous system of information; and, finally, the inability of the communist leadership to foresee and consequently to adapt to this evolution. These structural forces had been at work since the mid-1970s and it is well known that, in 1981, the Socialist Party of François Mitterrand appeared to represent an alternative means of renewal for the French Left which, up to then, had been polarized round the PCF.

Structural causes, which are not dissimilar but which have much earlier historical origins, explain why French trade unionism has become so weak. The myth of the hegemony of the working class or, more prosaically, that of trade union countervailing power, was becoming less seductive even without the death of those regimes in which the proletariat was deemed to hold power. In France, such hegemony has never existed except among small groups of militants. Periodic strong protests and demonstrations seem to contradict this reality, but in appearance only. In reality, the connection between these demonstrations – in any case not particularly characteristic of workers – and trade union organization is extremely loose.

The blow supposedly dealt to the idea of socialism in 1989 cannot easily explain the splintering in all directions – Greens, Trotskyists, National Front, Bernard Tapie and abstentions – of the socialist electorate in the 1986 and 1988 legislative elections, in the various elections of 1993, in the 1994 European elections when the Socialist Party scarcely reached 15 per cent, and even in the presidential elections of 1995 or the parliamentary elections of 1997. The concept of the 'union of the Left', broadly accepted by the socialist electorate since the establishment of the Fifth Republic because of the majority ballot system in two rounds, never signified to this electorate that the socialism of the party of François Mitterrand, Lionel Jospin, Laurent Fabius or Michel Rocard had much in common with the real socialism of eastern and central Europe. The gradual weakening of orthodox socialist ideas as represented for a century by social-democratic or Labour parties is a European phenomenon which pre-dates 1989. In France, the socialist electorate, always structurally unstable because of the weak cultural ties between political socialism and the labour and trade union movements, had been further thrown into confusion by the policies of socialist governments after 1981.

This chapter focuses on the post-1989 period, which corresponds, approximately, to Mitterrand's second presidential term and the three governments of Rocard, Edith Cresson and Pierre Bérégovoy which preceded the second *cohabitation* of 1993–95.[2] It is nevertheless important to re-examine to some extent Mitterrand's first seven-year term and the governments of Mauroy and Fabius which preceded the first *cohabitation* because the current unease clearly dates back to these years, including the period pre-1983. In 1986 the Socialist Party gained 32.8 per cent of the vote, the highest percentage gained in its history without the benefit of a preceding presidential victory. But even these positive results should be interpreted as merely a reprieve. It is clear that at the time the socialist electorate wanted to give itself time to reflect on whether the political line followed after 1981 had been a digression or had actually become party policy. The second seven-year term continued in line with the first but, despite the fact that, as this chapter will demonstrate, the measures taken by the government at that time were more left-wing than those taken at the end of Mitterrand's first term, the disarray among the socialist electorate became manifest in 1993 and 1994. The majority of socialist voters in fact were still attached to the idea of what they believed socialism to be and to what they thought the party believed socialism to be. Since then, the substantial recovery of Jospin's party and its victory in 1997 can be explained by the fact that a significant proportion of these formerly disillusioned socialists is prepared to familiarize itself with the new brand of socialism, not the pre-1981 socialism of ideas but the post-1981 realistic socialism.

The reader may be surprised to see the origins of the turmoil among the electorate traced back to 1981 and not just to 1983, when the Mitterrand experiment appeared to turn to the right. It must be understood that in France the left-wing electorate, from its most radical to its most moderate tendencies, was permeated with the memories of the Popular Front of 1936 elevated by subsequent generations to the status of myth. It was imagined that an electoral victory followed by the rapid adoption of a series of social measures constituted at one and the same time a fundamental break with the past and an indestructible basis for the future. The situation appeared to parallel that of 1936 when paid holidays and the generalization of collective agreements allowed the working class to pass from gross exploitation to an entirely different 'social partnership'. In 1981, Mitterrand's success and the landslide socialist victory in the ensuing legislative elections awakened

eschatological expectations of similar reforms. People were not sure
what these reforms might be, but they assumed they would equal the
historical significance and magnitude of those of 1936. Of course, the
left-wing electorate, but also that of the Right which had lived through
the 1981 elections in a state of anxiety, may not have realized the full
significance of the great structural reforms which resulted from 1936,
the Liberation and several post-war right-wing governments. These had
propelled France from the savage capitalism of the nineteenth century
and the absolute rule of the bourgeoisie to the welfare state and the
social and political integration of the working class. But, after these
achievements, all that a left-wing government could do was to add
quantitative improvements to these structures. This is exactly what it
did in the years to 1983: there were additional nationalizations, the
length of the working week was further reduced along with a lowering
of the retirement age. But nationalizations, limitations on working hours
and the principles of retirement were already in existence whereas, in
1936, paid holidays and collective agreements were entirely new. The
irony of history was that the only reform which was truly new was the
least known. This was contained in the Auroux laws whose aim was to
introduce elements of industrial democracy. This reform, which could
have brought about structural changes in the sense that it could lead to
the co-management of companies, left French wage-earners, whose
culture was alien to such aspirations, almost totally indifferent.

While the Right felt overwhelmed by a sense of dread and professional observers thought that the policies of the Mauroy government
between 1981 and 1983 were dangerously radical, left-wing opinion was
rapidly disillusioned (the concept of 'illusion' fits very well with the
state of mind of the Left since 1936). The fact that the long-awaited
left-wing government had finally arrived signalled a transition from the
lyrical socialism of hope to the prosaic socialism of administration. The
sobering effect on the electorate was like a cold shower. By-elections in
autumn 1981 went extremely badly for the Left. The municipal elections
of 1982 went even worse, particularly in left-wing strongholds. They
took place just after the adoption of measures which will go down in
history as typical of the voluntarism – in the sense of an imagined
absence of major constraints – of the early Mitterrand years. The effects
on left-wing opinion of the February 1983 shift in policy 'to the right'

came to light more slowly. As we have already noted, this section of public opinion was in a state of uncertainty in 1986 and was still cautious in 1988 after the Mitterrand–Chirac *cohabitation*, but the incredible blunders of the right-wing government, including the abolition of the wealth tax, caused anti-right-wing reactions. In the short term, the greatest shock was due to the *de facto* de-indexation of salaries from prices resulting in a drop in real wages.[3]

In the medium term, another shock for the Left, this time more protracted and less sharply focused, was the decision of the socialist government to accept a large-scale restructuring of manufacturing industry. What this entailed was perceived only gradually. Yet it had major implications because it was accompanied by a fundamental cultural break in the traditions of French socialism and republicanism. This was the irreversible decision made in 1983 by Mitterrand, Mauroy, Bérégovoy, Delors and the Socialist Party that France should be fully integrated in the global capitalist market. French socialism, fed on a diet of widely shared Jacobin views, had been convinced, up to then, that the struggle to contain and domesticate capitalism, including any unavoidable compromise with it, was a national affair. The economic constraints of capitalism could be dealt with through changes in internal politics while protecting the French model from external economic constraints. After the 1983 shift in policy, the discourse of French socialists on competition and external constraints – so overdue that to some it seemed pedagogical, to others naive – appeared scandalous and scarcely credible because it struck at the heart of the two strongest elements of left-wing culture: political voluntarism and republican nationalism. Since the principal constituent of the Right, Gaullism, also broadly shared these ideas, the political complications were embarrassing for all. As a result, the central question concerning France's integration into the global economy was not a campaign theme in the 1986 and 1988 elections. Indeed, even in 1995 Chirac won because he suggested during his campaign, contrary to his predecessors from the socialists to Balladur, that France could extricate itself from external constraints.

A non-native reader may find it hard to comprehend how French people at the end of the twentieth century could consider economic issues and questions in a purely national context, or how they could imagine themselves subject to aggression and plots when constrained and forced to recognize globalization. But this is, indeed, the case, on the Left as well as the Right. This explains the flood of votes for the National Front which originates in roughly equal measure from a working-class left-wing electorate and from right-wing voters who fear globalization even more than immigration. This also explains why in the referendum on the Maastricht Treaty, the Left–Right split was eclipsed by a split between the so-called elites and the people.

Except on the margins (the Communist Party and the socialist Chevènement on the Left; Le Pen, the 'euro-sceptic' De Villiers and to a certain extent the other 'euro-sceptic' Séguin, now leader of the Gaullists, on the Right), no political force can any longer seriously aspire to govern on the basis of even a partial isolation of France from the global economy. The 1983 shift in policy was inevitable; it so happens that it was the socialists who brought it about. However, this leaves entirely open key questions without which it is not possible to understand the programmes and policies which were really followed by the different parties:

1. How much room to manoeuvre do national governments still have as far as economic policy is concerned?
2. To what extent are the social policies of national governments independent of economic policy? At issue here are crucial questions facing socialist governments supposed to be more 'socially' oriented than right-wing ones.
3. Are there other areas in which Right and Left can be differentiated from one another? French history over the last ten years, having seen an alternation between left- and right-wing governments with a duration of equal length in both camps, constitutes a textbook example illustrating the convergence and divergence of left- and right-wing governments at a time when it is appropriate to predict an effective end to the relevance of these two categories in the future.

To recognize that there is no choice but to integrate with the global market, such as it is – that is to say, in the absence of anything resembling a planetary state with a market open to regulatory interventions comparable to those undertaken up until now by nation-states – implies that the free circulation of goods is accepted. Of course, as far as France was concerned, this had been the basic rule since the 1950s, in spite of resistance from various sectors to which both Left and Right responded similarly (but selectively, since their electoral clienteles differed). But the other implication of liberal globalization is the free circulation of capital. It follows from this that nation-states must give up exchange controls, allow free competitive play between interest rates and must stabilize currencies. This is indeed what all the socialist governments since 1983 did as a logical consequence of the 1983 shift in policy, continuing what the right-wing governments had done, and for good reason. Nevertheless, the depressionary effects of such stringency on growth and employment, coinciding with a global economic depression and the voluntarily agreed sacrifice of control over capital movements and financial markets, ran counter to one of the convictions which define French socialism: the power of the *mur d'argent* (the wall of money) deployed against the Left by national capitalists. Combined with the threat of a flight of capital, this represented a modern symbolic equivalent of the counter-revolution, the emigration and the flight of the King which occurred during the great revolution after 1789. The Left could no longer count solely on its executive for controlling capital or repressing capitalists. The socialist governments even went beyond the bounds of realism in their obstinate pursuit of a strong franc policy which could not be explained rationally. This was doubtless connected to the personality of Pierre Bérégovoy and did not really imply a stable franc. This policy was so rigorous that it incurred the dissatisfaction of a number of employers. The government also erred on the side of liberalization by an excessive deregulation of the internal financial market in the illusory hope that Paris might become a financial centre to rival London and Frankfurt.

Elsewhere, and here the Socialist Party of Jospin is committed to important corrective measures, the socialist governments have not used even the weapons at their disposal which, if used, would have been entirely compatible with integration into the global market: indicative planning, for example, though increasingly neglected during the '30 glorious years', was well suited to moments of crisis and austerity; the utilization of specifically national institutions to regulate the effects of the market, such as those concerning national and regional development, which were well suited to industrial restructuring; the use of the banking sector, nationalized in 1982, to transform credit into an instrument of economic development instead of being inexplicably requested by socialist governments to behave like the rest of the private system.

It is always dangerous to resort to counter-factual history, asking 'What would have happened if ... ?', but it is not an unwarranted intellectual exercise to imagine a perspective for a positive use of external constraints. There were several nostalgic challenges including the Communist Party's vain hopes of restoring its fortunes by becoming a focus of protest; but none of them actually explored more realistic perspectives. Everything occurred as if the Socialist Party, by renouncing its past dogmas, had been vaccinated and that the dose required could not be subject to any modification whatsoever.

An economic policy of this kind, common to both Right and Left, prevented a Keynesian approach to unemployment – boost through demand. There is no doubt that the socialist governments further contributed to the growing consensus of the political establishment and the experts supporting it, by placing all their hopes into a supply-led boost primarily through a reduction in labour costs. Of course, the most severe legal blows to the protection of jobs were dealt by the Chirac government of 1986–88, when it abolished the legal requirement for mass redundancies, and by the Balladur government of 1994 when it limited overtime payment by increasing the flexibility of working hours. Nevertheless, the fact that socialist governments increased business exemptions from social security contributions and other taxes, and developed artificial incentives for taking on the unemployed, led to an increase in capital's share of added value to the detriment of employment, and to an increase in job insecurity.

If this aspect of our assessment of socialist economic policy is accepted, French socialism would appear to be abandoning its identity altogether. But this is not the case because, in its social policy, the socialist governments have behaved quite differently from the three governments of the Right: Chirac (1986–88), Balladur (1993–95) and Juppé (after 1995–97).

It is true that it was only late in the day – in September 1992 – that Martine Aubry, Minister for Employment in the Bérégovoy government, introduced legislation allowing trade unions to challenge mass redundancy programmes (euphemistically called 'social programmes') in the courts. Since then, in the majority of cases where this procedure has been used – some of these extremely significant because of the size of the enterprises and the number of employees concerned – the unions have won their cases either totally or partially. As a result, many firms have been forced to revise their 'social programmes' and sometimes abandon them altogether. This represents a far-reaching innovation because it compels companies to 'factor in' the notion of risk before rushing into making redundancies.

The socialist governments, however, have not touched the two main pillars of the social compromise erected at the time of the Liberation and during the '30 glorious years' of capitalism (1945–75): a legally enforceable minimum wage (SMIC or *salaire minimum interprofessionel de croissance*), in spite of the desire of the majority of employers and of those on the Right to see it repealed; a system of social welfare which is funded by contributions from employers and employees and not by the state budget and which is subject to the control of both without state interference. The Juppé plan of November 1995 aimed at dismantling some of these features.

Without doubt, to protect the old system amounts to a defensive social policy which adds nothing to the existing welfare state while its preservation seems so obviously necessary to those who use it that it is unlikely to arouse their enthusiasm. But such protection did make a difference because when the Right returned to power in 1993 its attempt to tinker with it explains in part the social movements of the winter of 1995.

In December 1990 the socialist government introduced the *contribution sociale généralisée* (CSG or general social contribution) in order to cover the social security deficit. This would have remedied one of the most reprehensible features of the French system of social protection: although it had become universal, it was still financed for the most part out of deductions from salaries, of which one portion was redistributed to independent businesses or retired people; what is more, among salaried workers, the rate of deduction was not progressive but regressive, with the highest salary bands being exempt. The CSG, as its name implies, is applicable to all revenues without exception (pensions and capital income) and with no upper limit. That the pro-communist union, the CGT (Confédération Générale du Travail), protested because the CSG impacted on salaried workers as well (on top of the contributions they were already paying elsewhere) should not conceal the fact that with the CSG incomes other than salary were hit at last. At first the Right conducted an angry campaign against the CSG. Eventually, in government, it decided to accept it. Indeed, it has had to expand it because its yield had become indispensable for maintaining the level of social welfare to which French public opinion, including right-wing voters, is deeply attached.

With the institution of income support or RMI (*revenu minimum d'insertion*) the Rocard government added a considerable new element to the social security system. The RMI is a universal benefit. It is not conditional on contributions, that is on paid work, and it is set at a relatively generous level (higher than the minimum wage in America). Inspired by a Christian philosophy of solidarity, it was regarded with suspicion by employees traditionally attached to the principle of work-related benefits. The RMI, however, is well suited to an economic and social situation where job insecurity leads increasingly to periods of joblessness which can last longer than unemployment benefits and thence to poverty pure and simple. Like the CSG, the RMI has become, and is likely to remain, an irreversible aspect of social reality in France. Moreover, the number of people benefiting from it has doubled in six years to over 2 million today.

Finally, one should not under-estimate the positive effects of what socialist governments have called a 'policy for the cities' (*politique de la ville*). This had suddenly materialized with the nomination of Bernard Tapie (an ecologist financier, later indicted for fraud) to a ministry created for this purpose. Undoubtedly this had been devised in a hurried and unsystematic way; nevertheless, it showed some awareness of the problem and of the method required to deal with it politically. This was a novelty: a policy for the cities which tried to deal with the causes and effects of the geographical concentrations of the unemployed, the poor and the immigrants. This situation is not unique to France, but it profoundly shocked even those not committed to an egalitarian culture. The *politique de la ville* initiated by the socialists was relatively free of bureaucracy. This, in France, is nothing short of a minor miracle.

As the cutbacks multiply, there is little doubt that the social policies of the socialist governments of 1988–93 will have a lasting impact and will appear entirely praiseworthy. But at the time, as indeed also today, it caused embarrassment on the Left. Except in its defensive dimension (that of the minimum wage and the welfare system), it did not really consolidate a wage-earning society by and for active workers, a project which both socialists and communists had been mobilized to achieve for a century. Socialist social policy thus is powerless to resolve unemployment or to improve a little the purchasing power of working people, because it is juxtaposed purely and simply with an economic policy that is almost entirely liberal. The social policy of present-day socialists was indisputably ambitious in its intent to reshape society as a whole and was not ineffectual when they were in power, but it is not capable of resolving the conflict which separates them from the world of work in its traditional sense. Indeed, it can sometimes revive it, even when adopting policies which are beyond reproach from the point of view of more general, let us say more republican, left-wing values, such as those of equality. An example of this is the CSG.

A few words on the concept of 'republican values'. In northern Europe, from the Nordic countries to Germany and Britain, the touchstone of the socialist identity of the social-democratic or Labour parties used to be the working class and the Labour movement. One needs only to look at the economic and social chapters of their programmes and of their actions in government to establish their role in relation to the rightwing parties, which it would not be out of place to term 'bourgeois'. This is not at all the situation in France where the historic identity of the Left also incorporates features which belong to spheres other than the economic and social. French socialism, which is not the whole of the Left, but with which it is generally and justifiably associated, is at least as much, if not more so, the party of the Republic rather than the party of Labour. In France the Republic is far from being simply a type of constitutional regime. It still remains linked to its revolutionary origins and to the century-old operation of the dual principles of liberty and equality. The republican regime has generated consensus only since the end of the Second World War, but the Left has for a long time regarded itself as the modern successor to a 'Republican Party' whose ideology and ethics were formed at the time of the 1789–93 revolution and revived by national conflicts which were not class conflicts: the Dreyfus affair; the secular principles of the state, especially in education; the Vichy–Resistance split. Given that the ties between political socialism and

French trade unionism are loose to say the least, the Socialist Party has always been fortunate in having a stronger possibility of finding a cross-class audience than in any other country in Europe. Of course, many of the original disputes between republicans and conservatives have been resolved, for example the exercise of civil freedoms which no one, not even the National Front, would dream of curbing. Other areas, however, which after the Liberation or under orthodox Gaullism appeared to have been resolved, have returned to be battlefields on which Left–Right confrontation is as intense as ever.

Thus, when French people speak of liberalism today, whether positively or negatively, they have in mind not so much economic concepts and practices as a universe of activities, economic or otherwise, which are opposed to the values of 'public service'. This term is difficult to understand outside France, but it is deeply significant for the French. Whether they love it or loathe it, public service for them includes all the activities which work towards the collective interest (the product accessible to everyone, free of charge if possible) and towards administration unencumbered by imperatives of economic profitability: education, health, culture, post and telecommunications. The Left unites almost unanimously in praise of public service to the point where it is probably the only issue on which the Socialist Party, however pro-Europe it may be, is prepared to clash with the Commission in Brussels. A section of the Right is undoubtedly sensitive to the defence of public service, a fact which provides the Left with ample strategic opportunities. It is therefore understandable that the socialist governments of 1988–93 took care – in spite of liberal tendencies among the non-left-wing ministers called on to support Mitterrand ('*ministres d'ouverture*'), and indeed among Rocard supporters – not to impair public services, even when some of its enterprises could not be sheltered from competition. Thus, while Paul Quilès, Minister for Post and Telecommunications in the Rocard government, was unable to preserve the state monopoly of telecommunications, he succeeded in preserving a fair pricing policy for consumers and maintaining the status of government employees for the workforce.

The conviction that the development of education, scientific research and national culture comes under the duties of the state is related to the republican identity of the Left. One needs only to recall that the National

Library, the Public Archives, the Louvre, the Museum of Natural History, the Museum of Arts and Technology were created by the Revolutionary Convention; that the Museum of Mankind, the Cinémathèque, the Museum of Popular Arts and Traditions and the National Centre for Scientific Research were created by the Popular Front governments. The fact that almost all French people immediately cite compulsory, free and secular education as the outstanding achievement of republicanism gives a measure of just how far the Left consíders these domains to be its own.

Although, since 1988, the 'great' intellectuals who aspire to a public role à la Voltaire, Victor Hugo, Zola and Sartre have refrained from partisan commitments, and although an interventionist and reformist education policy has provoked the corporatist resistance of teachers and students, education and culture are sectors which, in the long run and in terms of the numbers of those involved, are likely to remain most faithful to the Left. And for good reason: in terms of funding, future projects and the public esteem enjoyed by cultural workers, the Jospin years at the Ministry of Education (1988–92) and the long tenure of Jack Lang at the Ministry of Culture were like a golden age. These two sectors were protected from external constraints. Education was undoubtedly very expensive: the education budget, the largest of all, accounts for 20 per cent of public expenditure. The budget for culture was so small that a significant increase brought spectacular results at minimum cost. In this respect, the socialist Left can rely on a certain enthusiasm, while right-wing blunders in particularly sensitive areas (the questioning of free higher education by Devaquet in 1986, and of the secular nature of education at the end of 1993) have done the rest. The Left is still prone to policies which can be expressed in simple formulas such as '80 per cent of each age group to sit the Baccalauréat', or 'University 2000'. It is significant that between 1988 and 1993, when the socialist government was several votes short of an absolute majority in the National Assembly and had to find majorities either among the communists or among a number of centrist MPs, the budgets for education, research and culture, along with transport, were the only ones to be voted for consistently by a left-wing majority.

Finally, since we are considering the remaining differences between Right and Left, it should not be forgotten that the two camps are not supported by the same pressure groups; along with the teaching profession, the radical and alternative 'lobbies' in France have infinitely greater affinity with the Left and in particular with the Socialist Party, many of whose members and leaders come from ecological or feminist groups, from the association of magistrates and from the League of Human Rights. This proximity has had positive consequences for the Socialist Party: it has facilitated the marginalization of political ecologism; its only remaining vaguely coherent organization is Dominique Voynet's Green Party which, having explicitly allied itself with the socialists, is now in the government. No alternative pole – like the German Greens – has been formed to compete fiercely with the socialists for the same votes. In fact, the Socialist Party born in Epinay is at least as much, if not more, the party of new cultural tendencies as it is the party of working people.

In the current state of affairs, in 1997, this last diagnosis may be the most useful for understanding the situation of the French Left. Now that the equivocations characteristic of Mitterrand's politics are over – they had served well for so long, but had become an obstacle in the end – and there is a lull in factional infighting thanks to the popularity of Lionel Jospin, the French Socialist Party, except in certain very specific geographical areas, has a cultural and ideological identity somewhat distant from traditional social-democrat and Labour parties. Perhaps it presents some similarities with the PSOE (Spanish socialist party) and the American Democratic Party.

The problem of popular support in the Socialist Party ('popular' in the French sense of working people) remains because traditional allegiances to Right and Left have become blurred above all by the question of Europe, which has become the closest symbol of the globalization of the economy. The Socialist Party is the most pro-European of all, but only in its cadres and leaders; its electorate is split down the middle on this issue, as the results of the referendum on the Maastricht Treaty demonstrated. That section composed of salaried workers, technicians and executives with a high educational level voted overwhelmingly yes, while clerical and above all blue-collar workers largely voted against. This was confirmed by the referendum results of the départements of the Nord and the Pas de Calais where the Socialist Party has a strong working-class base. When in opposition, the Socialist

Party can allow pro-Europeanism to lapse a little, but not when it is in power.

While routine forecasts of the obsolescence of the Right–Left distinction seem wrong, there is no denying that, as far as France is concerned, the Left is still seeking a new identity. The culture of the world of labour contributes decreasingly to such identity while the myth of socialism as an alternative model can no longer inspire it. Right–Left ideological splits are still strong in France, but the Left appears as a 'federation' of a number of ideologies, while the Right increasingly expresses a single unified ideology. The Left is both strengthened and weakened by this diversity: strengthened because the federative strategy of coalescing ideologies can compensate for its losses among the working classes, but it is weakened because it no longer has a great, quasi-prophetic project, such as those depicted by republican or socialist orthodoxy. This is, no doubt, the situation confronting the Left throughout Europe, but in France the shock is greater because the collapse of the idea or of the myth of radical change in favour of the banality of reformism is more recent and is taking place in a country where in the past ideologies had a quasi-religious status.

6

The transformation of German social democracy

THOMAS MEYER

In 1989 two distinct processes of transformation, completely independent of each other, marked the history of German social democracy. The first was the fall of the Berlin Wall on 9 November which paved the way for German unification. This changed the agenda of and the conditions for social-democratic politics in Germany. The second was the adoption, in December 1989, of the new Basic Programme of the SPD, the Berlin Programme, to replace the famous Godesberg Programme of 1959, a document which had helped the SPD to edge its way towards political power over three decades ago. In this respect, 1989, the year of the 'Democratic Revolution' in Europe, marked a major step in the development of the German Left.

So far these altered conditions, far from bringing about new political successes, have heralded a period of stagnation and confusion at the national federal level. However, the SPD party has been relatively successful at the regional or *Länder* level where it has often been able to form governments, usually in coalition with other parties. This ambiguous situation – success in the *Länder* and defeat at the centre – requires some explanation. Any account of the transformation of German social democracy in the years since 1989 necessitates the casting of some light onto this ambivalence and its causes.

The Basic Programme of the SPD, as issued at the end of 1989, a few weeks after the collapse of communist rule over the eastern part of a then divided country, was supposed to help overcome a discouraging crisis of identity which had affected the party since its last years in government in the early 1980s. This crisis of identity, as it has been termed by outside observers as well as by concerned party activists, was in turn a consequence of the unforeseen crisis of the traditional model of technological and economic progress which made itself felt in the early 1970s in its dual aspect: an economic crisis and an unprecedented threat to the ecological foundations of industrial civilization.

In 1973 the oil crisis and publications such as the Club of Rome's famous report *Limits to Growth* signalled in no uncertain terms that the period of economic optimism had come to an end. The era of ever-expanding prosperity, near-full employment, a constant increase in incomes, and high economic growth rates was abruptly terminated. A new period of stagnation, mass unemployment and high state budget deficits commenced. It was accentuated by a process of economic globalization which seemed to set unparalleled narrow limits to all national policies of economic regulation. In addition, for the first time in modern history, public opinion became aware that the established model of quantitative economic growth could endanger the very survival of humanity by undermining its ecological foundations. It was above all in Germany that, from the middle of the 1970s and to the 1990s, these issues arose to dominate public discourse.

In response to all of this, the social-democratic Left in Germany underwent momentous strategic changes which amounted to a redefinition of its very political identity. This occurred in response to the development of the so-called New Social Movements (NSMs) of the early 1970s: the peace movement, the women's liberation movement and the environmentalist movement with their numerous citizens' initiatives, all of which had exercised a particularly crucial influence within the democratic Left in Germany. It was estimated that, at their peak, these movements had more members than all the political parties put together. Throughout the 1970s and even later there was a remarkable overlap between the SPD and all these movements. This came to an end in 1989 when the Green Party became well established. Henceforth, a majority of those active in the NSMs turned to support the Green Party while a minority tried to shift the SPD towards a greater sensitivity on ecological issues.

The deepening economic crisis drove the SPD – in government until 1982 – increasingly towards austerity policies accepting, albeit reluctantly, cuts in social welfare and education and adopting supply-side economics. At the same time the growing ecological movement inside and outside the SPD urged a radical revision of the economic growth policy model of the Godesberg type and a full reconsideration of the concept of economic and social progress.

A new and unprecedented division emerged to replace the historic split between communists and democratic socialists which, since the division of the country, had no great relevance to the West German Left in terms of numbers. This amounted to a two-fold split within the democratic Left.

1. A split between the SPD in government and the trade unions. The party in government was prepared to accept that, given the structural economic crisis and the ensuing globalization, some concession to neo-liberal economic policies was unavoidable. This was expressed symbolically in the early 1980s by Oskar Lafontaine's initiative in favour of more flexible working hours including regular weekend work. This was bitterly opposed by the trade union wing which was fervently committed to the protection of all the the social rights workers had achieved in the course of the class struggles of the last century.

This split between those who were prepared to endorse more liberal economic policies and those who opposed them contributed – at least to some extent – to the fall in autumn 1982 of the SPD–FDP coalition government led by Helmut Schmidt, though this fall was directly brought about by the abrupt neo-liberal turn of the hitherto 'social-liberal' FDP. The party–union split was caused by what seemed to be the unavoidable effects of a globalizing economy and the perplexing question of how the party should respond to it. This question has haunted the party ever since.

2. The *alternativist* versus *traditionalist* or ecological–industrial split. This was even more crucial than the first. It was triggered off by the discourse on the ecological limits to growth which had developed since the early 1970s. In its turn it was tremendously dramatized by a series of related catastrophes such as those at Harrisburg (USA), Bhopal (India) and Seveso (Italy) in the course of the subsequent decade. In

Germany, the anti-nuclear movement, which spearheaded this alternative position on the Left, attracted a considerable section of the younger generation, particularly those with a middle-class background, a high level of education and strong connections in social and cultural affairs. In an earlier period these would have been supporters and voters of the SPD.

Since the late 1970s the peace movement had gathered momentum, particularly when the NATO decision to site a new generation of nuclear missiles (the famous dual-track decision) heightened the suspicion that Germany had been designated by US strategists as the main theatre in the case of nuclear war. Pacifist and anti-industrialist positions within growing parts of the leftist SPD activists and voters were in sharp contrast to the traditionalist orientation of the mainstream of the party. The newly emerging rift between the traditionalists, who wanted to go on pursuing the classical path of technological and economic progress, and the alternativists, who feared that this path would lead to environmental self-destruction, became sharp and bitter. At the end of the 1970s it appeared irreconcilable. It still runs through the very core of the party.

By the end of the 1970s, almost 40 per cent of the delegates to federal party meetings were influenced by the political orientations of the alternativists and this influence was continuously increasing. Once the Green Party was founded the SPD appeared to be caught in an electoral trap. If it did not embrace ecological policies the party would lose voters to the Greens. If it neglected issues bound up with economic growth it was bound to lose votes in favour of the CDU or the FDP. And so it did in the course of the 1980s, sometimes in both directions at the same time.

These historically unprecedented splits and the political issues underlying them constituted for more than a decade what has been called the 'crises of identity' of the SPD. It was not clear whether the conflicting factions within the party would be able to find a working compromise or whether the party itself was destined to fragment or plunge into irrelevancy. Prominent representatives of the traditionalist current, such as Richard Löwenthal, urged the party to take a clear stand against the alternativists and stick to its traditional positions unambiguously.

Advocates of alternativism, such as the former minister Erhard Eppler, exhorted the party to undergo a radical shift and abandon its anti-ecological industrialism if it wanted to maintain its credibility and remain in contact with the values of the younger generation. It fell to Willy Brandt, the SPD chairman, to make the most serious, determined and, eventually, successful attempt to integrate these rival tendencies after the party was forced into opposition in the Bundestag in 1982.

From its inception in 1981, the Green Party had turned out to be a formidable electoral competitor of the SPD. Its party programme combined a sharp anti-industrial thrust with a basic democratic concept of socialism. This, inevitably, attracted many former members of various small left-wing radical groups as well as left-leaning liberals with strong ecological values. The Green Party even swayed a significant proportion of the existing social-democratic electorate and voters. For some time the SPD seemed to run the risk of losing the bulk of its supporters among the young generation and professional middle classes operating in sectors concerned with culture, education and welfare.

This trend had become obvious in elections at the *Land* level from the beginning of the 1980s and had established itself unambiguously since the 1983 federal elections when the SPD obtained a meagre 38.5 per cent (down from 42.9 per cent in 1980) against the 5.6 per cent achieved by the Greens.

Many social and political indicators pointed to a scenario where the SPD and the Greens would have to compete for an almost constant and finite proportion of the votes; a zero-sum game which would never resolve itself in losses for parties to their right. This strengthened those within the SPD who had advocated a fundamental renewal of the programme and the politics of the party, hoping that these would shift decisively towards the issues and demands of the NSMs. This should not be seen as a mere tactical move dictated only by electoral requirements because many activists of the pacifist, ecological and feminist movements had been active within the SPD for a considerable period of time.

Once it was realized that these unresolved internal crises threatened the credibility of the party and continued to have negative public effects, the SPD Congress of Essen (1984) unanimously decided to give the go-ahead for a major consultation process leading to the drafting of a new

Basic Programme. A programme commission was set up with Willy Brandt and Erhard Eppler as its guiding spirits. Brandt and Eppler stressed that the drafting of a new basic programme was meant to be, above all, a process which would enable the different tendencies within the party to reach a political understanding. In so doing it was hoped that the party would find a new political identity round a long-term vision able to guide the day-to-day policies of the party.

In order to achieve such ambitious results it was necessary to appoint the most outspoken and influential representatives of all the contending factions of the party as members of the programme commission, presided over by Willy Brandt as party chairman. Members of the commission thus included representatives of the peace and ecology movements such as Erhard Eppler and Johano Strasser, of the women's liberation movement such as Heidemarie Wieczorek-Zeul and Inge Wettig-Danielmeyer, trade union leaders such as Franz Steinkühler and Hermann Rappe, and intellectuals who stressed the necessity of a new economic policy to confront the ongoing globalization of the economy.

The process of drafting the new programme by involving the whole party at all levels took almost five years. The New Basic Programme of the SPD was adopted at the Berlin Congress of 18 December 1989 with only one vote against. Present at the congress were, for the first time since the country had been divided in 1949, delegates of the East German Social Democratic Party, founded illegally in the GDR in August 1989, when the communists still ruled the eastern part of the country.

In terms of the objectives established, the Berlin Programme was a success. It contained a new paradigm of social-democratic policies endorsed by all the main tendencies within the party. The new programme therefore seemed to have the potential to unite the party on a new political platform and bring it back on the offensive in the public political debate about the future of the country in a radically changed situation. In terms of political programmes, the SPD had undergone a substantial transformation. The main idea of the new programme was to prepare a broad 'reform alliance' between the SPD, the NSMs and parts of the new technocratic elite on the basis of the concept of an ecologically and socially responsible society. Its detailed policies were based on new political guidelines intended to merge the core concepts

of the social-democratic tradition with the central realistic concepts of
the NSMs such as:

- *common security* by ending the arms race and establishing international institution for peaceful cooperation
- a *fair world economy* which provides development opportunities for
  the Third World
- *social equality* in which all women and men have a right to decent
  employment and equal treatment
- a political framework for *shaping technological development* to enhance
  the quality of working life and reduce the risks posed by new techno-
  logies
- a policy of *qualitative economic growth* and *technological innovation* in
  which decisions on how much should be produced are taken demo-
  cratically
- *qualitative rather than quantitative progress* in which the principle of
  the quality of life selects and structures all developments in technology, trade and industry
- new forms of *democratic politics* beyond state actions through social
  dialogues, citizens' initiatives and civil society activities

In a nutshell: a new vision of modernization and progress.

It is important to bear in mind that this new party programme was
not designed by a tiny group of spin-doctors to help a handful of party
leaders to win elections. Nor was it the product of an isolated small
drafting group. It was rather the outcome of a highly inclusive discussion process involving a very large and representative proportion of the
party membership for a prolonged period of time. It reflected a new
party consensus about modern social democratic politics. It purported
to appeal not only to the groups which traditionally supported the SPD,
such as the trade unions, but also to the more realistic components of
the NSMs and to those members of the liberal and professional social
milieux eager to combine their professional pursuits with the modernization of the country within parameters of ecological and social
responsibility.

Considerable research had been commissioned and a great many
debates had been conducted in the course of drafting the new
programme in order to achieve the desired objectives and root the

programme as deeply as possible in society. As Erhard Eppler explained, the programme was meant to become the platform for a new 'reform majority'. When it was adopted, at the end of 1989, in Berlin, it looked very much as if it could play such a role in the political practice of the party. Unfortunately, very soon it became clear that in the following years it was unlikely to perform such a hoped-for integrative function or play any substantial role in the politics of the party leadership.

The reasons for this are manifold. One was connected to the question of leadership. In the SPD the office of chairman (the equivalent of party leader) is normally not held by the party candidate for Chancellor – the eventual Prime Minister. Willy Brandt had withdrawn as party chairman in 1987 and was succeeded by Hans-Jochen Vogel, the defeated party candidate for the chancellorship in the 1983 federal elections. Vogel, a moralist and a statesman, was not, like Brandt, a charismatic leader of great vision. He had no skills as a persuasive media communicator but he had been quite successful in holding together the centrifugal forces inside the party and finalizing the draft of the new party programme. The SPD nominated Johannes Rau as its new candidate for the post of Chancellor in the federal elections of 1987. The results were disappointing. The party obtained 37 per cent – a loss of 1.2 per cent since 1983 when Vogel had been the candidate and of 5.9 per cent since 1980 when the party was led by Helmut Schmidt. In the same period the Green Party constantly gained in support, advancing from 1.5 per cent in 1980, to 5.6 per cent in 1983 and 8.3 per cent in 1987. An electoral zero-sum game between the SPD and the Greens appeared to be in operation. What the SPD lost, the Greens won but the Left as a whole did not seem to increase in size.

After 1989, far from deriving any benefit from its new image as a modern socio-ecological reforming party, the SPD went on losing electoral support and credibility. The fact that it succeeded in taking power in many *Länder* during the 1980s and 1990s does not modify this generally negative picture because nearly all these local governments were coalitions: in Hesse, North Rhine-Westphalia, Lower Saxony, Bremen and Schleswig-Holstein with the Greens; in the Rhine-Palatine with the FDP (the Liberals), in Berlin, Bremen and Baden-Württemberg with the Christian Democratic Union (CDU), and there was even a minority government supported by the post-communist PDS.

Table 6.1 SPD share of the vote in selected *Länder* elections, West Germany 1978–96

Baden-Württemberg		Bavaria		Berlin	
1980	32.5	1982	31.9	1981	38.3
1984	32.4	1986	27.5	1985	32.4
1988	32.0	1990	26.0	1989	37.3
1992	29.2	1994	30.0	1990	30.4
1996	25.1			1995	23.6

Hamburg		Hesse		Lower Saxony	
1982	51.31	1982	42.8	1978	42.2
1986	41.7	1983	46.2	1982	36.5
1987	45.0	1987	40.2	1986	42.1
1991	48.0	1991	40.8	1990	44.2
1993	40.4			1994	44.3

North Rhine-Westphalia		Saarland		Schleswig-Holstein	
1980	48.4	1980	45.4	1983	43.7
1985	52.1	1985	49.2	1987	45.2
1990	50.0	1990	54.4	1988	54.8
		1994	49.4	1992	46.2
				1996	39.8

The electoral data in Table 6.1 may provide an overall impression of the performance of the SPD in *Länder* elections. Obviously, in some of these *Länder* the SPD was able to hold its positions either at a low level, as in Bavaria, or at a relatively high level, as in Lower Saxony and the Saarland. In other *Länder* it lost support, either slightly, as in Hesse and in North Rhine-Westphalia (between 1985 and 1990) or very severely, as in Hamburg and Berlin. In no *Land* did it make significant gains. On the whole, the SPD was unable to maintain its positions.

The most surprising electoral results, however, occurred in the new *Länder* which had been formed out of the territory of the former GDR, some of which, particularly Saxony and Thuringia, had been SPD traditional strongholds in the decades preceding the Nazi seizure of power. Table 6.2 shows the electoral results since unification.

Table 6.2 SPD share of the vote in the new *Länder* (former GDR) 1990, 1994

	1990	1994
Thuringia	22.8	29.6
Saxony	19.1	16.6
Upper Saxony	26.0	34.0
Mecklenburg	27.0	29.5
Brandenburg	38.2	54.1

Only in Brandenburg, where the SPD leader, Dietrich Stolpe, was suspected to have been a collaborator of the communist regime, did the SPD manage to play a leading role. Everywhere else in the former GDR it was in a clear minority position; in Saxony it was even weaker than the PDS.

There were several reasons behind the electoral failure of the party in the 1980s and early 1990s. The SPD was unable to present itself to the German public as a credible alternative to the ruling CDU–FDP coalition mainly because of four different factors.

1. In the period immediately after the unification of the country the SPD candidate for the office of Chancellor, Oskar Lafontaine, emphasized the obstacles to full monetary, economic and social unification, giving little sign of euphoria about the unexpected event, in direct antithesis to the mood of the majority. As a consequence, the party was defeated in the first all-German elections of 1990. The underlying negative mood towards the SPD has prevailed until recently in the new *Länder* as it was felt the party had lacked enthusiasm about immediate and unconditional unification. It was no consolation and no help to the party that, later, it turned out that almost all of Lafontaine's reservations and warnings had been correct.

2. There had been an excessively high turnover of party leaders and candidates for the chancellorship. After the resignation of Willy Brandt, Hans-Jochen Vogel was party leader from 1987 to 1991. He was followed by Björn Engholm (1991–93), Johannes Rau (temporarily in 1993), Rudolf Scharping (1993–95) and Oskar Lafontaine (since 1995). The candidates for the chancellorship in the federal elections were replaced

with the same rhythm: Vogel in 1983, Rau in 1987, Lafontaine in 1990, Scharping in 1994. Almost certainly someone else again will be the candidate in the 1998 elections. As a consequence of this unsteady performance, it was difficult to counter the general impression that the party was substantially lacking in seriousness, reliability and continuity. A damaging connection was established between electoral failure at the top, negative media image and the hectic replacement of leaders.

3. None of the party leaders and candidates after Vogel whole-heartedly accepted the Berlin Programme as his own personal political position. Each of them underlined selected issues from the new programme or emphasized his own policies, but they all stopped short of espousing its full vision. A vague impression of what the party really stood for emerged instead of a clear message on key economic, social and ecological issues. Moreover there were doubts whether it would strive to pursue its official policies unwaveringly

4. The uncertainties, irritation and electoral failures which occurred as a consequence of all of this contributed to the lack of solidarity and collaboration which characterized relations at the top of the party. The leaders fought out their rivalries in the mass media using any eventual weakness of their competitors to their own personal advantage.

To sum up: instead of presenting itself as a renewed party with a new reform programme which combined in a convincing manner the economic, ecological and social policies required for the years ahead, the SPD, after 1989, acquired the image of a helpless party with no clear vision and no attractive leadership. The transformation so far achieved had been concentrated on the programme, but the body of the party lagged far behind. It remained on the defensive, was unable to make inroads in the young generation and continued to be unable to hold the electoral positions it had achieved in the 1970s under the leadership of Willy Brandt. In West Germany many of its former voters turned to the Green Party, or abstained from voting, and some even supported the right-wing populism of the Republican Party. In East Germany large portions of its potential electorate supported the CDU or even the PDS.

In the 1990s the party was unable to play a more offensive and successful role along the lines advocated in the Berlin Programme because it accepted the dominant neo-liberal discourse of economic globalization and the necessity of national competition for optimal investment conditions as a framework for its own economic and social policies. It did not succeed in communicating a plausible and clear-cut economic alternative.

At the end of the 1970s, when the SPD was still in government, the idea of Germany as an 'investment centre' and the accompanying neo-liberal discourse had begun to become accepted in academic and political circles. Keynesian policies did not play a major role in the Berlin Programme; in the succeeding years, the SPD no longer referred to them. The economic spokesmen of the party tried instead to adopt the framework and the argumentation of globalization as best they could and formulated proposals for a social-democratic alternative within this framework.

In the course of the 1990s four key policies were formulated to define the economic alternative of the SPD:

• reduction of labour costs by means of lowering not wages but the indirect costs of labour
• the introduction of an ecological tax while lowering labour taxes and other costs in the same proportion
• public efforts to support research and innovation which could bring about new technologically sophisticated goods and services to increase the competitiveness of the German economy in global markets
• the overall protection of the welfare state which was meant to serve two purposes at the same time: to maintain minimum standards of social dignity and security for the losers in the new process of modernization and to strengthen the domestic demand for goods and services in order to stabilize the economic cycle

In the 1990s, particularly in the 1994 elections and thereafter, two policies were particularly stressed to highlight symbolically the social-democratic combination of economic and ecological reform and the SPD's determination to protect the welfare state against the neo-liberal attacks of the government parties: an ecological reform and an increase in family allowances. In the Berlin Programme itself the idea of a continuous and substantial reduction in working hours had been advanced as the main pillar for a social-democratic policy for full employment. The main reason for this proposal was the realization that the very high rate of unemployment in Germany (around 10 per cent) could not be substantially reduced in the foreseeable future only by economic growth. This idea, however, was never pushed forward decisively in public during the 1990s. There was no debate over whether it should be renounced altogether or kept on the shelf for a more favourable situation.

Obviously this economic policy was serious and realistic but lacked the power of attraction of a big new idea, nor could it present itself as a convincing recipe for full employment and wealth creation. It was also not a fundamental alternative to the policies of the governing parties. It contributed to the widespread public impression that the political framework within which both government and opposition were operating was similar and that their disputes were all about minor points. In this situation the impression made by the top leaders and the party was all the more crucial.

In addition there was always a certain amount of disagreement among party leaders about economic and social policies. The low point of these public disputes occurred in 1995 with the controversial remarks of the economic spokesman of the party in 1995, Gerhard Schröder, a contestant for the post of candidate for Chancellor in the federal elections of 1998. He declared that there could no longer be distinctive social-democratic economic policies but only a more or less 'modern' economic policy. Though he had to withdraw from the contest immediately after these remarks, his views contributed to the general impression that the party was in some confusion about its economic policy.

There was always an irritating amount of argument among the leaders or differences between their public pronouncements and the programme, even on important issues such as green taxes, or symbolic ones such as speed limits on motorways.

Those social democrats who held office as prime ministers in SPD-led *Länder* governments were facing fiscal crises and had to implement rigid austerity policies, such as reductions of public services, which seemed to run counter to the declared policies of the party. This added to the party's lack of credibility.

The overwhelming impression – exploited and magnified by most of the mass media – was that there was a deep split in the party between a group of responsible realists who had more or less accepted the basic position of neo-liberalism and others who still nurtured typical social-democratic illusions about redistribution.

This scenario was only the beginning of what turned out to be a totally inadequate media performance by the party and its leadership throughout the 1980s with the lowest point being reached in the first half of the 1990s. In 1993, immediately after the party had selected Rudolf Scharping as its candidate, his competitors for leadership – above all the Prime Minister of Lower Saxony, Gerhard Schröder – started a kind of private media campaign in order to diminish Scharping's authority. In interviews and background briefings to journalists Schröder voiced openly his doubts about the capabilities of the candidate of his own party and emphasized in a provocative manner political differences between the party line as a whole and his own point of view, representing himself as a realist who, as a *Land* prime minister, was much closer to the real problems of the economy of the country. As a consequence, the public image of the party and its leadership was tarnished and brought down to a deplorably low level.

The consequence of this image problem was that, in the course of the party conference of November 1995 at Mannheim, Oskar Lafontaine made a surprise challenge against Scharping and convinced a majority of the delegates (who had not been forewarned) to back him on the grounds that only a change in leadership could bring the party's misery to an end and provide it with a new opportunity for recovering.

The crisis of the public image of the party in the 1990s revealed the difficult problems social-democratic parties face in modern media-dominated societies. Social and political reality are filtered through the mass media. As a consequence, the party's own political vision cannot be adequately conveyed through media channels. Party representatives striving to achieve media prominence or, at least, a presence, cannot do so if all they try to do is to communicate the political message contained in the party reform programme. They have to cater to the media code – what one might call the 'aesthetic' requirement of the media – by playing up conflicts, differences, personalities, controversial behaviour, eccentric opinions and the like.

As a comprehensive reform message is even today an essential part of the political identity of social-democratic parties, a two-way trap opens up. To get access to the media and achieve a regular media presence, the party leader has to adapt his public performances and messages in terms of the 'aesthetics' demands of the media rather than in terms of the requirements of the party programme. If he fails, he is almost automatically excluded from access. It follows that a significant media presence requires a personal image design and appropriate symbolic actions addressed to the media.

Each difference and conflict relating to the party is almost invariably inflated according to media rules, whereas the political message itself, the party policies and programmes, constantly appear as a non-event. This media-structured scenario makes it quite easy for competitors of the party leader to gain media presence and prominence by stressing differences and staging conflicts with the official party representative in a way that suits the media.

It is particularly difficult for social-democratic parties to avoid this trap without neglecting the media and their crucial influence altogether or alienating important parts of their own following in the party.

An example will elucidate this: when Björn Engholm was still party leader in 1992, there was a populist media campaign instigated from conservative right-wing quarters, but in tune with popular feelings, to stop what was called 'the flood' of incoming foreigners, particularly applicants for political asylum. This campaign contributed to a widely shared media image of the party, namely, that it was not fit to rule the country unless it joined those who were determined to stop immigration immediately by changing one of the basic rights laid down in the constitution.

Engholm convinced a small group of party leaders to abandon this position overnight and to go along with right-wing efforts to do away with the constitutional protection of political refugees in Germany – contrary to what the party had campaigned for in the previous two years. The party derived some short-term advantages from this media-induced tactical turnaround: the media campaign against the party stopped. At the same time, among many intellectuals and in the more rational sections of society, it seemed as if the party would abandon even its basic values in order to gain political power. The impression which prevailed was that the party had betrayed some of the moral

foundations of the Federal Republic. Anxieties which had been in existence for a long time now turned into alienation from the party, a process
which benefited the Green Party.

Another example which demonstrates the negative effects of the
media trap for a social-democratic party is the image strategy party
leaders adopted after Hans-Jochen Vogel. None of them tried to enhance
his public profile by using the programme of the party or by connecting
particular features of his own personality to it to win credibility and
influence. Instead of personifying the programme they all developed an
image strategy which stressed their own independence and personal
capacity. They tried not to be seen as merely the spokesmen of their
party. Consequently, the hectic change of leaders appeared as a hectic
change of policies in the eyes of public opinion.

Between 1992 and 1994 a party commission called 'SPD 2000' discussed this dilemma and tried to develop a comprehensive strategy in
order to overcome it. Two different options emerged within the party.
Those who were close to the party leader or themselves active in the
mass media system endorsed a strategy which would give the party
leader as much independence from the party as possible. This would
require considerable funding for a professional public relations campaign
advertising in the media the strategy of the leaders, their images and
their messages. Those who opposed this American model declared it
acceptable only for conservative and liberal parties. These parties, they
argued, were not interested in communicating through political debates
or mobilizing party members as part of a process of interaction between
the party and society; a social-democratic party would want its own
reform message to be communicated and this could not be done through
an American-type campaign.

They pointed out that analyses of the behaviour of potential SPD
voters had shown that its electoral success depended considerably on
the decision of a large group of middle-class voters who take fresh
decisions with each election and scrutinize rationally the positions and
arguments of several parties. This group gets rather alienated by political commercials and wants a proper political debate.

The German case shares some of the general problems social-democratic
parties face everywhere in post-industrial societies and it exposes in

addition some problems which arise from the German government system. To the latter category belongs particularly the federal structure of the governmental system. Each of the 16 *Länder* has sovereign powers which are exercised by its parliament and government. The Bundesrat has substantial prerogatives in the legislative process so that no bill concerning the administration of the *Länder* or cultural affairs can pass without the consent of the majority of that body in which the *Länder* government are represented.

A major consequence of this institutional pattern is the strong position of the heads of government or prime ministers of the *Länder*. They are elected in the *Länder* and are obliged to cater to the particular needs of their *Land* above all. This is one of the main reasons why party leaders who are *Land* prime ministers can always legitimize a conflict with the federal party chairman or the top candidate by referring to their constitutional duties on behalf of their *Land*. No federal party leader would find it easy to compel a whole group of party leaders to speak with one voice with respect to the key issues of building up the public image of the party.

This German particularity compounds the general difficulties social-democratic parties face in media-dominated societies. As there is almost no direct way of communicating reform projects directly through the mass media, indirect channels for the communication of political messages have to be found. *Either* there is a charismatic communicator who does not subjugate himself and his message to the 'aesthetic' requirements of the media but succeeds in being acceptable to the media *and* getting a political message across. *Or* the whole group of party leaders must act in unison on the basis of full loyalty to party policy.

If neither of these happens, as is the case in Germany, the whole party becomes a toy of the media. The problem is aggravated substantially by the fact that leaders who have a particularly high visibility in the media have considerable freedom and scope to deviate from the party consensus and even exhibit disloyal political behaviour. Notwithstanding dissent and even anger from substantial quarters of their party, they are almost invariably supported because the prevailing opinion inside and outside the party is that there is no alternative to media prominence if the party want to gain power.

The increasing convergence of the rules of behaviour of the political system with the requirements of the media fosters the separation between the media-charismatic party leader and the proper discourse of the party. At the time, continuous media presence fosters rivalries between party leaders as long as the media-charismatic supremo has not yet emerged. Moreover, the mass media are given a substantial share in the decision as to who will be accepted as the supremo. This is exactly what happened with the SPD after the retirement of its acknowledged leader Willy Brandt in 1987.

Like all the other social-democratic parties in post-industrial societies, the SPD is confronted with an historically unprecedented situation. Four factors contribute to it.

1. What were once relatively homogeneous working-class communities have been replaced, in course of recent decades, by a large number of sub-cultures, none of which exhibits a tendency to support social democracy as an automatic reflex. In present-day Germany both the working class and the middle class are represented by a broad range of socio-ethical sub-cultures with very different attitudes and ideas about life, work and politics. The split between materialists, post-materialists and post-modernists – as these currents of opinion are called by various research institutes – contains many sub-groups which are liable to support different parties depending on their political image and performance. The traditional working class, defined in terms of attitude and political orientation, amounts to 5 per cent only of the adult population. The SPD has to perform political somersaults to integrate four or five of these sub-cultures if it wants to gain more than 40 per cent of the votes. This is a much harder task for the SPD than for other German parties which have to target only one or two sub-cultures.

2. The glorious welfare state record of the SPD seems destined to become an ever greater burden in the new arena of global competition unless the party finds new answers to old questions.

3. Many new political issues have emerged in the political arena during the last two decades, from nuclear energy to genetic engineering, from the deployment of armed forces in UN-sponsored missions to immigration policies. The traditions of the SPD do not automatically provide guidance. The party has to develop new concepts for its entire

membership; this is often achieved only after considerable internal struggles.

4. The party has to fight on many different fronts: the Green Party gains from SPD failure in the ecological field; the CDU gains if the SPD accentuates ecology at the expense of economic growth and increasing prosperity; right-wing populists gain if the party position *vis-à-vis* immigration is too tolerant; the Greens gain if that position is too harsh; and the camp of the non-voter grows to the detriment of the party if its profile and performance as a reform party are unclear.

The squaring of the circle under these complicated conditions can be achieved only if the party selects two or three 'integrative' issues which are felt to be vital by all the sub-cultures it can target, and campaigns on them in such a way that its message can be received with trust. This is the German experience of the last two decades.

It seems that after one and a half decades of abortive attempts the party leadership is about to learn from its past mistakes. Since Lafontaine took over as party chairman in November 1995 he has tried to overcome the main handicaps of the party, with some signs of success. He refused to accept the neo-liberal discourse about globalization and the iron law of cost minimization as compulsory preconditions for realistic economic policies. As a social-democratic alternative he offered a policy aiming at internationalizing the ecological and social framework for international markets. At the same time, maximum use is to be made of existing national possibilities for economic innovation by supporting the process of 'ecologizing' the economy with state support. The green tax reform is the symbolic priority of that programme. To counter the past disastrous media image of the party Lafontaine has started to coordinate the media communication of the entire leadership with the aim of using the media for diffusing the social-democratic message instead of being used by them.

7

The post-communist socialists in Eastern and Central Europe

PETER GOWAN

One of the most unexpected features of contemporary European politics is the continued strength of the post-communist parties. In the five countries of East Central Europe the formerly ruling communist parties emerged from the elections in 1989–90 as the dominant parties of the Left.[1] In six of these first elections they gained the largest vote of any party. Subsequently, in Poland and Hungary they became the most popular national parties. Seven years after the beginning of the transition to capitalism, the ex-communist parties remained the dominant parties of the Left in all the countries of the region except one – the Czech Republic. In four of them – Poland, Hungary, Bulgaria and Romania – they have been the leading party at a national level, though in Romania and Bulgaria they were defeated in presidential elections towards the end of 1996.

These former ruling communist parties had swiftly repudiated the political system of the Soviet Bloc, especially the principle of 'the leading role of the communist party'. All changed their names to 'socialist' or 'social-democratic' parties except the Czechoslovak communists, who kept their name, and the Romanian communists, who organized themselves in a 'National Salvation Front' before re-christening themselves 'Social Democrats' in 1993. These transformation decisions in some cases led to splits with minorities attempting to maintain the old party or with minorities wishing to go further than the majority and form explicitly pro-capitalist social-democratic parties.

Table 7.1 The share of the vote in East and Central Europe 1989–96 (post-communists, independent social democrats and liberal parties, first three elections)

Hungary	March 1990	June 1994
HSP	10.9	33
HSDP	3.6	0/1
HSWP	3.7	3.2
AFD	21.4	19.8

Key: HSP: Hungarian Socialist Party; HSDP: Hungarian Social Democratic Party; HSWP: Hungarian Socialist Workers' Party, later renamed Hungarian Workers' Party; AFD: Alliance of Free Democrats.

Bulgaria	June 1990	October 1991	December 1994
BSP	47.1	33.1	43.5
SDP	0.1	–	–

Key: BSP: Bulgarian Socialist Party; SDP: Social Democratic Party.

Poland	June 1989	October 1991	September 1993
SLD	11.0	12.0	20.4
Dem. Union	–	12.3	10.6
Lab. Solid/UL	–	2.1	7.3

Key: SLD: Democratic Left Alliance, led by the Social Democrats of the Polish Republic (SDPR); Dem. Union: Democratic Union, later called the Freedom Union; Lab. Solid./UL: Labour Solidarity which became the Union of Labour.

Romania	May 1990	September 1992
NSF	67	27.5
SDP	1.1	

Key: NSF: National Salvation Front, later renamed the Party of Social Democrats of Romania; SDP: Social Democratic Party.

Czech Rep	June 1990	June 1992	June 1996
CP	13.5	14.3	10.3
SDP	4.1	7.7	26.4

Key: CP: Communist Party; SDP: Social Democratic Party.

Slovakia	June 1990	June 1992	June 1996
CP/PDL	13.8	14.4	10.4
SDP	1.9	6.1	–
AWS	–	–	7.3

Key: CP/PDL: Communist Party, later renamed the Party of the Democratic Left (PDL) after its fusion with the Social Democratic Party (SDP); AWS: the Association of Workers of Slovakia, a Left split-off from the Communist Party after its fusion with the SDP.

Germany, East	March 1990
PDS	16.3
SPD	21.8

Key: PDS: Party of the Democratic Socialists; SPD: Social Democratic Party of Germany.

Attempts were also made after 1989 to establish new social-democratic parties hostile to the post-communists. These parties were initially encouraged by the Socialist International, notably in the case of the Czechoslovak and Hungarian social democrats and later in the case of the Polish Union of Labour. Others joined with free market liberals in the centre, notably in the Hungarian Free Democrats and the Polish Democratic Union. Yet with the exception of the social democrats in the Czech Republic, all these parties, both social-democratic and liberal, have been less successful than the parties of the former communists.

This chapter will explore first the possible reasons for the strength of the ex-communists, the general environment in which the ex-communist parties have found themselves in the first half of the 1990s and, finally, the ways in which they have sought to respond to this environment with policies aimed at strengthening, or at least not weakening, their support.

After looking generally at the evolution of the Left throughout the region, we will then examine more closely the politics of the four main post-communist socialist parties: the Social Democrats of the Polish Republic (SDPR), which is the main successor party of the Polish communists (i.e. the Polish United Workers' Party); the Hungarian Socialist Party (HSP) which is the main successor party of the Hungarian 'communists' (the Hungarian Socialist Workers' Party); the Bulgarian Socialist Party (BSP), the successor of the Bulgarian Communist Party; and the Party of Social Democracy of Romania (PSDR), the main successor party, initially via the National Salvation Front, of the Romanian Communist Party.

The sources of comparative strength of the post-communist socialists

There are widely diverging opinions as to why the post-communist socialists have become so strong. Some hold that these parties, at least in the Visegrad countries, were more or less wiped out in the so-called revolutions of 1989 and that their 'resurrection' is the result of protest votes against the painful costs of transition to capitalism combined with moods of nostalgia for the security of the communist past.[2] The implication of such a view is that the post-communist protest vote may fade in the future. At the other extreme, some analysts argue that the post-communists are strong because the basic structures of the old communist states throughout the region have changed only superficially.[3] The implication of this view is that unless there is more vigorous western political intervention, authoritarian post-communist regimes will be consolidated throughout most of the region.

Both these opposed views share the following widely held assumptions: that the ruling communist parties had negligible popular support in the last phase of communism; that the substance of the collapse of 1989 was a revolt by the 'people' or 'civil society' as a more or less homogeneous group on the one hand against the (communist) state on the other; and that these societies were not significantly polarized between left-wing and right-wing tendencies.[4] Such assumptions were, of course, a product of the dominant paradigm in the field of Soviet studies: totalitarian theory, viewing communism as a state-repressive system of managerial control without socio-political roots. The initial but ephemeral appearance of anti-communist coalitions calling themselves civic fronts of various kinds in some countries seemed to give substance to these preconceptions. The collapse of 1989 was thus seen as a popular anti-statist revolution and analysis of the politics of the region was then largely assimilated to a supposedly general field of transitions from dictatorship. The initial electoral strength of the post-communists was viewed as ephemeral and there was an expectation that the political forces that had been linked to the previous regime would sink without electoral trace as they did in, for example, southern Europe in the 1970s.

The subsequent electoral evidence of continued ex-communist strength thus leads those determined to stick to the paradigm towards the view that the 'revolution' of 'civil society' must have been superficial; communist statism has been able to survive the 'revolution' throughout most of the region. Others have stressed contingent (and thus perhaps temporary) factors behind the revival: backlash protests against the temporary hardships of shock therapy, nostalgic protest votes for the old security, or the initial rightist rejection by voters of the non-communist social democrats after 1989.

There is, however, a simpler solution to this puzzle produced by the preconceptions of totalitarian theory: it is that the socialist constituency inclined to support the communists has been fairly strong, though in a minority in the Visegrad countries, throughout both the 1980s and the 1990s.

The ignored socialist electorate

Opinion surveys during the 1980s in the Visegrad countries (Poland, Hungary and Czechoslovakia) and the GDR showed that significant minorities of the population supported the ruling parties. Even in Poland after the imposition of martial law, polls in 1984 showed that 25 per cent supported the Communist Party leadership, 25 per cent were hostile to it and 50 per cent had no opinions or did not wish to express them.[5] Furthermore, the 25 per cent supporting the party tended to

hold socialist values, particularly egalitarianism and support for nationalized property, while those hostile tended to be anti-egalitarian and in
favour of the free market. Polish society was thus politically polarized
on a Left–Right basis, with the PUWP supporters on the left. The
same poll evidence shows majorities of the population supporting
various central aspects of the social principles of state socialism.

Similar evidence is available for neighbouring countries. From 1985,
competitive elections were taking place in Hungary, and these demonstrate that, as late as 1989, the Hungarian communists were gaining 30
per cent or more of the votes and that these votes were indicative of
support for left-wing political and social values.[6] Polling in the GDR
tells a similar story. Polls conducted there between 20 and 27 November
1989 showed the SED as having the largest percentage of support of
any party: 31 per cent.[7] In Czechoslovakia polling in December 1989
showed majority support not only for socialized property but also for
central planning.[8]

A further important feature of political developments in the late
1980s and early 1990s has been the survival of the official unions of the
state socialist period. They have become the dominant trade union
confederations during the transition to capitalism.[9] They did so despite
concerted efforts on the part of governments of the Right and of
western bodies such as the ICFTU and the AFL-CIO to weaken them.
In Hungary, the main trade union federation retained some 3 million of
its 4.5 million 1988 membership in 1991.[10] The Polish official unions
emerged with 4.5 million members in comparison with Solidarity's 2.3
million members. The same pattern emerged in Czechoslovakia.[11] In
Bulgaria the official unions faced a serious challenge with the emergence
of an initially strong new union but this challenge had faded by 1993.
The old official federation's membership also declined, from 3 million
at the end of 1990 to only 1.6 million at the end of 1992, but its
dominance within the trade union field was maintained. In Romania,
the official unions also remained the strongest although they fragmented
into competing centres in the early 1990s.

The official unions of the communist period had not been mere
transmission belts for a 'totalitarian' state without a significant social
base. It follows that there was a substantial trade union constituency to
be won by parties of the Left.[12]

If, then, there was a core socialist electorate of 25 per cent or more at the time of the regime collapse, the strong showing of these parties during the first part of the 1990s as the strongest parties on the Left is scarcely surprising. Indeed, the puzzle is why these parties did not do much better in the first post-1989 elections than they did, why their votes were lower in the GDR and the Visegrad countries than polling evidence from the 1980s would have suggested.

One explanation could be that erstwhile communist supporters were temporarily swept up in the wave of enthusiasm for a transition to capitalism in 1989–90 and switched their support to the parties of the free market Right. This does seem to have been an important factor in the GDR elections of March 1990. Polling in early 1990 showed over 60 per cent of the GDR electorate holding social-democratic or socialist political and social opinions and yet Kohl's campaign promises swung a big majority for the Right precisely in the traditional social-democratic Saxon strongholds, leaving the PDS with only 16.3 per cent and the SPD with only 21.8 per cent.

On the face of it, the same effect seems to have operated elsewhere. In 1990 and 1991 opinion polls showed large majorities in favour of so-called 'market economies' in Poland, Hungary, Czechoslovakia and Bulgaria, with a majority the other way only in Romania. This support had dropped massively by 1994 (except in Romania where there was a reverse trend).[13]

This evidence of enthusiasm for the market among large parts of the electorate does not explain why the still large minorities hostile to the introduction of capitalism and market forces did not fully support the post-communists. The reality is that there were many abstentions. Indeed, these were so large that even many of those who told pollsters they favoured a market economy must have decided not to vote. In the 1989 Polish elections, less than 50 per cent of the electorate voted for Solidarity: the turn-out in this first competitive election was low, with high levels of abstentions. In 1991 when the first full parliamentary elections in Poland were held, total turn-out was 43 per cent. In the 1993 parliamentary elections both the turn-out (52 per cent) and the vote for the SDPR went up substantially and detailed analysis has shown that this correlation was central to the success of the SDPR.[14] Parties of the centre and Right in Hungary also failed to gain support from over 50 per cent of the electorate in a low turn-out; and the party calling fairly explicitly for free market capitalism, the Alliance of Free Democrats, gained only 21 per cent of those who voted. In Czechoslovakia, the Civic Forum did not campaign on a free market programme in the 1990 elections.

Thus, a more likely explanation for the limited support for the post-communist parties is that many of their supporters decided not to vote at all. This explanation is reinforced by the fact that the post-communist parties with the smallest percentage of the vote were those of Poland and Hungary where electoral participation was lowest. In Hungary, only 58 per cent of the electorate turned out and the figure was roughly the same in Poland – hardly a sign of a popular revolution for freedom against 'totalitarianism'.

The high abstention rate in Poland and Hungary suggests another puzzle: why was it that in the only two countries where the ruling Communist Party leadership took autonomous decisions (in February 1989) to move towards pluralist democratic political systems, and where they had been campaigning for years for 'market reform', did the communists perform worst of all the communist parties in the region? If the great issue of these elections was freedom (and the free market) against totalitarianism, why did these two parties perform worse than the two parties that resisted democratic change and the market: the East German and Czechoslovak parties?[15]

This points to the possibility that the poor performance of the Polish and Hungarian parties had little to do with freedom versus totalitarianism, but was linked to another feature that distinguished these two parties from the Czechoslovak and East German parties: the fact that their party leadership had for some years been vigorously promoting policies of increasing marketization and social differentiation, with increasingly negative effects on those sections of the population in whose name they ruled; policies which were not being promoted by the Czechoslovak and East German parties whose economies under centralized planning were more successful than those of either Poland or Hungary.[16]

Evidence from the results gained by smaller parties in the Hungarian elections tends to confirm the view that the low vote of the HSP was partly the result of its pro-market orientation. While the HSP gained 10.9 per cent of the vote, a further 8.8 per cent of votes went to small,

Table 7.2 Communist Party transformations

Old name	Year of change	New name
Polish United Workers' Party	February 1990	Social Democrats of the Polish Republic
Hungarian Socialist Workers' Party	September 1989	Hungarian Socialist Party
Bulgarian Communist Party	April 1990	Bulgarian Socialist Party
Yugoslav League of Communists	February 1990	Party broke up
Albanian Workers' Party	June 1991	Albanian Socialist Party
Romanian Communist Party	January 1990	National Salvation Front
National Salvation Front	July 1993	Party of Romanian Social Democrats
Socialist Unity (GDR)	February 1990	Party of the Democratic Left
Slovak Communist Party	1990	Party of the Democratic Left
Montenegro Communists	1991	Democratic Party of Socialists

mainly anti-market parties. The Hungarian Socialist Workers' Party gained 3.7 per cent, and a single issue group which opposed the break-up of agricultural cooperatives gained 3.2 per cent of the vote.

What I offer here is nothing more than a set of hypotheses with some empirical evidence. They explain the rather general revival of the fortunes of these parties as the 1990s progressed; their levels of support were simply returning to previous trends despite strenuous efforts by anti-communist parties and the media to delegitimize them. It may also suggest another conclusion: that a significant minority of electorates may have held social values to the Left of the post-communist party leadership and may indeed still do so.

In most of the Balkan countries, the post-communists tended to emerge from the first elections as the strongest parties. This occurred in Romania, Bulgaria, Serbia, Montenegro and later Albania.[17] These initial successes were not ephemeral. These parties retained strong support even if they were, as in Bulgaria and Albania, subsequently to go into opposition.

The fate of the non-communist social-democratic parties

Some have suggested that the principal cause of post-communist strength in the Visegrad zone lay in mistakes made by the independent social democrats.[18] In most of the countries of the region, non-communist socialists created new social democratic parties, backed initially by the Socialist International (SI). In Poland after some false starts such a group emerged from Solidarity and was called the Union of Labour (UL).[19] In Czechoslovakia a social-democratic party was re-established. This then divided into a Czech and a Slovak party, respectively the CSSD and the SDSS. In Hungary a similar party, the Hungarian Social Democratic Party, was formed. The Slovene Social Democratic Party also emerged and similar small parties were created in Bulgaria, Albania and Romania.

All these parties swiftly gained political support from the SI. The German and Austrian parties were particularly active in ensuring financial support for these groups as were the French socialists.[20] It was not unusual for almost the entire funds of these parties to be supplied from the West.[21] Yet except in two cases – the Czech Republic and Slovenia – these parties failed to compete successfully with the post-communists for leadership of the Left. They gained between 0.1 per cent and 7.5 per cent of the votes. In most cases they failed miserably. The reason for this is not obvious: standard accounts of popular revolution against communism would lead us to expect the opposite. Some have suggested that the social democrats failed because their names were tainted by their historical and ideological links with communism.[22] This may explain why they did not obtain support from the right-wing electorate, but not their failure with left-wing voters. Others have suggested an historic–cultural explanation: that social democracy was historically important only in inter-war Czechoslovakia and therefore there was no cultural tradition elsewhere.[23] This may be true of parts of the Balkans but it ignores the dominance of this tradition on the Left in both inter-war Poland and Hungary.

A more straightforward explanation is that these parties failed because they made no serious appeal to the socialist section of the electorate we identified above. Many of these parties simply stressed the free market programme which the West European social democratic parties were arguing for within East Central Europe in the early 1990s: the western socialist parties tended to insist upon support for a thorough-going free market transformation combined with strong anti-communism in East Central Europe. Arguing for policies that entailed first dismantling the egalitarian and welfare arrangements to build capitalism so that one could later construct welfare capitalism seemed disingenuous. These policies wiped out the social democrats in the Balkan zone and in Hungary.[24] In Poland, on the other hand, within Solidarity there emerged a left opposition (later the Union of Labour) to the neo-liberal Balcerowicz Plan of mainstream Solidarity. This tendency raised real issues of concern to working-class people against Solidarity-based governments, breaking with Catholic connections, vigorously championing abortion rights in 1993 while the neo-liberals in the Democratic Union sought to appease the church hierarchy on the issue. As a result, the Union of Labour gained a genuine base on the Left in the 1993 elections, polling 7.3 per cent. At the same time, this leftist orientation was combined with anti-communism. The German SPD supported the Union of Labour financially in the hope that the organization could be used to split the Polish ex-communists. A prominent post-communist intellectual, Lamentowicz, was drawn over to the party and efforts were made to open a split within the post-communists. However, these tactics failed and instead the UL itself was split in the 1995 presidential elections, as Lamentowicz was expelled for supporting post-communist leader Kwasniewski's candidacy while other leaders of the UL campaigned on behalf of Democratic Union candidate Jacek Kuron. The result was that the UL candidate received negligible support.

Non-communist social democrats did succeed in out-distancing the post-communists in two countries in the region: the Czech Republic and Slovenia. The Slovene dynamics were governed by the break-up of Yugoslavia. While the Yugoslav League of Communists was the biggest party in the April 1990 Slovene elections, its support evaporated during the Slovene drive to secede from Yugoslavia. The Slovene social democrats became the dominant Left party on the basis of a strong nationalist appeal. The really significant exception to the pattern outlined above was the Czech case, and it tends to confirm the explanation offered above for the failures of social democracy elsewhere in the region. In the Czech Republic the social democrats initially gained only 4.1 per cent of the vote in June 1990 (against the Communist Party's 13.5 per cent). In the June 1992 elections the social democrats' vote rose to 7.7 per cent (while the Communist Party's vote also rose to 14.3 per cent). But in the 1996 elections the social democrats decisively established themselves as the dominant party on the Left, gaining 26.4 per cent of the vote against the Czech communists' 10.3 per cent.

The three crucial factors operating in the Czech case were: (1) the decision of the Communist Party not to occupy the centre-left ground by transforming itself into a socialist party; (2) the decision by the social democrats to make a leftist appeal to the electorate; and (3) the capacity of the social democrats to establish a serious trade union base. Of course, financial support from the West helped, but without the other factors, the money would have been useless.

The decline in support for the Czech communists was not only the result of their continued adhesion to the communist tradition; indeed, after 1990 their support actually rose and in local elections they gained almost 18 per cent of the vote, the highest vote of any communist party in continental Europe in the early 1990s. But in 1993 the Communist Party was riven by internal conflict, which turned the party inwards and involved both the expulsion of a neo-Stalinist group and the defection of groups on the party's right. The majority forces in the party were at the same time unable to develop a coherent strategic identity for the party.[25] Simultaneously, the Czech social democrats were able to present themselves as a serious grouping to the left of the neo-liberals. In the first place they recruited the economist Komarek (Vaclav Klaus's boss before the 'Velvet Revolution') who had become a household name throughout the country in 1990 because of his economic reform ideas against the communists and who then criticized Klaus's neo-liberal economic ideology in a detailed, well-informed way, offering his own alternative economic strategy. This was unique in the region: the best-known non-communist economic expert with impeccable political credentials offering an authoritative alternative to neo-liberalism.

The second important achievement of the Czech social democrats was their ability to develop influence with the former official trade union confederation, CSKOS, through a strong social-democratic representation on its leadership. These links were no doubt strengthened by the assistance given to CSKOS by the German DGB. These advantages were consolidated when Zeman took over the leadership of the party and swung its policy more to the left.

A further factor in the Czech case, reinforcing all the others, was undoubtedly the country's geo-political and geo-economic environment. Wedged between Vienna and Berlin, the Czech Republic had received very strong signals from the German government that it was at the head of the queue for membership of the EU. Its highly skilled workforce and advanced engineering traditions as well as its geographical location offered its population the hope of a substantial rise in living standards in the future. All these circumstances helped a social-democratic party pragmatically focused upon concrete problems facing working-class people. It is also worth noting that the large increase in the vote of the Czech social democrats in the 1996 elections was not principally at the expense of the Czech Communist Party. It was much more the result of winning back from centrist parties that large part of the Czech socialist constituency who had been drawn towards the centrists or who had abstained in the 1990 and 1992 elections.[26]

The environments confronting the post-communist socialists

The most basic contextual problems for the four parties we shall discuss (the Polish, Hungarian, Romanian and Bulgarian) have been: (1) the terrible economic slump that hit their economies at the start of the 1990s, in part due to the collapse of Comecon trade and payments networks and the break-up of the USSR; (2) the debt burdens and financial crises of the region; and (3) the slump-deepening demands of the International Financial Institutions (IFIs) reflecting the goals of western governments for the region.[27]

The economic crisis was most severe and protracted in Bulgaria which had very strong economic links with the USSR and had to default on its very heavy debt repayments. The country remains in a profound depression. The Hungarian economy has been recovering from the slump very slowly and its debt problems are severe and deepening. Both the Polish and Romanian economies have been growing fairly strongly since 1993. Within this general context, the states of the region faced more or less severe resource crises in the form of chronic and acute fiscal problems and debt repayment difficulties and few opportunities for tackling these problems through borrowing on private capital markets at home or abroad. Romania had paid off its foreign debt in the 1980s, but faced acute shortages of hard currency as well as budget difficulties. Poland was uniquely able to have much of its debt written off and, combined with economic growth, this has given the parties of the Left in government some room for manoeuvre. But both Bulgaria and Hungary have faced more or less continuous financial crises.

Solutions to many of these problems could have been facilitated if the European Union had opened its markets widely for the region's exports, particularly those of its more advanced industrial sectors. But the governments of the EU had no economic interest in taking such a step against a background of long-term stagnation and saturated domestic markets within the EU combined with high levels of un-employment. At the same time, the economic and the state financial crises gave the western powers a quite extraordinary degree of leverage over the governments of the region: they could deny them access to finance and a trade substitute for Comecon simply by maintaining the Cold War embargoes used previously against the Soviet Bloc.

This leverage was placed in the service of an extremely ambitious western campaign for thorough social engineering within the region to establish a new social system: the replacement of regimes of strong social and economic protection in these countries with regimes with less social protection than those of the EU and with a 'globalized' institu-tional face to the outside world, in other words an extreme form of open door for products and capital, including hot, short-term money flows. These regime goals were given the label 'market economy' but were in reality geared towards ensuring that these economies occupied subordinate places in the projected new European international division of labour. The guidelines were mainly derived from US tactics since the 1980s for reorganizing international economic relations in ways that favoured their own capitalism. The Soviet crisis and the collapse of the state socialist regimes enormously enhanced this drive by disorienting and disorganizing the Left on a global scale. In such conditions, the USA, backed by the main West European states (though with a partial and half-hearted attempt at resistance by the French government) felt able to attempt to impose this programme on the East Central European states in the midst of their crisis. The campaign initially sharply exacerbated the economic crisis, thus strengthening further western leverage.

It was an agenda that offered very handsome rewards to those within the region with access to capital or with the possibility of partnership with western capital; but it tended to make losers of the majority of the population and to impoverish a significant minority. These were, of course, the natural constituencies of the socialist parties. It follows that, from the point of view of US strategy, the post-communist parties were bound to be a potential obstacle and vigorous efforts were to be made to weaken them. But these global regime goals promoted especially by the USA and the IFIs were potentially modified by the geo-political interests of the main West European states. From the start of the transition to capitalism, the Visegrad countries could hope to enjoy some geo-political advantages over their neighbours to the East and South: their location on Germany's eastern periphery meant that the German government was interested in drawing them firmly under German influence (mainly indirectly through EU mechanisms). This offered the hope that for Germany a modicum of stability in these countries would be essential and could over-ride the general regime goals. Slovenia and Croatia also hoped to gain from German foreign policy by separating from Yugoslavia, but for Croatia these gains have been postponed by the war.

Romania and Bulgaria initially lacked much geo-political interest for the western alliance and during 1990 the latter took an especially tough line towards them. But the development of the Yugoslav war (as well as the resurgence of Greek–Turkish rivalry) has given Bulgaria an increased political salience and the western powers softened their stance towards it in what might be called the field of symbolic politics. Romania, on the other hand, has remained, so far, in a political limbo.

Against this background, the domestic political agenda was more about 'state refounding' than about what might be called 'normal politics'. What was debated were the social principles of the new state and its economy; its institutional structures and, above all, the composition of the new, emergent capitalist class (that is, the principles and forms of privatization). In this complicated environment all parties were seeking to find ways of enhancing their own legitimacy and authority, principally through gaining authoritative approval from the West. Here, the most important source of support for parties to the left of centre was the Socialist International, but during the first five years of the transition only the Hungarian Socialist Party could gain minimal recognition from that quarter by being granted observer status in 1992. On the other hand, the evolution of the PCI in Italy was a powerful indirect source of inspiration for many intellectuals from the ex-communist parties, as it transformed itself in 1989–91 into the PDS and obtained full membership of the Socialist International.

These international conditions and constraints would have been extremely onerous for any government. They proved near-catastrophic for those of the Left. In a different international environment their behaviour would undoubtedly have been very different and it is not easy to distinguish the endogenous policy impulses within these parties from the exogenous international constraints, or indeed positive external diktats in analysing their behaviour, especially while in government. But I shall attempt to do so below.

The policy orientations of the post-communists

I shall try to examine some aspects of the politics of the post-communist parties in Poland, Hungary, Romania and Bulgaria. Three of these parties have had a continuity of name and structures since early 1990: the Social Democrats of the Polish Republic (the SDPR), the Hungarian Socialist Party (HSP), and the Bulgarian Socialist Party (BSP). In Romania the pattern of organizational evolution has been very different. The Romanian political transition was carried through by a combination of potentially radically opposed forces: a popular uprising against the Ceauşescu dictatorship and a palace coup by Ceauşescu's praetorian guard. Political leadership was seized by the pro-Soviet wing of the Communist Party under Iliescu. This group then successfully stabilized a new regime by simultaneously banning the Communist Party and transferring its forces into a new National Salvation Front (NSF).[28] In 1992 the NSF split into two separate movements, one led by Iliescu; the other, by his former Prime Minister, Petre Roman. The Iliescu group then, in 1993, formed the Party of Social Democracy of Romania and claimed to support the Socialist International. Meanwhile, another group established a Socialist Labour Party, claiming allegiance to the traditions of Romanian communism. The Iliescu group has remained the dominant party in all elections up to the autumn of 1996.[29]

Today in all four countries, the post-communists claim allegiance to the Socialist International, declare support for the principles of the Council of Europe on human and civil rights, and defend the notion of a 'market economy' and pluralist liberal democratic principles. They all also declare their goal to be eventual membership of the European Union. Yet these declaratory commitments tell us little and obscure the substantial differences between these parties.

Differences on systemic change

From an institutional point of view, after the political collapse of the single-party regime, the states of the region could be described as forms of social democracy in the strict sense of combining socialized property forms with political democracy. But to what extent were these parties prepared to dismantle existing institutions in the direction of capitalism? How far to retreat from socialized property and political intervention in economic life?

The Polish and Hungarian post-communist parties assumed that their countries were going to be absorbed into western Europe and that they had to accept the fate of being on the left within a capitalist country. In the Polish case the outgoing PUWP leader Mieczyslaw Rakowski clearly spelled this out in a series of speeches in the autumn of 1989: the new party should become the dominant centre-left force in Polish politics, counter-balancing a centre-right party[30] and accept a new market economy.[31] In Hungary, acceptance of a transition both to pluralist democracy and to capitalism had been universal within the top leadership since the autumn of 1989.

For the Romanian and Bulgarian post-communist parties, the international conjuncture in 1989–91 was far less easy to read. There was always the possibility that Gorbachev's effort to renew socialism in the USSR might succeed; and there was little indication of a strong western

drive to integrate their countries into the West. In Romania, President
Iliescu assumed at first that Gorbachev would succeed. Therefore he
was ready to enter a security pact with the USSR, despite strong
western opposition, and embraced 'market socialism' defined as the
continuation of a non-capitalist economy, thus rejecting the regime
programme set out by the West.

When the Soviet Union collapsed at the end of 1991, so did the
perspective of Romanian development within a Soviet-centred geo-
political and economic space. The erstwhile Prime Minister, Petre
Roman, responded in 1992 by splitting from the NSF and creating a
new NSF ready to embark upon a transition to capitalism and merging
with the smaller Democratic Party. The following year, Iliescu also
shifted ground with the transformation of his NSF into the Party of
Social Democrats of Romania oriented towards the introduction of
capitalism, though a strongly national one rather than the 'globalized'
variety. This has remained a strong aspect of the politics of the Romanian social democrats.

The Bulgarian Socialist Party (BSP) faced a more difficult international context. Its economy was closely linked with that of the USSR;
yet, unlike Romania, Bulgaria was located at the intersection of two
potentially explosive crises that the US government has been strongly
focused upon and involved with: that in Yugoslavia and the rivalry
between Greece and Turkey. At the same time Bulgaria was facing a
desperate debt crisis with western creditors. The BSP sought to maintain some element of ambiguity, favouring privatization and 'market
reform' in general public statements, but remaining unenthusiastic in
practice. The efforts of the party leadership were directed towards
preserving a powerful state sector and cooperatives in agriculture, resist-
ing western pressure to 'globalize' the economy, stressing the importance
of maintaining national control over capital assets.

Party organizational transformation

The Polish SDPR, the Hungarian HSP and the Bulgarian BSP were all
formed at congresses of the former communist parties. The new ideological and political parameters were openly debated. New organizational
arrangements were set up. Regular party congresses have subsequently

been held, with real debates and evident differences within the parties. But the Romanian pattern was very different.

The formation of the Romanian National Salvation Front (NSF) indicated the profound ambivalence of the new political order emerging out of the combined revolt from below and the palace coup from above. The Iliescu leadership group tried to offer a political identity which could somehow be accepted by both these potentially antagonistic forces, hence the formation of the amorphous NSF. The subsequent formation of the Party of Social Democracy of Romania (PSDR) was not the result of an organic process of political differentiation within the NSF but, rather, an initiative taken from above by the Iliescu government. The congress that founded the new party did not adopt sharply defined political principles and the new name was decided after the congress by the leaders. As a result, the PSDR resembled a loosely defined group of supporters of President Iliescu himself, not fully autonomous from the state executive. The evident divisions within the PSDR were not clearly reflected in open debates at party congresses. As a result the PSDR resembles what might be called a Leader Party, which substitutes the leader's will for strongly defined programmatic parameters.

The abandonment of the principle of 'the leading role of the party' entailed also the sociological separation of the ex-communist parties from the large managerial layers of the old regime – both state officials and economic managers. This process of organizational differentiation was massive and swift in both Poland and Hungary in 1989–90 and was accepted by the SDPR and the HSP as they went into opposition. Their party organizations became western-style parties devoted to electoral political activity.

In Bulgaria and Romania, where the ex-communists remained in power after the first elections, the process of differentiation of the party from managerial groups was far less pronounced. The NSF and the BSP continued to exercise large powers of state patronage and remained a focus for the pursuit of managerial interests. This has subsequently marked the evolution of the BSP, some of whose members have simultaneously been linked to powerful business groups (both state and private). Nevertheless, the BSP's organizational transformation into an autonomous organization for political communication and deliberation developed more or less along the lines of the parties in the Visegrad countries, especially once it too went into opposition in 1991.

Here too the Romanian case was unique. The collapse of the party–state complex of the Ceauşescu regime left a state elite in place without any real party at all. The process of post-communist party formation was both slow and was led by Iliescu from his state presidential office. The highly elitist official ideology put forward by the NSF reflected this socio-political reality. The boundaries between state and party activity were never fully drawn, making the Romanian situation in the early 1990s somewhat similar to the kind of 'party of power' that operated in parts of the Commonwealth of Independent States (CIS) after the collapse of the USSR. Even when the 'Social Democratic' party (the PSDR) was created, it had little internal life of its own and no real programme. The party appeared more as an appendage of the state leadership than as an autonomous collective political actor. Nevertheless, as the competitive party system has evolved, the PSDR has had to define its political references and organizational structures more clearly. The major test will come if the party is faced with the prospect of going into opposition.

Domestic political rifts and party policy

The various post-communist parties have defined themselves through overlapping political splits at a national level during the 1990s. In three of the four countries the impact of these polarizations on the party system have been to produce divisions on Left–Right lines, but in Romania this spectrum has been blurred by the impact of nationalism.

Communism versus anti-communism The first great polarization in all four countries was that between communism and anti-communism. At an electoral level, the anti-communist appeal of the first phase of the transition had largely played itself out in all four countries as it was being overlaid by other polarizations. Nevertheless, this rift remains at deeper structural levels a very important one in all four countries because it still divides their socio-political elites and because of the uncertain futures of the countries themselves.

In all the countries concerned, parties are identifiable by reference to the political origins of their elites. In all of them, the last five years have seen the construction and legitimation of new capitalist classes. This process has been in large measure a matter of political decisions, connected to privatizations rather than simply a 'spontaneous' accumulation of private capital within a separate economic sphere. Thus party splits also reflect social splits at the elite level. If this does emerge as a significant fissure, it may make the emergence of an elite consensus on national strategy more difficult.

In all these countries a vast gulf remains on key historical questions: on the Right, the period of state socialism is presented as one of enslavement, while the inter-war years of the Pilsudski regime in Poland, the Horthy regime in Hungary and of monarchism and dictatorship in Romania and Bulgaria are seen as phases of national authenticity and autonomy. For the post-communist parties, on the other hand, the period of state socialism had positive, developmental features, not least in ending the legacies of inter-war authoritarianism and fascism.

One bridge across this gulf could have been constructed by strong and modern centrist parties inspired by political liberalism, without ties to inter-war regimes or to the state socialist period. This possibility has emerged in Hungary with the willingness of the Alliance of Free Democrats to cross the anti-communist divide and enter a coalition with the HSP. In Poland, on the other hand, the political liberals have so far remained allied with the anti-communist Right which draws on the traditions of Catholic and nationalist rejection of all Polish history since 1944. Similar rifts apply in Bulgaria.

In Romania, both the ex-communist camp and the anti-communist camp contain the same ideological tendencies. The ultra-nationalist parties which were allied with the PSDR have promoted themes and symbols reminiscent of the Iron Guard and of the Antonescu dictatorship, while the anti-communist camp has contained strong monarchist elements. Both liberal and socialist themes are promoted in both camps.

Neo-liberalism versus social protection   The second great polarization has been between supporters and opponents of neo-liberal 'economic reform'. This split appeared first in Hungary and cut across the communist/anti-communist divide by placing both the HDF on the right and the HSP in opposition to the Free Democrats and the Young

Democrats. In Poland the division opened through the impact of the Balcerowicz plan and as it worked itself through, it fragmented the anti-communist front and enabled the SDPR to take the leadership of a broadening coalition of interests and parties. The same basic pattern appeared in Hungary where the supporters of neo-liberalism became minoritarian as its economic and social consequences strengthened the HSP. In Bulgaria the neo-liberal rift remained superficial because the UDF did not coherently defend this political stance. In Romania the advocates of neo-liberalism remained weak.

A much more difficult issue, however, is to define the kind of socio-economic alternative to neo-liberalism which the post-communist socialists are seeking to promote. The source of this analytical problem arises largely from the extreme practical constraints facing these parties in power and thence from determining where the boundary lies between external constraint and autonomous political will on the part of these parties.

While in opposition, the SDPR, HSP and BSP all formed strong alliances with the main trade union confederations. In Poland the SDPR formed a Democratic Left Alliance with the OPZZ and as a result some 61 OPZZ candidates were elected to parliament in 1993. The HSP placed Sandor Nagy, the head of the trade union confederation, number two on its national party list. Similar links were established in Bulgaria. In Romania, dozens of small trade union confederations sprang up in 1990 (according to some, with deliberate encouragement from the government), but shortly after the formation of the PSDR in the spring of 1993, the main successor group from the Ceauşescu era merged with other large groups to form a new, dominant trade union confederation.[32] PSDR leaders welcomed this development which brought some order into industrial relations.

Thus the post-communist parties have sought to include the trade unions as important partners in national political life. At the same time, there have been conflicts between the parties in government and the trade unions, especially over wages and welfare issues and in no case have the parties been prepared to allow the trade union leadership a veto on matters of concern to Labour.[33]

In both Poland and Hungary, the post-communist socialist parties have felt the need to reassure the international financial markets when they formed their governments. In Hungary the HSP formed a coalition with the Free Democrats despite having a majority in parliament, though it held the Finance Ministry. In Poland the SDPR appointed a non-party academic, Kolodko, a critic of the Balcerowicz plan but also an orthodox champion of low inflation and low budget deficits, as Finance Minister.

There have been constant tensions between the finance ministers and other government departments over key aspects of economic and social policy, with the finance ministers generally reflecting the pressures of the international financial institutions and markets. The typical pattern has been for the finance ministries to win on specific issues, while the President (in Poland) and the Prime Minister (in Hungary) have signalled their dissatisfaction with the general approach of the Finance Ministry.

In Poland, the SDPR combined defence of the idea of a universalist welfare state with an orthodox stress on financial stringency. It was able to do so because of the strong growth of the Polish economy and the debt forgiveness won under previous neo-liberal governments. Kolodko sought to offer a longer-term perspective of future prosperity for Polish voters by producing a medium-term economic plan. He ended the sharp discrimination against state enterprises, providing them with a more favourable legislative framework. He also committed Poland to improving trade and economic links with countries further east as well as with the West.

In Hungary, the HSP government, unlike that of Poland, has been constantly faced by acute financial strains, which reflected both its lack of debt forgiveness and the very sluggish economic recovery from the deep slump of the early 1990s. These problems have been used by western financial institutions to undermine the HSP's credibility as a defender of a social-liberal welfare state.

The crisis began in early 1995 when Prime Minister Horn accepted the resignation of the neo-liberal Finance Minister Bekesi rather than accede to his demands to sell off state hotel chains cheaply to western buyers. The International Monetary Fund responded to Bekesi's resignation by making two dramatic demands: first, that Hungary's public utilities be privatized into mainly western hands; and secondly, demanding the introduction of fee-paying elements in health care and education and cuts in old-age and disability pensions. The Mexican-style utilities privatization bonanza was a unique development for the region, offering a large, continuous stream of profits for western investors and the welfare cuts package was designed in such a way as to break brutally with the values championed by the HSP.[34] Prime Minister Horn made a direct appeal to Chancellors Kohl and Vranitsky (of Austria) for their intervention against the package but was rebuffed.

There followed a succession of resignations from the government, combined with a string of Supreme Court rulings declaring unconstitutional various aspects of the package. As large protests and strikes involving employees in education and health continued into November 1995, the Free Democrat Minister of Education felt bound to resign over the changes in education policy.

The political dimension of the package was fairly transparent: either the HSP would swing decisively to the right, losing credibility, or its government would be engulfed by a financial crisis as western (particularly American) funds pulled out of Budapest while other international financial institutions withdrew their support. The expectation in western financial circles and among US policy-makers was that the HSP would be structurally weakened, unless it replaced Horn with a neo-liberal as leader. But the HSP has continued to support the leadership while being strongly opposed to the policies forced upon it. At the same time, the government sought to rebuild understanding with the trade unions by offering substantial wage increases and by raising the minimum wage.[35]

For different reasons, the governments of Romania and Bulgaria have not been susceptible to the kind of pressure faced by the HSP in Hungary. In Romania, the absence of a debt burden coupled with the government's tight control over the domestic financial system gave the IFIs and western financial multinationals little market leverage, while the strong domestic nationalist consensus in Romania has meant that the ideological linkage with domestic neo-liberalism has been very weak. The Romanian government's search for access to western capital markets has therefore produced IMF packages focused mainly upon purely financial retrenchment rather than social engineering.[36] The PSDR privatization programme has been geared towards passing the ownership of the bulk of enterprises into Romanian hands rather than offering them to foreign buyers. The party has been committed to preserving a welfare state and to building a policy dialogue with the trade unions on wages and social issues.

In Bulgaria, as the economic crisis in the country has steadily deepened during the 1990s, crisis management has dominated domestic policy-making. The economy is burdened by very heavy debt repayments in conditions of continuing domestic depression. Out of a GDP of just over $10 billion, western creditors are expecting to receive $1.27 billion in 1996 and $1.7 billion in 1997.[37] The Bretton Woods institutions have viewed these huge repayments strains as a means of persuading the BSP government to sell the most valuable of the country's enterprises to western buyers, thus producing a short-term injection of hard currency to pay western banks (while incurring long-term dividend obligations to western share-holders.) Therefore, when, in 1996, it became clear that Bulgaria would once again be unable to continue to service its debts, the IMF refused to provide assistance until the government had agreed both to asset sales to foreign investors and to closing down non-profitable state enterprises making at least 40,000 workers redundant. The Bulgarian government's own programme of mass privatization via domestic voucher sales was no longer enough for the International Monetary Fund.

One factor which may have been of concern to western policy-makers is the fact that up to now the Bulgarian private sector has been dominated by a few conglomerates, built largely by former officials of the communist regime, with links to both the main political parties and in many cases also with strong links to powerful Russian business groups.[38] This pattern of power has developed in parallel with increasingly close links being re-established between Bulgaria and Russia not only in the important energy sector but also in the field of military procurement.

The deadlock between the IMF and the BSP government in early 1996 produced a currency collapse on international money markets and this in turn generated rapid domestic inflation. The BSP government then felt compelled to comply with IMF demands in the summer of 1996. In so far as the IFIs' programme is implemented it will conflict with the general public hostility towards such 'structural reform', hostility that extends far beyond the BSP's own electorate. On the other hand the Bulgarian electorate is now so impoverished that political activity has tended to give way to the daily struggle for existence. Furthermore, while the Dayton Agreement remains in place, Bulgaria's stability is of lesser concern to US policy-makers. It is too early to predict the political consequences of the crisis for the future direction of the BSP. The future shape of both economic and social policy remains obscure.

Nationalism versus Europeanism Both the Polish SDPR and the Hungarian HSP have remained strongly identified with an anti-nationalist, Europeanist and internationalist orientation. In Poland, nationalist anti-Europeanism has been overwhelmingly a phenomenon of the Right and it has divided the Solidarity political camp. But the hostility of the SDPR's ally, the PSL, to the European Union's external agricultural policies has turned it towards a more nationalist economic policy. For the SDPR, unlike the Democratic Union, Europeanism has not been linked to support for neo-liberal socio-economic nostrums but has rather meant a defence of democratic, secular and civil rights against xenophobia and Christian nationalist authoritarianism. But the SDPR's stance has also involved the priority of integration into western institutions.

Following the SDPR's electoral success in 1993 there were attempts by politicians on the Right to claim that the SDPR was not fully committed to membership of the EU and NATO. Walesa's Foreign Minister Olechowski claimed to have resigned on this issue in January 1995, but such charges have cut little ice either in Poland or abroad. Kwasniewski's election as President, which gave the SDPR full control over foreign policy for the first time, brought no significant shift on these core issues. The priority of western integration commands all other concerns.

While Kwasniewski has been as vigorous as Walesa in promoting Polish NATO membership since becoming President, the SDRP and PSL leadership initially accepted the possible enlargement of NATO without genuine enthusiasm. Both parties would have preferred a greater emphasis on the development of pan-European collective security structures. In accepting NATO enlargement they have stressed that they are talking about a new, reformed NATO. They, like many others, doubt the wisdom of effectively excluding Russia from the politics of European security which a NATO enlargement could mean. At the same time the Polish Left will not oppose enlargement if it appears to be the will of the main NATO powers.[39]

In relations with the EU, the SDPR continues the stress laid down by former Foreign Minister Skubiszewski in desiring Polish membership of a strongly institutionalized, political EU, rejecting the loose free market concepts of British provenance.[40] But the Left coalition's ascendancy will mean an attempt at a more robust defence of Polish agricultural interests by the PSL, being prepared to take stronger protectionist measures against EU-subsidized agricultural exports to Poland, and seeking to combat what the PSL believes to be the aim of some EU groups and states: the weakening of Polish agriculture. More generally, the leaders of the Polish Left share the widespread cynicism among Polish policy-makers about the conduct of EU policy towards Poland over the last six years, but this cynicism does not in the slightest weaken their resolve to make the attainment of full EU membership the country's over-riding priority.

In Hungary the Socialist Party has taken a stance on the broader ideological issues more or less identical to that of the SDPR but, more than in any other of the four countries, the split between nationalism and Europeanism has been of central policy significance because of its connection with central aspects of Hungarian foreign policy: the recognition of Hungary's borders and the question of the rights of Hungarian minorities in neighbouring states. The governing centre-right coalition had taken a strongly nationalist stance on these issues which included an undertone of irredentism while the HSP and the Europeanist camp repudiated this approach. The erstwhile neo-liberal camp of the Free Democrats and Young Democrats increasingly polarized on this issue as the nationalist theme became more prominent in the latter party. The agreement, on this issue, on the other hand, between the Free Democrats and the HSP, was an important element in enabling these parties to work together subsequently, in contrast with Poland where the Democratic Union's anti-communism and commitment to neo-liberalism led it to make concessions to the Right.

The foreign policy dimensions of this split have been far more pronounced in Hungary than in Poland. A triangle of issues has dominated foreign policy debate: integration into western institutions, inter-state relations with Hungary's neighbours and defence of the interests of Hungarian minorities living in neighbouring states. Left and Right have differed on each of these issues and they have also differed on the sequence of priorities in tackling them.[41]

The HDF and its coalition partners, the Smallholders and the Christian Democrats, tended, in office, to present the task of defending Hungarian minorities abroad as an historic mission. Improving relations with neighbouring states – Slovakia, Romania and Serbia – has been made conditional upon those states improving the position of minorities. Hungarian integration into NATO and the EU has sometimes appeared to be an instrument for helping the minorities.

The HSP has sought to reverse these priorities: the aim is integration within the EU. Settling disputes with Hungary's neighbours is a necessary step towards western integration. Protecting the rights of Hungarian minorities in neighbouring states has been viewed as being strengthened rather than weakened by achieving friendly relations with Hungary's neighbours.

The HDF-led coalition had consistently rejected the idea of new treaties being signed with Slovakia and Romania repudiating any change in those countries' borders with Hungary. They cited the existing Helsinki Final Act as sufficient border guarantee, ignoring the fact that the Final Act is not a legally binding international treaty. They also frequently gave the impression of harbouring irredentist hopes, notably through the HDF prime ministers' insistence that they were the leaders of all Hungarians including those outside Hungary's borders. The HSP not only accepted the idea of treaty-based border guarantees for neighbouring states, but pledged to seek an historic settlement with these neighbours. The HSP–AFD government moved swiftly to achieve such treaties after coming into office.[42] The HSP accused the Right of seeking to promote its own ideology within the Hungarian minority movements in Slovakia and Romania, rather than seeking to achieve adequate guarantees of their rights from neighbouring governments.

Finally, the HSP criticized the HDF coalition for trying to use its western links for narrow national advantage over neighbouring states. Thus, it suggested that the Right's enthusiasm for swift entry into NATO was governed by the hope that, in the event that Slovakia and Romania were not integrated into NATO, Hungary could use its position within the organization to strengthen its leverage against these states. By contrast, the HSP has sought to argue that any NATO expansion should be preceded by a longer phase of broad NATO cooperation with all the countries of the region.

On the general issue of NATO enlargement eastward, the Hungarian socialists, like the Polish socialists, have not been enthusiastic. There is little doubt that they would have favoured other kinds of security arrangements in East Central Europe, arrangements more inclusive of Russia (and Ukraine). But they have silenced their doubts. The Hungarian Prime Minister Horn did, however, insist upon visiting Moscow to discuss and explain his orientation towards NATO membership and to seek Russian acquiescence. And unlike other parties, the HSP has pledged that it will put Hungary's NATO membership (as well as its EU membership) to a referendum.

The HSP leadership has also been less than enthusiastic about the EU's own policies in trade and other fields. But this, of course, only strengthens their determination to enter the Union. HSP leaders also hope this will enable Hungary to be less vulnerable to the Bretton Woods institutions. And both the SLD and the HSP have some hopes that they may be able to use their links with EU social democratic parties to achieve some leverage of their own in defence of their domestic social goals.

In Bulgaria, the BSP has also increasingly adopted a Europeanist stance after initially being accused of playing upon anti-Turkish sentiment and for much of the 1990s it has been allied with the largely Turkish third party. On the other hand, the anti-communist Union of Democratic Forces has become more pronouncedly nationalist, with far-right elements in its ranks supporting irredentist positions towards Macedonia. But in foreign policy, Bulgaria differs from the Visegrad countries. Like them, Bulgaria joined the Partnership for Peace and wishes to join NATO, but for the BSP leadership this is purely to avoid Bulgarian exclusion in the event of NATO enlargement.[43] EU membership, along with EU–Bulgarian relations generally, is not yet viewed as within reach. The West's trade embargo against Yugoslavia hampered the development of EU–Bulgarian trade. Bulgaria remains a long way from being on the threshold of EU membership. There has been a great deal of resentment among political elites in the country at the lack of priority given by the EU to Bulgaria since 1989.

In Romania, President Iliescu initially stressed nationalist themes while the opposition held up the banner of Europeanism and universalism. The state executive encouraged the development of ultra-nationalist parties on the far-right and Iliescu was prepared to form a governing coalition with them (as well as with the nationalist Socialist Labour Party). This domestic dimension was linked to evident irredentist tendencies on the part of the Romanian government in the early 1990s: in particular efforts to reincorporate Moldova into Romania, and a refusal to accept the legitimacy of North Bukovina's continued incorporation within Ukraine.

From the spring of 1993, Iliescu's orientation switched in an increasingly Europeanist direction, the first sign of this being the formation of the PSDR itself. Romania's acceptance into the Council of Europe in November 1993 seemed to strengthen this turn.[44] The government gave up its earlier attempts to re-annex Moldova. In October 1995 the PSDR broke its alliance with the extreme-right Greater Romania Party and, during a visit to Washington, Iliescu called the leader of this party and the leader of another allied far-right party 'Romania's Zhirinovskies'.[45] Hand in hand with this has been Iliescu's positive response to the election of the HSP in Hungary in 1994, expressed in his desire to settle disputes with Hungary over minority and territorial issues, through an 'historic reconciliation' treaty between the two countries.

While the opposition parties have increasingly sought to emphasize their nationalist profile, the PSDR government declared in 1993 membership of the EU and NATO to be its 'strategic goal' and has worked vigorously to try to ensure that Romania is allowed to enter NATO at the same time as any Visegrad countries. The government evidently has two serious fears: first, that the first enlargement of NATO may also be the last, with the result that Romania will be left in a security void that Russia would seek to fill and that would in turn pull the country away from being able to join the EU; second, the government fears that Romania's exclusion from NATO's first enlargement at the same time as Hungary is included, could generate a new and perhaps serious deterioration of relations with Hungary over Transylvania which could also make Romanian entry into NATO and the EU much more difficult.[46]

Secularism versus Church This division has been especially important in Poland. In predominantly orthodox Romania and Bulgaria the involvement of the church in secular and political affairs has not been a major issue of contention between parties, while in Hungary divisions over the role of the Catholic Church have generally been subsumed under other differences.

In Poland, however, Catholicism versus secularism has been a major political issue and the SDPR has, together with the Union of Labour, championed secular rights. The Polish Catholic hierarchy obtained support not only from the Right but from the liberal centre for an anti-abortion law in 1993. This was opposed both by the Union of Labour and the Social Democrats. The new Social Democratic government reversed the law after it entered office in 1993. The presidential elections of 1995 brought the issue of secularism to the fore again as the church hierarchy threw its weight behind Walesa by calling upon Poles to reject the 'neo-pagan' Social Democratic candidate Kwasniewski. The Social Democrats also indicated that the Concordat between Poland and the Vatican, drawn up before they came into office, had made too many concessions to the church. For important sections of the Polish intelligentsia and urban populations, this defence of secularism and liberal rights provides them with a good reason to endorse the SDPR, given the church hierarchy's record not only on the issue of anti-Semitism but also in promoting authoritarian values and ultra-conservative views on important aspects of social policy.

Domestic ethnic minority rights   In Poland, these issues have not seriously divided the main parties; there has been a broad consensus on the stance towards both the western territories and the German minority. Apart from some remarks by the Primate, Cardinal Glemp, anti-Semitism has been confined to the far-right fringe in the 1990s.

In Hungary the main issue of minority rights has concerned racism against gypsies and Romanies. Their cause has been taken up seriously only by the parties of the Left, not only the HSP but also the small Marxist Hungarian Socialist Workers' Party.

In Bulgaria the civil rights of the Turkish minority was a major issue in the last phase of the communist regime as the Bulgarian Communist Party leadership sought to bolster its support by encouraging anti-Turkish sentiment. Despite accusations against the BSP that its leadership was also playing upon such sentiments in 1991, the Turkish minority party has felt more comfortable allying with the BSP than

with the UDF on the Right. The plight of the gypsies and Romanies
is also very difficult in Bulgaria but it has not been taken up seriously
by the main parties. The same problem exists in even more acute form
in Romania.

The most politically contentious issue in this field among the four
countries is that of Romania's Hungarian minority. This is an extremely
complicated problem. Antagonism between the 2-million-strong Hungarian minority in Transylvania and Romanian political movements has
deep roots, going back to the days of the Austro-Hungarian Empire
when the Hungarian landowners in Transylvania treated the subject
Romanian population there more or less like personal chattels. During
the war, the German government handed Transylvania back to Horthy's
Hungary.

The contemporary leadership of the Hungarian minority is strongly
nationalist and contains right-wing irredentist trends within it. On the
other hand, in Romania the NSF and the PSDR have given support and
encouragement to far-right nationalist allies up to 1994 while the latter
have taken stridently anti-Hungarian stances reminiscent of fascism.[47]
At the same time the PSDR sought to present itself as a centrist force
on the issue, while claiming, with some justice, that irredentist political
trends within the Hungarian minority were being encouraged by the
HDF-led coalition in Budapest. It argued that once the Hungarian
government fully guaranteed Romania's existing borders in a binding
treaty, tensions between the Hungarian minority and the Romanian state
could be quickly resolved. Meanwhile, Iliescu included the extreme
Nationalist Party of Romanian National Unity led by Gheorghe Fumar,
the Mayor of Cluj, in the governing coalition.[48]

One of the main flash-points has been the issue of educational rights
for the Hungarian minority. The main party of the Hungarian minority,
the Hungarian Democratic Federation of Romania (HDFR), has claimed
that Hungarian educational rights have been restricted in comparison
with the Ceauşescu period. In parliament, despite vigorous lobbying by
the HDFR, it was unable to get either most of the liberal opposition or
Petre Roman's Social Democrats to support its amendments to the
education legislation, and despite promises from Iliescu to look favourably on the amendments only 30 of his party's deputies supported them.
At the same time the OSCE Commissioner for Minorities Rights

declared that there was nothing wrong with the new law. Other issues, particularly over cultural symbols in the city of Cluj, have brought sharp conflicts with the Hungarian minority.[49] The main issue raised by the Council of Europe has been the refusal of the Romanian government to grant collective autonomous political rights to the Hungarians. But with the election of the HSP government in Budapest in 1994, substantial progress has been made in combining a firm Hungarian guarantee of Romania's border with a satisfactory set of autonomy arrangements for the Hungarian minority. At the same time, the tensions on this issue are too deep-rooted to be expected to disappear even after the ratification of such a treaty and they may be exacerbated by the nationalist Right in both countries.

Conclusion

Both the SDRP and the HSP have transformed themselves into western-style social-democratic parties and can be seen as bulwarks of the democratic integration of their polities. The PSDR has evolved from authoritarian and oligarchic origins buttressed by a strident nationalism in the direction of a western-style social-democratic party. The BSP has also evolved as an authentic socialist party committed to democratic development, though it is locked into a desperate economic crisis and unstable political situation in the midst of terrible impoverishment of large parts of the population.

Yet in no case is the future of these parties secure. In Poland, a Christian nationalist Right with deep reserves of anti-socialist authoritarianism remains a potentially powerful force if it can unite, while the liberal centre is weak and tends to ally with the Catholic Right against the SDPR. A deep elite division thus remains. In Hungary the populist far-right is today the most dynamic political force and western financial pressures, utilizing the economic crisis inherited by the HSP, have deeply divided the forces of the Left, threatening to destabilize the government. In Bulgaria the prospect of a breakdown of the political order cannot be excluded. Paradoxically, economic growth and the wide base of popular support for a gradual transformation towards a western-oriented national capitalism seems to offer the most secure prospects for the development of a centre-left in a fairly stable political context, now that the far-right nationalists are weakened, at least for the moment. But the test of governmental alternance has yet to occur and must be an important one, given the authoritarian origins of the PSDR.

All these issues will be profoundly influenced by the direction of policy on the part of the EU and other western institutions. Much of the instability in the region over the last five years is a direct consequence of western policy. If this policy trend continues, the evolution of West-European-style democracies, which rest very largely on the existence of a strong Left and Labour movement, will probably be called in question.

It would appear that an influential group in American foreign policy circles wishes to see the post-communist parties destabilized, viewing them as the main obstacle to the consolidation of what, in their view, democracy should be about. They regard the authoritarian populist Right in the region as far less threatening.[50] The source of these judgements seems to be a new conception of democracy now being promoted within US foreign policy: one that is concerned to promote a kind of polyarchy in which the link between popular opinion and policy formation should be entirely broken and indeed where the whole conception of the state serving collective goals is viewed as a throwback to the age of European collectivism. This conception may be serviceable for consolidating globalized peripheral polyarchies in Mexico but it has nothing to do with overcoming the division of Europe.

Notes

1. The British Labour Party since 1989

This chapter was written well before the British General Election of 1997. The only significant revisions made to it immediately following the election have been to alter tenses where the sense required it, and to add the final paragraph, replacing a discussion of the prospects for electoral reform which the unexpected scale of Labour's parliamentary majority seemed to have made less likely.

1. Eric Shaw, *The Labour Party Since 1979* (Routledge, London, 1994), esp. pp. 59–67.

2. Other closely related changes included the practice of submitting policy statements to party conferences for adoption or rejection as a whole, with no possibility of amendment; ending the trade union sponsorship of individual MPs; rewriting Clause 4 of the party's constitution to eliminate any commitment to public ownership and to endorse markets and competition; and introducing 'The Road to the Manifesto', a pre-manifesto statement of policies to be submitted for prior endorsement to the membership as a whole. For a fuller account, see Shaw: *The Labour Party Since 1979*.

3. Tony Blair, speech to the Keidanren, Tokyo, 5 January 1996.

4. Seumas Milne, 'My Millbank', a review of Mandelson and Liddle's *The Blair Revolution*, in *London Review of Books*, 18 April 1996, p. 3.

5. Peter Mandelson and Roger Liddle, *The Blair Revolution: Can New Labour Deliver?* (Faber and Faber, London, 1996), p. 185. As Labour's unchallenged chief spin-doctor, Mandelson's views on this subject should carry weight.

6. Borrie Gordon (ed.), *Social Justice: Strategies for National Renewal* (Vintage, London, 1994), is actually a comprehensive programme of economic and social reform for national competitiveness.

7. See especially Stuart Weir and Wendy Hall (eds), *Ego Trip: Extra-governmental Organizations in the United Kingdom and Their Accountability* (Democratic Audit of the United Kingdom and Charter 88, London, 1994); and the same authors' *The Untouchables* (Scarman Trust and Human Rights Centre, University of Essex, 1996). See also Anthony Barnett, *The Defining Moment* (Charter 88, London, 1995), setting out constitutional issues.

8. From the statement 'Why Demos?', in Demos's brochure.

9. Geoff Mulgan, interview, 11 August 1995.

10. The *Guardian*'s political commentator Hugo Young claimed that the word 'new' occurred 137 times in Blair's speech to the 1996 Labour Party conference.

11. I am grateful to Neal Lawson for the information on Nexus's origins and plans described here.

12. *The Need for Nexus*, published by Nexus, 'The *Renewal* Ideas Network', summer 1996.

13. Mandelson and Liddle: *The Blair Revolution*, p. 7.

14. Tony Blair, 'The Rights We Enjoy Reflect the Duties We Owe', The Spectator Lecture, 22 March 1995.

15. Tony Blair, speech to the Labour Party conference issued by the Conference Media Office, 3 October 1995. The whole speech was a prose poem written in this format.

16. The term originated in debates about corporate governance and applied to the various parties such as employees and suppliers, as well as shareholders, who had an interest or 'stake' in company policy. Will Hutton, who was then the *Guardian*'s assistant editor and leading economic columnist, broadened the concept to one of 'stakeholder capitalism' in his best-selling book, *The State We're In*, first published in March 1995. It may be surmised that Blair's speechwriters, to whom Hutton had ample access, were not unaffected by his thinking; but Blair's Singapore speech used the narrower expression 'stakeholder economy', and in general New Labour conspicuously refrained from endorsing Hutton's general ideas, which argued for a British version of 'Rhineland' capitalism, with a radically re-regulated financial sector and far-reaching social and constitutional reforms. Mandelson's views, as evidenced in his book *The Blair Revolution*, completed shortly before Blair's Singapore speech, seem likely to have been more directly influential.

17. Tony Blair, speech to the Singapore business community, 8 January 1996.

18. Blair, The Spectator Lecture.

19. It was noteworthy that in his last pre-election annual conference speech in October 1996, Blair made no reference to stakeholding, but only to being a united national 'team' in the global race. It is clear that whatever other influences are at work on New Labour as a whole, the most important source of Blair's politics is a relatively conservative version of Christian ethics.

20. Tony Blair, 'Faith in the City – Ten Years On', speech at Southwark Cathedral, 29 January 1996.

21. Henry Porter, 'Zealous Moderate', *Guardian*, 18 July 1995 (emphasis added).

22. Ibid. 'Quangos' are 'quasi-autonomous non-governmental organizations', appointed and largely unaccountable bodies whose number and membership (consisting largely of Conservative supporters) increased dramatically during the Thatcher years, to the point where they had many more members than the total of the country's elected councillors, and were responsible for spending roughly as much money.

23. Tony Blair, 'The Flavour of Success', based on a speech made on 5 July 1995 to the Fabian Society, *Guardian*, 6 July 1995.

24. Gordon Brown, 'Labour's Macroeconomic Framework', speech, 17 May 1995.

25. The third Maastricht criterion, that public debt should not be more than 60 per cent of GDP, Britain was well-placed to meet. Mandelson emphasizes the benefits of EMU, while acknowledging that without much bigger subsidies for poorer regions EMU 'could soon set up intolerable social and political strains that might undermine the legitimacy of both the single currency and the EU as a whole' (Mandelson and Liddle: *The Blair Revolution*, p. 179), and says the decision whether to join the EMU 'should be a pragmatic one. We should weigh the costs of staying out against the risks of participation' (p. 170).

26. Tony Blair, speech to the British American Chamber of Commerce, New York, 11 April 1996.

27. Tony Blair, speech to the annual conference of the Federation of Small Businesses, 29 March 1996.

28. Gordon Brown, 'Labour's Tax Principles', speech, 20 November 1995; at the 1996 party conference he reiterated the aim in terms which suggested it could be policy within the next parliament.

29. Tony Blair, speech to the CBI, *Guardian*, 14 November 1995.

30. Tony Blair, speech to the Scottish Labour Party conference, 8 March 1996.

31. Tony Blair, speech to the Labour Party conference, 3 October 1995.

32. Brian Wilson MP, in a letter to all prospective investors in the privatized railways, *Guardian*, 17 November 1995.

33. Clare Short, Labour's transport spokeswoman, referring to Railtrack, in a speech reported in the *Independent*, 30 March 1996.

34. Mandelson and Liddle: *The Blair Revolution*, p. 108.

35. Tony Blair, speech to the Scottish Labour Party conference, 8 March 1996.

36. Noel Thompson, 'Supply Side Socialism: The Political Economy of New Labour', *New Left Review* 216 (March–April 1996), pp. 53–4.

37. Iain Macwhirter, *Observer*, 19 November 1995.

38. Tony Blair, speech to the Singapore business community, 8 January 1996; and 'Faith in the City – Ten Years On', speech at Southwark Cathedral, 29 January 1996.

39. Labour Party estimates of the potential yield of such a tax were initially reported as £1 billion, but had risen to over £3 billion by late 1996.

40. Preview of speech to the National Association of Schoolmasters/Union of Women Teachers at Glasgow, reported in the *Guardian*, 11 April 1996. The merchant banks' possible motives for lending for this purpose were not explained.

41. Labour's education proposals are contained in *Diversity and Excellence*, published in May 1995, and *Excellence for Everyone*, published in December, 1995.

42. According to Labour's 1995 policy document, *Renewing the NHS*, the proportion of the NHS budget spent on administration had risen by over 100 per cent, and spending on managerial and administrative staff by £1 billion, as a result of the internal market introduced in 1990. Top managers alone now cost an additional £450 million a year, and £70 million a year was being spent on cars.

43. *Renewing the NHS*, p. 20. As the members of the boards were also to be drawn from 'people with experience in health and social care' and 'those with the expertise to oversee a large organization', these bodies were not to become representative either.

44. Details of Labour's official proposals are contained in *Security in Retirement*, 1996; counter-proposals calling for raising the standard state pension, re-indexing it to average earnings, and restoring the State Earnings-Related Pension Scheme (also emasculated by the Conservatives) are contained in Peter Townsend and Alan Walker, *New Directions for Pensions* (Spokesman/European Labour Forum, Nottingham, 1995).

45. Tony Blair, the John Smith Memorial Lecture, 7 February 1996.

46. 'The first right of a citizen in any mature democracy should be the right to information ... Why, apart from obvious exceptions like national security, should people not know what is available on file about them? It is a great irony that in a democracy where people have increased information about almost everything else, they often cannot find out the simplest thing from government. If trust in the people means anything then there can be no argument against a Freedom of Information Act which will give people rights to public information' (ibid., p. 11). What is the meaning of 'public' here?

47. In his John Smith Memorial Lecture, Blair endorsed the idea that 'if [note: not when] there was a move to an elected second Chamber, provision for people of a particularly distinguished position or record could be made', adding that 'we are masters of our own rules and procedure'.

48. Tariq Ali, *Guardian*, 28 October 1996.

49. See, for example, Paul Hirst and Grahame Thompson, 'Global Myths and National Policies', *Renewal* 4/2 (1996) pp. 57–65; and their *Globalization in Question* (Polity Press, Cambridge, 1996).

50. This in turn made it seem unlikely that Tony Blair, as Prime Minister with an overall parliamentary majority of 179 seats and hence in no need of Liberal Democrat support, would reverse his oft-stated personal objections to proportional representation and support that option in the promised referendum on the subject.

2. The Italian Left after 1989

Translated by Amy Rosenthal.

1. See Giulio Sapelli, *Sul Capitalismo italiano. Trasformazione o declino* (Feltrinelli, Milan, 1993).

2. Giulio Amato and Luciano Cafagna, *Duello a Sinistra* (Il Mulino, Bologna, 1987).

3. For the distinction between the Left organized around political parties and the generic non-party Left, see Paolo Farneti (ed.), *Il sistema politico italiano* (Il Mulino, Bologna, 1973).

4. For Europe, see Donald Sassoon, *One Hundred Years of Socialism: The West European Left in the Twentieth Century* (I.B.Tauris, London, 1996); on Asia, see the interesting analytical approach of P. Lyon and J. Manor (eds), *Transfer and Transformation: Political Institutions in the New Commonwealth* (Leicester University Press, 1983).

5. See A. Mastropaolo, *La Repubblica dei destini incrociati. Saggio su cinquant'anni di democrazia in Italia* (La Nuova Italia, Florence, 1996, pp. 80ff); see also Otto Kirchheimer, 'The Transformation of the Western European Party Systems', in J. La Palombara, and M. Weiner (eds), *Political Parties and Political Development* (Princeton University Press, 1966). I should also mention the last contribution of P. Farneti, *Stato e mercato della sinistra italiana: 1946–1976* (Edizioni della Fondazione Giovanni Agnelli, Torino, 1980).

6. These themes are stressed in M. Flores and N. Gallerano, *Sul PCI. Un' interpretazione storica* (Il Mulino, Bologna, 1992).

7. See Donald Sassoon, *The Strategy of the Italian Communist Party: From the Resistance to the Historic Compromise* (Frances Pinter, London, 1981); and Giuseppe Vacca, *Saggio su Togliatti e la tradizione comunista* (De Donato, Bari, 1975).

8. P. Ignazi, *Dal PCI al PDS* (Il Mulino, Bologna, 1992), p. 49; also Giuseppe Vacca, *Tra compromesso e solidarietà. La politica del PCI negli anni '70* (Editori Riuniti, Rome, 1987).

9. S. Hellman, *Italian Communism in Transition: the Rise and Fall of the Historic Compromise in Turin 1975–1980* (Oxford University Press, 1988).

10. See these theories, now falsified by history, in Palombara and Weiner, (eds): *Political Parties and Political Development.*

11. M. Degl'Innocenti, *Storia del PSI. Vol III. Dal dopoguerra a oggi* (Laterza, Rome-Bari, 1993).

12. Sassoon: *One Hundred Years of Socialism*, pp. 730ff.

13. Giulio Sapelli, *Southern Europe since 1945. Tradition and Modernity in Portugal, Spain, Italy, Greece, and Turkey* (Longman, London, 1995), pp. 111ff.

14. This was a theme very dear to my old 'autonomist' friend, Guelfo Zaccaria, who tragically disappeared in the 'neo-caciquista' storm of the transformation of the PSI: I would like to remember him here with regret and affection.

15. See the main and 'classical' text on these themes: M. Degl'Innocenti, *Geografia e istituzioni del socialismo italiano* (Guida, Naples, 1983); see also Gino Giugni, *Socialismo: l'eredità difficile* (Il Mulino, Bologna, 1995).

16. K. R. Legg, *Politics in Modern Greece* (Stanford University Press, 1969);

Jean Meynaud, *Les forces politiques en Grèce* (Études des sciences politiques, Geneva, 1965).

17. Sapelli: *Southern Europe since 1945*. Much support for my thesis can be found in R. S. Katz and P. Mair (eds), *How Parties Organize. Change and Adaptation in Party Organizations in Western Democracies* (Sage, London, 1994). See also P. Mair, *Party Organizations: A Data Handbook on Party Organizations in Western Democracies, 1960–1990* (Sage, London, 1992).

18. On this, see Mauro Calise (ed.), *Come cambiano i partiti* (Il Mulino, Bologna, 1992) – still the most important work to understand the party situation at present.

19. See A. Pizzorno, *I soggetti del pluralismo* (Il Mulino, Bologna, 1980).

20. L. Weinberg, *The Transformation of Italian Communism* (Transaction Books, New Brunswick and London, 1995).

21. Giulio Sapelli, *Cleptocrazia. Il meccanismo unico della corruzione tra economia e politica* (Feltrinelli, Milan, 1994).

22. For an examination of the concept of political institutionalization see Samuel Huntington, *Political Order in Changing Society* (Yale University Press, New Haven, 1968).

23. Charles Lindblom, *Politics and Market* (Basic Books, New York, 1977).

24. Renato Mannheimer and Giacomo Sani, '1994: dalla decomposizione alla ristrutturazione?', in Mannheimer and Sani, *La rivoluzione elettorale. L'Italia tra la prima e seconda repubblica* (Anabasi, Milan, 1994).

25. For the concept of 'quasi-groups' see Sapelli: *Southern Europe since 1945*.

26. Giuseppe Vacca, *Per una nuova costituente* (Bompiani, Milan, 1996) – essential for the understanding of the historic significance of the 'transition' of the 1990s.

27. S. Warner and D. Gambetta, *La retorica della riforma. Fine del sistema proporzionale in Italia* (Einaudi, Torino, 1994).

28. On this, see the interesting essay by F. Cicchitto, *Il PSI e la lotta in Italia dal 1976 al 1994* (Spirali/Vel, Milan, 1995).

29. Maurizio Cotta uses the term 'meso-political' to define competitive party policies which 'significantly modify economic, social and institutional life.' I use the term 'meso-governmental', instead, to show that the parties attempting such policies do so in the context of governmental policy-making, as government actors rather than as agents of mobilization and opinion. See M. Cotta, 'La crisi del governo di partito all' italiana', in M. Cotta and P. Isernia, *Il gigante dai piedi di argilla* (Il Mulino, Bologna, 1996), p. 29. This important volume is an unconventional contribution to the current debate. The text supports my view relating to the pervasive weakness of Italian political parties. It is not an accident that this scholar belongs to the 'realistic' tradition of Italian political science.

30. P. Ciofi and F. Ottaviano, *Il fattore Craxi. Dalla prima elezione a segretario agli anni Cossiga* (Datanews, Rome, 1992).

31. For an analysis of the 1994 elections see the December 1994 issue of the

Rivista italiana di scienza politica; see also the April 1994 issue of *Polis*, in part devoted to the referendum and local elections of 1993.

32. Ignazi: *Dal PCI al PDS*.

33. On these themes, see the essays by Stephen Gundle in S. D. Bell (ed.), *Western European Communists and the Collapse of Communism* (Berg, Oxford, 1993); and P. Daniels and Martin Bull, in M. Bull and Paul Heywood (eds), *West European Communist Parties after the Revolution of 1989* (St. Martin's Press, New York, 1994).

34. Vacca: *Per una nuova costituente*, p. 22.

35. Ignazi: *Dal PCI al PDS*; see also C. Baccetti and M. Caciagli, 'Dopo il PCI e dopo l'URSS. Una subcultura rossa rivisitata', *Polis* (December 1992), pp. 537–69.

36. Giulio Amato, a socialist, had in effect become Prime Minister instead of Bettino Craxi because the President of the Republic had refused to appoint for such a high position someone whom the magistrates were investigating.

37. L. Ricolfi, *L' ultimo parlamento. Sulla fine della prima repubblica* (La Nuova Italia Scientifica, Florence, 1993).

38. Vacca: *Per una nuova costituente*, p. 22.

39. L. Verzichelli, 'Le politiche di bilancio: il debito pubblico da risorsa a vincolo', in Cotta and Isernia (eds), *Il gigante dai piedi di argilla*, pp. 189–239.

40. J. M. Bull, 'The PDS, the Progressive Alliance and the Crisis', *Modern Italy* (autumn 1995), pp. 30–39.

41. On these themes, see Massimo Caciagli and David I. Kertzer (eds), *Politica in Italia. Edizione 1996* (Il Mulino, Bologna, 1996).

42. R. D'Alimonte and A. Chiaromonte, 'Il nuovo sistema elettorale italiano: quali opportunità?', *Rivista italiana di scienza politica*, 23/3 (December 1993), pp. 513–47; see also R. D'Alimonte, 'From Polarized Pluralism to Moderate Pluralism: Sartori's Model and the Italian Transition', *Estudios. Working Papers*, Instituto Juan March (March 1996).

43. Pietro Scoppola, *La repubblica dei partiti* (Il Mulino, Bologna, 1991).

44. I am thinking above all of the 'Dossettiani'; see Giuseppe Dossetti, *La costituzione, le radici, i valori, le riforme* (Edizioni Lavoro, Rome, 1996).

45. See G. Davie and D. Hervieu-Leger (eds), *Identités religieuses en Europe* (La Découverte, Paris, 1996).

46. L. Ricolfi, 'Quali Italie? Vecchie e nuove fratture territoriali', *Rassegna italiana di sociologia* (June 1996), pp. 267–78.

47. On these themes, see my *Le borghesie per la crescita senza sviluppo. Riflessioni sull' Italia che decade* (forthcoming).

48. The elimination of these earnings, the so-called *rendite parassitarie*, protected by thousands of laws, was an issue long debated in the past, but now under a disquieting theoretical silence. For the origins of the discussion, see R. Bellofiore, *La passione della ragione. Scienza economica e teoria critica in Claudio Napoleoni* (UNICOPLI, Milan, 1991).

49. Sassoon: *One Hundred Years of Socialism*, ch. 24.
50. See V. Saba, *La questione dell'unità sindacale oggi*, mimeo, Turin, 23 May 1996.
51. M. Cotta and L. Persichelli, 'La classe politica: cronaca di una morte annunciata?', in Cotta and Isernia (eds), *Il gigante dai piedi di argilla*, pp. 379ff.

3. The Left and the crisis of the Third Hellenic Republic, 1989–97

I would like to thank Donald Sassoon for helping me with some crucial methodological premises assumed in this paper. I am grateful to Nicos Mouzelis and Tolis Malakos for their perceptive remarks and many stimulating conversations. I am also indebted to Sheila Blankfield for her prompt and excellent editing.

1. By 'Third Republic' I refer to the historical period stretching from 1974 to the present *metapoliteussi* or 'post-regime'; the Second Hellenic Republic was the inter-war period (1924–35); whereas the First was the war of independence against the Ottoman Empire (1821–29).

2. Pouliopoulos was the first general secretary of the Greek Communist Party and one of the most distinguished Greek Marxists of the inter-war period. He was the first translator of Marx's *Capital* (the first volume). Expelled from the party because of his Trotskyist beliefs, Pouliopoulos was executed by the Nazis and fascist troops at Nezero, near Athens, in June 1943. The extract is from his *Democratic or Socialist Revolution in Greece?* (in Greek; Protoporiaki Bibliothiki, Athens); 1980, p. 69 (first edn, Govostis Publishing House, 1934).

3. Turkey's recent custom union agreement with the European Union underpins the argument further; see, *inter alia*, J. F. Brown, 'Turkey: Back to the Balkans?', in G. E. Fuller and I. O. Lesser (eds), *Turkey's New Geopolitics* (Westview Press, Oxford and Boulder, CO, 1993), pp. 141–62; G. Sapelli, *Southern Europe since 1945. Tradition and Modernity in Portugal, Spain, Italy, Greece, and Turkey* (Longman, London, 1995), p. 23, passim; J. Barham, 'Turkey: the Customs Union with Europe', *Financial Times*, 22 January 1996.

4. C. Simitis, 'Introduction', in C. Simitis (ed.), *Populism and Politics* (in Greek; Gnossi, Athens, 1989), pp. 16–17 (emphasis added).

5. For such one-sided accounts, see A. Elefantis, *In the Constellation of Populism* (Politis, Athens, 1991); D. Charalambis, *Populism and Clientelism* (in Greek; Exantas, Athens, 1989); J. Petras et al., 'The Greek Socialism: the Patrimonial State Revisited', in J. Kurth and J. Petras, *Mediterranean Paradoxes: The Politics and Structure of Southern Europe* (Berg, Oxford, 1993), pp. 160–224. The thesis I put forward is that PASOK's populism has extended political democracy and civil rights, and guaranteed mass participation in politics. As we shall see below, PASOK also protected the labour market against the neo-liberal trends

in the 1980s; see V. Fouskas, *Populism and Modernization: The Exhaustion of the Third Hellenic Republic, 1974–1994* (in Greek; Ideokinissi, Athens, 1995).

6. Nicos Mouzelis has convincingly argued that the dictatorship of the Colonels (1967–74) was a response to this upheaval, the establishment being afraid of the power enjoyed by the movement and that the conflicts might possibly end up in anarchy and communism. Thus, the dictatorship worked somehow as a 'safety valve' in order to prepare a 'mildest' possible transition to full democracy. Consequently, the old dilemma dominant in Greek politics from the beginning of the century, namely the dilemma 'Monarchy or Democracy', could be solved; see N. Mouzelis, *Modern Greece: Facets of Underdevelopment* (Macmillan, London, 1977). No doubt, during the junta years the Greek economy witnessed the most rapid rates of growth. The absence of a mass anti-dictatorial movement strongly contributed to it. The regime collapsed chiefly because of its internal contradictions as well as from the failure of foreign policies adopted; see, *inter alia*, N. Poulantzas, *The Crisis of the Dictatorships: Spain, Portugal and Greece* (New Left Books, London, 1975).

7. The KKEes split from the KKE after the Soviet invasion of Czechoslovakia in 1968. It followed the Italian Communist Party's line of *Eurocommunism*. Although lacking the dogmatic and rigid character of the pro-Soviet KKE, the KKEes did commit serious political mistakes. For instance, it attempted an *instrumental* application of Berlinguer's historic compromise notion in the Greek socio-political and historical conditions. Thus, it claimed an alliance with the ND *vis-à-vis* the 1977 general election because, according to the then leading party group, the danger for a fascist coup in Greece was possible (the famous line of National Anti-dictatorial Unity, in Greek, EADE). This strategic notion had been utterly defeated both electorally and politically. It is worth noting that many Greek intellectuals, such as Nicos Poulantzas and Sakis Karagiorgas (the latter being the major contender for PASOK's leadership in 1974), had opposed EADE's political line. S. Carillo's PCE made the same blunder when he tried to outdo even the socialist Gonzàlez in extolling the Moncloa Pact (institutional negotiations with the UCD Right of Soares) as a formula for '"a government of national concentration" in which the communists would work shoulder to shoulder with the UCD'; see P. Camiller, 'Spain: the Survival of Socialism?', in P. Anderson and P. Camiller (eds), *Mapping the West European Left* (Verso, London, 1994), p. 246.

8. Greece's entry into the EEC was seen as a serious blow for Turkey. As Hershlag put it: 'The extension of EEC membership to Greece ... put Turkey at a disadvantage and required readjustments on the part of both sides', Z. Y. Hershlag, *The Contemporary Turkish Economy* (Routledge, London, 1988), p. 86.

9. Quoted in the original research conducted by A. Kalafatis, H. Koliopoulos and G. Maroussis, *Redundant Working Population in Lame-duck Enterprises* (OAED, Athens, 1990), p. 11.

10. See, OECD Economic Surveys, *Greece 1989–90* (OECD, Paris, 1990), pp. 48–51, passim.

11. Total employment accounted for almost 30 per cent of total dependent employment in 1990; see OECD Economic Surveys, *Greece 1993* (OECD, Paris, 1993), pp. 39, 66, passim.

12. Up to 1984, lay-offs – even for economic reasons – were very difficult and required approval by the Ministry of Labour, which was not granted easily. After 1984, this strict system was eased somewhat and firms could theoretically dismiss up to 2 per cent of their personnel per month without government authorization. (Authorizations for dismissals in excess of 2 per cent continued to be subject to long procedural delays until recently.) Wages were strictly protected, although the 1985–87 *stabilization programme* tended to reverse the situation. In addition, the national health system, generous pension schemes, the official recognition of the National Resistance, the enactment of civil marriage and other welfare issues, were all achievements of PASOK.

13 . OECD Economic Surveys, *Greece 1993*, p. 45.

14. On this fascinating topic, see the perceptive sociological analyses of K. Tsoukalas, *State, Society and Labour in the Post-War Greece* (in Greek; Themelio, Athens, 1986).

15. See, C. Offe, '"Crisis of Crisis Management": Elements of a Political Crisis Theory', in J. Keane (ed.), *Contradictions of the Welfare State* (Hutchinson, London, 1984), pp. 35–65.

16. It is worth noting here that the KKEes, two years before the Italian communists launched their transformation in November 1989, had transformed itself into a post-communist political formation, the Hellenic Left, EAR. A minority faction, following the theses of left-wing Eurocommunism alongside Pietro Ingrao, split and gave birth to the Communist Party of Greece Interior-Renewed Left (KKEes–aa). The pro-European and revisionist EAR agreed to ally with the KKE, the KKEes–aa being virtually left out as it did not espouse the common programmatic declaration between EAR and KKE.

17. See, *inter alia*, G. Mangakis, 'The Repeal of the Scandals: an Unrepealed Crime', *Sunday's Vima*, 25 June 1989; D. Spinellis, 'Suspension of Repeal? Interpretation Problems Concerning the Ministerial Liability Law', *Sunday's Vima*, 30 July 1989.

18. For an analysis, see Fouskas: *Populism and Modernization*, pp. 267ff.

19. Similar categories were used by the Spanish United Left; see V. Agathidou, *The Isquierda Unida in Spain: From the Internal Divisions to a European Political Project*, BA Thesis, University of North London, May 1994; also my 'The *Boulevard* and the *Tortoise*: History and the Greek Communist Party', *Communist Review* 6, December 1990, pp. 40–46.

20. An excellent account on this topic is given by Costas Dimoulas in an unpublished research paper presented in the Centre of Marxist Research (KME), the Research Institute of KKE in Athens; see C. Dimoulas, *The Crisis of the Greek Communist Party* (KME Studies, Athens, February 1991).

21. ND, *The Programme of the New Democracy* (ND Press Office, Athens, 1989). ND presented no programme *vis-à-vis* the 1993 election.

22. On these points, see also the critique advanced by Manolis Drettakis, ex-Minister of Economic Affairs in the 1982 PASOK cabinet and then deputy elected on the lists of KKE and SYN, *Greece and the Maastricht Treaty* (in Greek; Odos, Athens, 1992), pp. 34–9, 45ff.

23. These loss-makers were: Halkis Cement Company, Piraiki Patraiki Cotton MFG, Greek Powder and Cartridge Co., the Hellenic Arms Industry, Asbestos Mines of Northern Greece, Piraiki Patraiki Spinning and Weaving Mills, LARCO, Elinda, Hellenic Shipyards, Eleussis Shipyards. Also all food industries controlled by cooperatives and supported mainly by the Agricultural Bank of Greece must always, according to Andrianopoulos, be totally privatized.

24. A. Andrianopoulos, 'For a liberal Greece', speech in the conference *Greece and Modernisation*, London School of Economics and Political Science, October 1994, mimeo. He had also considered the pension law quite improper, since the transition period provided in order for significant savings to be brought was very long; see also my account of the conference, 'A Conference in London: How Much Utopia is Greece's Capitalist Modernisation?', *Utopia* (14, November–December 1994), pp. 123–31.

25. Recorded unemployment in 1993 was around 11 per cent; for young people below 25 years and for women, it reached about 30 per cent and 16 per cent respectively. See, OECD Economic Surveys, *Greece 1993*, p. 67, passim.

26. Ibid., p. 57.

27. FYROM: Former Yugoslavic Republic of Macedonia, See also S. Economides, 'Nationalism and Foreign Policy: Greece and the "Macedonian Question"', in *Brassey's Defence Yearbook* (London: King's College, 1995), p. 115, passim; V. Agathidou, *Macedonia: Real Myths and Real History; the Dynamics of a Crisis*, MSc Dissertation, London School of Economics and Political Science, September 1995.

28. In 1943, Marshal Tito had recognized the existence of a Macedonian nation through his Anti-Fascist Council of National Liberation.

29. In order to succeed in its quest for recognition, the FYROM had to: (1) abandon the name of 'Macedonia' which denotes a geographical area not an ethnic identity; (2) recognize that it does not have any territorial claims against Greece; (3) recognize that no 'Macedonian' minority is to be found in Greece.

30. On this topic, see the perceptive essay by Tolis Malakos, 'Modernization via Nationalism: the Peculiar Character of the Re-unification of Greece', paper presented to the conference *Greece and Modernisation*, London School of Economics and Political Science, November 1994, mimeo.

31. The Portuguese Minister of Foreign Affairs Pinheiro (Portugal was then President of the European Union) had attempted to persuade Greece to accept a qualified version of the name, thus avoiding identification with the name 'Macedonia'.

32. Mitsotakis resigned after the defeat. On 3 November 1993 Miltiades Evert won the party leadership with 141 of the 182 votes cast. He was elected by the ND's electoral college, which includes MPs, MEPs and regional party activists.

33. The nationalistic thesis was also inserted in his programme; see PASOK, *The Programme of PASOK; for the Present and the Future of Greece-Regeneration Everywhere* (in Greek; PASOK Press Office, Athens, 1993), p. 4; hereafter: *PASOK 1993*.

34. See, D. Sassoon, *One Hundred Years of Socialism* (I.B.Tauris, London, 1996), pp. 534ff, 691ff.

35. Ibid., p. 79.

36. Ibid., pp. 30, 124–5 (emphasis in the original).

37. Part of ND's electoral campaign against the PASOK was based on the ill-health of the socialist leader. In fact, this benefited, instead of damaging, PASOK.

38. See *inter alia*, J. Charalambous (Minister of Transport), 'We have satisfied the claim of citizens', *Economicos Tachidromos* 2079/10 (10 March 1994), pp. 23–4.

39. See, K. Hope, 'Telecoms flotation is delayed', *Financial Times*, 14 November 1994, ('Survey on Greece').

40. These increases concern the 1994 budgeted policies and were of 5 per cent in January and July. In the 1995 and 1996 budgets, they were to be restrictive (3 per cent).

41. In July 1994 the Community Support Framework was signed, providing government with over ECU 40 billion.

42. The Skaramangas shipyards were bought from the famous Greek shipowner Stavros Niarchos in 1986 by the PASOK government. They had an extremely backward infrastructure. Since then, neither the PASOK nor the ND has taken any major step to improve it; see, among others, P. Klavdianos, 'Shipyards: from investment project into another investment project', *O Politis*, 10 (15 September 1995), pp. 35–8.

43. In a run-off ballot, 87 out of the 169 PASOK deputies opted for Simitis, after he and Tsohatzopoulos tied in the first round. Surprisingly, Arsenis was beaten in the first round by Tsohatzopoulos.

44. Simitis had to fend off charges of betrayal, inasmuch as he agreed with the American President Bill Clinton to leave the islets without the Greek flag and, in his speech in the Parliament, thanked the Americans for their help in the defusion of the crisis. See the daily *Eleftherotypia*, 31 January 1996 and 1 February 1996.

45. See, in particular, Arsenis' and Tsohatzopoulos' speeches in *The 5th Session of the Party's CC*, Athens, February 1996, pp. 31–40 and 101–11 respectively.

46. On the top of these, ex-PM Ciller faced allegations of corruption (April–May 1996) because of illegal contracts fixed with the state electricity giant *Tedas*, in order to promote the project of new power lines in 32 cities; see M. Demirsar-R. Rollnick, 'Ciller fights back as the divisions widen', *The European*, 8 May 1996.

47. ND's electoral campaign, which was entirely based on a populist discourse both on economic matters (promises for state subsidies) and national

matters (allegations against Simitis' moderate stances in dealing with the Aegean crisis and events in Cyprus), should be severely criticized.

48. Papandreou died early Sunday morning, 23 June 1996, only a few days before the PASOK Congress and while working on a draft for the congressional debate.

49. PASOK, *Fourth Congress: Ideological and Political Theses* (in Greek; PASOK Press Office, Athens, 1996); hereafter: *4th Congress*.

50. Ibid., pp. 62–3.

51. Ibid., p. 14, passim.

52. Ibid., pp. 75–6.

53. As Tsohatzopoulos put it: 'Dear comrades, I have been a member of PASOK for 21 years. Permit me to say that I have not been taught to separate the party from the government', in his speech in *The 5th Session*, p. 106.

54. Ibid., pp. 68–72.

55. Ibid., p. 25.

56. For this concept, Sassoon: *One Hundred Years of Socialism*, pp. 730–54.

57. The Congressional Theses state: 'Greece and Cyprus are two sovereign and independent entities in the South-east Mediterranean' and the 'united defence doctrine is sanctioned by international Treaties'; see *4th Congress*, p. 44; also the information package delivered by Simitis during his visit in London in April 1996. The material was kindly given to me by journalist George Pelarghidis.

58. In support of PASOK's pro-Keynesian behaviour, another two cases taking place under the new Simitis-led cabinet should be mentioned: that of national air-transport company Olympic Airways and the Athens casino affair. In April 1996, the European Commission blocked state aid worth Dr 23 billion to the air company, until it received assurances that the PASOK government would not be involved in management of the airline beyond its usual obligations as a shareholder. The Transport Minister blamed the company's managing director, who had resigned, for misinforming the European Commission. As far as the Athens casino was concerned, a project to build a resort complex aimed at attracting high-spending tourists to Athens was blocked by PASOK. The government's tourism policy was being revamped under Development Minister Papandreou, who opposed the previous administration's plans to raise Dr 40 billion in revenues by awarding 14 casino licences around Greece. All this, of course, confused investors and prompted a fall in Athens share prices; see N. Buckley, 'Halt ordered Olympic Airways aid', *Financial Times*, 1 May 1996; P. Anastasi, 'Greece faces Olympic trial', *The European*, 8 May 1996 and *Financial Times*, 25 April 1996.

4. The PSOE

1. See Martin Bull and Paul Heywood (eds), *West European Communist Parties After the Revolutions of 1989* (Macmillan, London, 1994).

2. John Gray, *After Social Democracy* (Demos, London, 1996).

3. Víctor Pérez Díaz, *The Return of Civil Society* (Harvard University Press, Cambridge, MA, 1993), pp. 93–4.

4. For a more detailed treatment see Paul Kennedy, 'Europe or Bust? Integration and its Influence on the Economic Policy of the PSOE', *International Journal of Iberian Studies* 9/2 (1996).

5. M. Galy, G. Pastor and T. Pujol, *Spain: Converging with the European Community* (International Monetary Fund, Washington, DC, 1993), p. 7.

6. Paul Heywood, 'Spain and the European Dimension: The Integrated Market, Convergence and Beyond', *Strathclyde Papers on Government and Politics* 94 (Glasgow, 1993), p. 14.

7. OECD, *Spain* (OECD Economic Surveys, Paris, 1991), p. 26.

8. S. González Fernández, 'Monetary policy', in Amparo Almarcha Barbado (ed.), *Spain and EC Membership Evaluated* (Pinter, London, 1993), p. 82.

9. OECD, *Spain* (OECD Economic Surveys, Paris, 1993), p. 81.

10. Economist Intelligence Unit, *Spain: Country Profile 1994–95* (EIU, London, 1994), p. 13.

11. A. Torrero, 'Problemas y Desafios de una Economía Abierta', in J. L. García Delgado (ed.), *Lecciones de economía española* (Civitas, Madrid, 1993), p. 470.

12. Pedro Montes, *La integración en Europa* (Trotta, Madrid, 1993), p. 183.

13. Heywood: 'Spain and the European Dimension', p. 24.

14. Economist Intelligence Unit, *Spain: Country Profile 1994–95*, p. 34.

15. Economist Intelligence Unit, *Spain: Country Profile 1995–96* (EIU, London, 1995), p. 15.

16. Eurobarometer Survey 43 (European Commission, Brussels, 1995), p. 5.

17. *Guardian*, 11 May 1996.

18. Patrick Camiller, 'Spain: The Survival of Socialism?', in Perry Anderson and Patrick Camiller (eds), *Mapping the West European Left* (Verso, London, 1994), p. 256.

19. Economist Intelligence Unit, 1995, *Spain: Country Profile 1995–96*, p. 20.

20. Interview with José María Aznar, *El País* (International Edition), 15 July 1996, p. 1 and 'Revista' Section, pp. 1–3.

21. William Chislett, *Spain 1996* (Banco Central Hispano, Madrid, 1996), p. 27.

22. Donald Sassoon, *One Hundred Years of Socialism: The West European Left in the Twentieth Century* (I.B.Tauris, London, 1996), p. 750.

23. Chislett, *Spain 1996*, p. 24.

24. José María Maravall 'From Opposition to Government: the Politics and Policies of the PSOE', in José María Maravall et al., *Socialist Parties in Europe* (ICPS, Barcelona, 1992), p. 26.

25. Eduardo Bandrés, 'Las Infraestructuras: Políticas y Realizaciones', in José Luis García Delgado (ed.), *España, Economía* (Espasa Calpe, Madrid, 1993), p. 1051.

26. Andy Robinson, 'Two Ways of going for Olympic gold', *Guardian*, 15 July 1996, p. 15.

27. *Resoluciones del 33 Congreso* (PSOE, Madrid, 1994), p. 232.

28. Sassoon: *One Hundred Years of Socialism*, p. 565.

29. Ian Gibson, *Fire in the Blood: The New Spain* (Faber and Faber, London, 1992), p. 99.

30. *Resoluciones aprobadas por el 31 Congreso Federal* (PSOE, Madrid, 1988), p. 84.

31. *El Mundo*, 23 February 1996, p. 18.

32. Gibson, *Fire in the Blood*, p. 71.

33. Maravall, 'From Opposition to Government', p. 21.

34. Paul Heywood, *The Government and Politics of Spain* (Macmillan, London, 1995), p. 227.

35. Chislett, *Spain 1996*, p. 106.

36. Otto Holman, *Integrating Southern Europe* (Routledge, London, 1996), p. 187.

37. Economist Intelligence Unit, *Spain: Country Profile 1995–96*, p. 23.

38. Quoted by Heywood, *The Government and Politics of Spain*, p. 227.

39. Jesús Mota, 'Pase lo que pase, continuarán las privatizaciones', *El País*, 1 March 1996, pp. 24–5.

40. Chislett, *Spain 1996*, p. 75.

41. Heywood, *The Government and Politics of Spain*, p. 227.

42. Sassoon, *One Hundred Years of Socialism*, p. 311.

43. Ibid., p. 748.

5. French socialists

Translated by Nicola Cotton.

1. This chapter was written before the election of June 1997. Some minor emendations were inserted after the results. The substance of the argument remains valid.

2. The first *cohabitation* took place in 1986–88. The term indicates a period in which the President of the Republic and the Prime Minister belong to different ends of the political spectrum.

3. In France there is no wage indexation, though the minimum wage is inflation-linked.

7. The post-communist socialists

1. By east central Europe we mean Poland, Hungary, Czechoslovakia, Romania and Bulgaria. With the break-up of Czechoslovakia they, of course, became six.

2. A sophisticated form of this view is advanced in the useful article by

Alison Mahr and John Nagle, 'Resurrection of the Successor Parties and Demo-cratisation in East Central Europe', *Communist and Post-Communist Studies* 28/4 (1995).

3. This view is promoted especially in publications of the US Council of Foreign Relations. See Anne Applebaum, 'The Rise and Fall of the Communists: Guess Who's Running Central Europe', *Foreign Affairs* (November–December 1994); and Michael Ignatieff, 'On Civil Society', *Foreign Affairs* (March–April 1995). A more sophisticated argument running along similar lines is found in Charles Gati, 'The Mirage of Democracy', *Transition*, 22 March 1996.

4. A good example of this dichotomization is George Schopflin, 'Obstacles to Liberalism in Post-Communist Politics', *East European Politics and Society* 5/1 (winter 1991).

5. Lena Kolarska-Bobinska, 'Myth of the Market, Reality of Reform', in S. Gomulka and A. Polonsky (eds), *Polish Paradoxes* (Routledge, London, 1991).

6. Bill Lomax, 'Hungary', in Stephen Whitefield (ed.), *The New Institutional Architecture of Eastern Europe* (St. Martin's Press, New York, 1993).

7. Dieter Segert, 'The SPD in the Volkskammer in 1990: A New Party in Search of a Political Profile', in Michael Waller, Bruno Coppieters and Chris Deschouwer (eds), *Social Democracy in Post-Communist Europe* (Frank Cass, London, 1994).

8. Sharon Wolchik, *Czechoslovakia in Transition* (Pinter, London, 1991); and James P. McGregor, 'Value Structures in a Developed Socialist System: the Case of Czechoslovakia', *Comparative Politics*, 23/2 (1991).

9. See the special issue of the *Journal of Communist Studies: Parties, Trade Unions and Society in East-Central Europe*, 9/4 (December 1993).

10. Ruth A. Bandzak, 'The Role of Labour in Post-Socialist Hungary', in the *Review of Radical Political Economy* 28/2 (June 1994).

11. For a valuable analysis of the Czech trade unions, see Anna Pollert, 'From Acquiescence to Assertion? Trade Unionism in the Czech Republic 1989 to 1995', paper presented to the Second Conference of the European Sociological Association, Budapest, August 1995.

12. See Waller et al. (eds), *Social Democracy in Post-communist Europe* for discussion of developments in the trade unions.

13. In 1994 the percentage of the electorate who said that they had previously supported the market economy but now rejected it were as follows: 21 per cent in Poland; 28 per cent in the Czech Republic; 29 per cent in Slovakia; 32 per cent in Hungary; and 47 per cent in Bulgaria. See Eurobarometer Survey (European Commission, Brussels, 1994).

14. See Larry L. Wade et al., 'Searching for Voting Patterns in Post-Communist Poland's Sejm Elections', *Communist and Post-Communist Studies*, 28/4 (1995), where it is stressed that the higher turn-out 'was perhaps the most important political reason for the strong emergence of the left in 1993'.

15. The Polish and Hungarian parties did worse than the PDS and the

Czechoslovak communists: respectively 10.9 per cent and 12 per cent as against 16 per cent for the PDS and 14 per cent for the Czechoslovak communists.

16. A further factor in Poland may have been the partial character of the June 1989 election: the electorate seemed to have a chance to protest against the PUWP government without facing the possibility of that government being removed.

17. In Macedonia the communists were the largest party but were not able to form the government.

18. Mahr and Nagle: 'Resurrection of the Successor Parties ... '.

19. On the non-communist Polish Left groups see Nowa Lewica, 'The Ex-Solidarity Left', *Labour Focus on Eastern Europe* 52 (autumn 1995).

20. Ulf Lindstrom, 'East European Social Democracy: Reborn to be Rejected', unpublished paper, University of Bergen, November 1990.

21. The Socialist International itself does not directly supply financial support. The Czechoslovak Social Democrats in exile were already members of the SI. The Hungarians were made members in 1990 but were later demoted to observer status.

22. See, for example, Michael Waller, 'Winners and Losers in the Early Post-Communist Elections in East-Central Europe', in Waller et al. (eds), *Social Democracy in Post-Communist Europe*.

23. See, for example, Lisl Kauer, 'Social Democracy in Eastern Europe', *Labour Focus on Eastern Europe* 50 (spring 1995).

24. In Hungary the Social Democratic Party's vote declined from 3 per cent in 1990 to just under 1 per cent in 1994 despite being accepted as a member of the Socialist International.

25. See M. A. Vachudova, 'Divisions in the Czech Communist Party', *Radio Free Europe/Radio Liberty Research Reports* 2/37 (17 September 1993).

26. See Adam Novak, 'Big Boost for Social Democracy', *International Viewpoint* 280 (September 1996).

27. Discussion of these issues is contained in Peter Gowan, 'The Theory and Practice of Neo-Liberalism for Eastern Europe', *New Left Review* 213 (September–October, 1995).

28. On the early development of the NSF see Tom Gallagher, 'Romania: The Disputed Election of 1990', *Parliamentary Affairs* 44/1 (January 1991); and Mark Almond, 'Romania since the Revolution', *Government and Opposition*, January 1991.

29. Petre Roman's Democratic Party–National Salvation Front has now set up an electoral alliance with the small Social Democratic Party of Romania. The alliance is called the Social Democratic Union.

30. See, for example, Mieczyslaw Rakowski, 'Our Actions are Defined by the Well-Being of Poland', speech on television, 13 September 1989, reprinted in *Contemporary Poland* 10 (1989).

31. See Ludwik Krasucki, 'On the Horizon – the 11th Party Congress', *Contemporary Poland* 9 (1989). This article, reporting preparations for the last

PUWP Congress, spells out that the PUWP leadership accepted the inevitability of a transition to capitalism.

32. See Dan Ionescu, 'Romania's Trade Unions Unite', *Radio Free Europe/Radio Liberty Research Reports* 2/28 (July 1993).

33. In Hungary Prime Minister Horn proposed Sandor Nagy as Industry Minister but this was blocked by the Free Democrats in the government as being financially destabilizing.

34. See Jeff Freeman, 'Hungarian Utility Privatisation Moves Forward', *Transition*, 3 May 1996.

35. See Zsofia Szilagyi, 'Communication Breakdown Between the Government and the Public', *Transition*, 22 March 1996.

36. The IMF did insist upon the opening of a stock market, but the result was a stock exchange with 12 quoted companies, only one of which was fully private. See Dan Ionescu, 'Romania's Stand-By Agreement with the IMF', *Radio Free Europe/Radio Liberty Research Reports* 3/18 (6 May 1994).

37. Michael Wyzan, 'Renewed Economic Crisis May End Foot-dragging Reforms', *Transition*, 23 August 1996.

38. See Kjell Engelbrekt, 'Bulgarian Power Games Give Way to Growing Competition', *Transition*, 26 January 1996.

39. See Jan B. de Weydenthal, 'Polish Foreign Policy After the Elections', *Radio Free Europe/Radio Liberty Research Reports* 32/14 (15 October 1993).

40. An important motive here is concern over Polish–German relations. As indicated in the 1990 Polish–German Treaty, the Polish government will take a more relaxed attitude towards its western territories only after Poland's full integration into a strong EU.

41. See Alfred A. Reisch, 'Hungarian Parties' Foreign-Policy Electoral Platforms', *Radio Free Europe/Radio Liberty Research Reports* 3/19 (May 1994).

42. See Alfred A. Reisch, 'The New Hungarian Government's Foreign Policy', *Radio Free Europe/Radio Liberty Research Reports* 3/33 (26 August 1994).

43. See Kjell Engelbrekt, 'Southeast European States Seek Equal Treatment', *Radio Free Europe/Radio Liberty Research Reports* 3/12 (1994).

44. See Dan Ionescu, 'Romania Admitted to the Council of Europe', *Radio Free Europe/Radio Liberty Research Reports* 2/44 (5 November 1993).

45. For the vituperative dispute which followed these remarks, see Michael Shafir, 'Anatomy of a Pre-Election Political Divorce', *Transition*, 26 January 1996.

46. See Dan Ionescu, 'Hammering on NATO's Door', *Transition*, 9 August 1996.

47. On the Romanian nationalist parties' background, see Tom Gallagher, 'Electoral Breakthrough for Romanian Nationalists', *Radio Free Europe/Radio Liberty Research Reports* 1/45 (13 November 1992).

48. After the 1992 parliamentary elections, the NSF lacked a majority in the parliament. It initially sought a grand coalition but, when unable to achieve

agreement with the anti-communist opposition, formed a coalition with ultra-nationalists.

49. See Michael Shafir, 'Ethnic Tension Runs High in Romania', *Radio Free Europe/Radio Liberty Research Reports* 3/32 (19 August 1994).

50. See Ignatieff, 'On Civil Society', on the supposedly crippled democracy that results from the continued strength of the post-communists; and Applebaum's argument ('The Rise and Fall of the Communists') as to why the populist Right should be looked upon more favourably than the post-communists.

Index

Adrianopoulos, Andreas, 73, 76
Alberdi, Cristina, 104
Ali, Tariq, 40
Amato, Giuliano, 55, 60
Andreotti, Giulio, 51, 53
Androulakis, Mimis, 74
Angelopoulos, Angelos, 68
Antonescu, Ion, 163
Aranzadi, 92
Arsenis, Gherassimos, 80
Aubry, Martine, 116
Aznar, José María, 95, 97, 99, 107

Balcerowicz, Leszek, 164, 165
Balladur, Edouard, 113, 116
Bekesi, 165
Benn, Tony, 23
Bérégovoy, Pierre, 111, 113, 115, 116
Berlinguer, Enrico, 46, 50, 51
Berlusconi, Silvio, 13, 15, 50, 53, 55, 56, 57, 58, 59
Bertinotti, Fausto, 55
Beveridge, William Henry, 3
Blackstone, Tessa, 23
Blair, Tony, 3, 10, 12, 15, 16, 19, 20, 21, 22, 23, 24, 25, 26, 27, 28, 29, 30, 31, 32, 33, 35, 38, 39, 40, 41, 42
Blunkett, David, 21
Brandt, Willy, 128, 129, 131, 133, 134, 141
Brown, Gordon, 32, 33, 36, 42

Camiller, Patrick, 98
Ceauşescu, Nikolai, 164, 174
Chevènement, Jean-Pierre, 114
Chirac, Jacques, 113, 116

Churchill, Winston, 2
Ciampi, Carlo Azeglio, 55, 56, 57, 61
Ciller, Tansu, 82
Clinton, Bill, 22
Cossuta, Armando, 54, 55
Craxi, Bettino, 8, 9, 46, 47, 50, 51, 52, 53, 56, 59, 62
Cresson, Edith, 111
Crosland, Tony, 23
Crossman, Richard, 23
Cunhal, Alvaro, 74

D'Alema, Massimo, 9, 15, 50, 57, 58, 61, 62, 63
De Villiers, Philippe, 114
Delors, Jacques, 113
Devaquet, 121
Díaz, Victor Pérez, 90
Diligiannis, Theodoros, 67
Dini, Lamberto, 57, 59, 61
Dragassakis, Iannis, 73, 74
Dreyfus, Alfred, 119

Engholm, Björn, 133, 138
Eppler, Erhard, 128, 129, 131

Fabius, Laurent, 110, 111
Farneti, Paolo, 51
Fini, Gianfranco, 13, 50, 55, 56, 58, 59
Fouskas, Vassilis, 8, 11, 12
Fumar, Gheorghe, 174

Garganas, Nicos, 69
Gennimatas, George, 73, 80
Glemp, Cardinal, 173
Gonzàlez, Felipe, 8, 70, 94, 102, 107

Gorbachev, Mikhail, 159, 160
Gowan, Peter, 7, 12, 13
Gramsci, Antonio, 45
Gray, John, 90
Guesde, Jules, 10

Hattersley, Roy, 21
Hewitt, Patricia, 23
Heywood, Paul, 95, 104, 106
Hincker, François, 12
Horn, Gyula, 165, 166
Horthy, Miklos, 163, 174
Hugo, Victor, 121

Iliescu, Ion, 158, 160, 161, 171, 172,
    174
Ingham, Bernard, 25

Jaurès, Jean, 11
Jospin, Lionel, 8, 16, 110, 111, 115,
    121, 122
Juppé, Alain, 116, 117

Karamanlis, Konstantinos, 64, 67, 68,
    69, 76, 77
Kennedy, Paul, 8, 11, 13
Keynes, John Maynard, 3
Kinnock, Neil, 10, 17, 18, 19, 21, 22,
    26
Kirchheimer, Otto, 45, 46
Klaus, Vaclav, 154
Kohl, Helmut, 149, 166
Kolodko, 165
Komarek, Valtr, 154
Koskotas affair, 72
Kuron, Jacek, 153
Kwasniewski, Aleksander, 153, 168,
    173
Kyrkos, Leonidas, 73

Lafontaine, Oskar, 126, 133, 134, 137,
    142
Lamentowicz, 153
Lang, Jack, 121
Le Pen, Jean-Marie, 114
Legg, 47
Lenin, Vladimir Ilych, 7
Leys, Colin, 3, 10, 11, 12, 15, 16

Liddle, Roger, 26, 34
Lister, General, 54
Löwenthal, Richard, 127

Macwhirter, Iain, 35
Major, John, 36
Mandelson, Peter, 25, 26, 34
Marchais, George, 74
Marx, Karl, 3, 11, 16
Mastropaolo, 45
Matutes, Abel, 97
Mauroy, Pierre, 111, 112, 113
Mendès-France, Pierre, 7
Metaxas, Ioannis, 72
Meyer, Thomas, 11, 15
Meynaud, Jean, 47
Michel, Robert, 47
Miliband, David, 23
Mitsotakis, Constantine, 71, 73, 74,
    76, 77, 78
Mitterrand, François, 7, 8, 70, 110,
    111, 112, 113, 120, 122
Mollet, Guy, 7
Moro, Aldo, 50, 51, 53
Mulgan, Geoff, 24, 25
Murdoch, Rupert, 26, 30

Nagy, Sandor, 164
Napolitano, Giorgio, 58

Occhetto, Achille, 14, 53, 54, 57, 62,
    63
Offe, Claus, 70
Olechowski, 168

Papandreou, Andreas, 64, 67, 69, 71,
    72, 76, 78, 80, 82, 85
Papandreou, George, 67
Papandreou, Vasso, 80
Philip II, 77
Pilsudski, Josef, 163
Pinheiro package, 78
Porter, Henry, 25, 30, 31
Pouliopoulos, Pantelis, 64, 86
Prodi, Romano, 9, 15, 58, 59, 61

Quilès, Paul, 120

Rakowski, Mieczyslaw, 159
Rappe, Hermann, 129
Rato, Rodrigo, 97
Rau, Johannes, 131, 133, 134
Rauti, Pino, 58
Reagan, Ronald, 69
Rocard, Michel, 110, 111, 118, 120
Roman, Petre, 160

Samaras, Antonis, 77, 78, 79, 85, 87
Sapelli, Giulio, 9, 12
Sartori, Giovanni, 51
Sartre, Jean-Paul, 121
Sassoon, Donald, 46, 100, 102, 106, 107
Scharping, Rudolf, 133, 134, 137
Schmidt, Helmut, 126, 131
Schröder, Gerhard, 136, 137
Séguin, Philippe, 114
Shaw, Eric, 18
Simitis, Costas, 8, 13, 65, 66, 69, 82, 84
Simpson, Alan, 21
Skubiszewski, 169
Smith, John, 10, 19, 25, 30, 38
Steinkühler, Franz, 129
Stephanopoulos, Costis, 74
Stolpe, Dietrich, 133
Strasser, Johano, 129

Tapie, Bernard, 110, 118
Thatcher, Margaret, 17, 25, 34, 35, 36, 38, 39, 69
Thompson, Noel, 34
Togliatti, Palmiro, 45
Torrero, A, 93
Trikoupis, Charilaos, 67
Tsovolas, Dimitris, 85, 87
Tzannetakis, Tzannis, 72, 73
Tzochatzopoulos, Akis, 80

Vacca, Giuseppe, 54
Varvitsiotis, Ioannis, 78
Veltroni, Walter, 15, 58
Venizelos, Eleftherios, 67
Vogel, Hans-Jochen, 131, 133, 134, 139
Voltaire, 121
Voynet, Dominique, 122
Vranitsky, Franz, 166

Walesa, Lech, 168, 173
Wettig-Danielmeyer, Inge, 129
Wieczorek-Zeul, Heidemarie, 129

Yeltsin, Boris, 1

Zola, Emile, 121
Zolotas, Xenophon, 73